Conferences that WORK

CREATING EVENTS THAT PEOPLE LOVE

ADRIAN SEGAR

Conferences That Work
Marlboro, VT 05344-0086
www.conferencesthatwork.com

ISBN 978-1-60145-992-3

Library of Congress Control Number 2009909766
Library of Congress subject headings:
Congresses and conventions—Handbooks, manuals, etc.
Congresses and conventions—Planning
Meetings—Handbooks, manuals, etc.

Printed in the United States of America.

Booklocker.com, Inc.
2010
Wholesale orders: https://secure.booklocker.com/booklocker/wholesale/order.php

Cover design by James F. Brisson
Interior design by Jeff Miller

Contents

Contents

Contents

About the Author

ADRIAN SEGAR has organized and facilitated conferences for over 20 years. Realizing that he loves to connect with people, and to create spaces for them to connect with each other, he created the first peer conference in 1992, and has been refining peer conference process ever since. Adrian was an independent information technology consultant for 23 years, taught college computer science for 10 years, and co-owned and managed a solar domestic hot water heating systems manufacturing company before that. He has an ancient Ph.D. in experimental high-energy particle physics, lives in Marlboro, Vermont, and loves to sing and dance.

Acknowledgments

This book owes its existence to changes in my life inspired by my wife Celia Segar, Jeannie Courtney, and Jerry Weinberg. People who contributed to the development of the peer conference approach include Esther Derby, Cory Doctorow, Naomi Karten, Kevin Kelly, Harrison Owen, Robert Putnam, Clay Shirky, David Weinberger, and the wonderful steering committee members, past and present, of edACCESS.

My editor, Anne Lezak, did a masterful job of keeping me on track, improving the clarity of my writing, and correcting my Briticisms.

Manuscript reviewers Laura Berkowitz, Elizabeth Christie, Virginia Corbiere, Mark Gerrior, Sherry Heinze, Leo Hepis, Naomi Karten, Pamela Livingston, Stuart Scott, and Celia Segar made suggestions that improved this book immensely.

I particularly want to thank all edACCESS attendees for putting up with my experiments over the years.

Finally, feedback from thousands of peer conference participants has proved invaluable for fine-tuning my work. Thank you everyone!

Preface

There is a widespread and unexamined assumption that the core purpose of a conference is to transfer knowledge from the learned few to the relatively uneducated many, and that this is best done through the familiar structures of pre-planned keynotes, presentations, and panels. In this traditional model, attendees are assigned a largely passive, secondary role with their spontaneous interactions relegated to mealtimes, socials, and perhaps a few "birds of a feather" sessions. Information is imparted, some good meals are eaten, perhaps some sightseeing occurs, and then attendees go home until next year, when the cycle is repeated.

I think we can do better.

Conferring: Isn't that what conferences should be about? Conferring: "To talk with somebody in order to compare opinions or make a decision." Traditional conferences attempt to disseminate information from a small number of speakers to the attendees. But suppose there was a conference where participants discovered and shared their collective body of knowledge in a way that was relevant and useful to each individual, creating a conference that directly responded to the needs and wishes of the participants; a conference where *the attendees themselves* created the kind of conference they wanted?

Such conferences exist; I call them *peer conferences*. Peer conferences focus on effectively exposing and sharing the vast body of knowledge that conference attendees collectively hold, knowledge that they are eager to share and thirsty to receive. *The goal of every peer conference is to provide a meaningful and useful experience for each attendee.* For this to happen, people need to learn about each other early in the conference. They need to discover the interests they share and the experiences that they want to explore with other attendees. They need support for the resulting discussions, and they need a way to integrate their overall conference experience into their lives.

A peer conference provides a safe and supportive framework for all this to happen.

This book describes and explains the process that I have developed to build interactive peer conferences. It contains much of what I have learned through designing and facilitating conferences for many years. Although the key elements have been central to my conferences from the start, this is still a work in progress. I continue to learn from every conference I run.

Attendees' evaluations of peer conferences are extremely positive. Participants comment on how much they prefer the format. Peer sessions, the heart of the conference, are invariably highly rated. Informal interactions, which this kind of conference encourages, are almost always described as excellent.

A peer conference is appropriate for any group of people who have a common interest and want to learn from and share with each other. There are hundreds of thousands of such groups that could coalesce, meet, learn, and grow via the structure of a peer conference. My intention is that this book both provides the practical details needed to hold a successful peer conference and inspires you to create and participate in these powerful and rewarding events.

A peer conference community story

I still remember the last state consortium meeting I attended, back in 1991. The facilitator asked us to share noteworthy events at our schools. Several attendees from a large university described with pride how they had finally selected a vendor to provide a piece of software for their school—for $250,000. Nancy, Mike, and I looked at each other. We knew we were all thinking the same thing. This school was spending more money on a software package—one that handled just a small part of the administrative needs of the school—than the entire information technology budgets of our two small colleges combined.

At that moment the three of us realized that we were living in a different world from the other educational institutions at the meeting. Five years earlier, none of our jobs had existed. There wasn't anyone around who knew more about what we did than us. Where could we find support for the problems that we faced?

After the meeting I felt dispirited, but Mike was undaunted. "I think we should organize a meeting for information technology directors at small schools like ours," he said. Nancy and I agreed to help.

Working together, we publicized a conference that was held June 3–5, 1992, at Marlboro College, Vermont. Twenty-three people came. We didn't know what participants wanted to talk about, or what knowledge they might have, so we asked them to tell us at an initial roundtable. The first evening, we set up a "topic board" where attendees could suggest and review topics for breakout sessions during the following two days.

The conference was an immediate success, and we decided to hold it again the following year. That year 45 people came. The following year, we held two conferences, one on the west coast and one on the east, with more than 80 people showing up.

At the eighth annual conference, I was watching everything going on, and suddenly realized that I had helped to create a community of genuine value, one that would endure for the foreseeable future, even if I stepped away at that point.

As I write this, we are gearing up for our 18th year of conferences. I am no longer an information technology director at a small college, but I still facilitate the annual conference. Each year, 20 to 40 percent of attendees are new, broadening our community ever further.

It is indescribably satisfying to be intimately involved in the formation of a community like this and to get to enjoy its success. May you be so fortunate.

Introduction

In October 2005, my wife and I were riding a hotel shuttle bus to San Francisco International Airport. Two women, seated behind us, started talking:

> WOMAN #1: "Did you go to the Austin conference last year?"
> WOMAN #2: "Yes."
> [*Pause*]
> Woman #2: "I don't remember a thing about the Austin conference."
> [*Long pause*]
> WOMAN #2: "Probably won't remember a thing about this one either."

As part of the research for this book, I interviewed numerous people about their conference experiences. Although most of them had some positive things to say, a solid majority had serious complaints about the quality and worth of the events they'd attended.

> "We sit there like lumps, basically . . ."

> "The conference turned out to be essentially the same as one I'd been to a couple of years before."

> ". . . being locked in a room with someone who doesn't know what he's talking about."

> "Most conferences I go to have the same format. They're all pretty bad."

"You might as well read a book."

"600 people, 450 vendors. Cattle call!"

—*Some interviewee descriptions of less than desirable conference experiences*

Over one hundred billion dollars is spent every year on conferences. And this figure does not include the value of attendees' time. With this level of expenditure of time and money you'd think that significant efforts would have been made to create conferences that were effective and memorable. I am not deprecating the significant work that creating a well-run conference requires, but far too much energy is expended on the mechanics of organizing the conference, *while far too little energy is spent creating a conference that meets attendees' needs.* We are informed about conferences by email, we arrive by airplane, and we gaze at fancy PowerPoint presentations, but, year after year, over a hundred million people experience a conference process that has changed very little since the 17th century.

What you're about to read will show you a better way to design and run a conference. I've divided the book into three parts. In Part I, *Reengineering the Conference*, I hope to convince you of two things:

- Certain key assumptions made about the format and structure used in most conferences today are fundamentally flawed; and
- There is a better way to structure what happens at a conference, a way that significantly improves the conference experience for each individual attendee.

Once you're convinced, naturally you'll want to know how to put my ideas to work.

In Part II, *Planning and Preparing for Your Peer Conference,* I'll take you step by step through everything you need to know to prepare for your conference.

And in Part III, *Running Your Peer Conference,* I'll cover conference setup and the nitty-gritty details of running a successful conference, from start to finish.

I wrote this book because I've found that peer conferences offer a truly superior conference experience that facilitates intimate connections, supports powerful peer-to-peer sharing and learning, and generates lasting impact. I want to share what I've found with you.

PART I

Reengineering the Conference

CHAPTER 1

What Is a Conference?

The people I interviewed about their conference experiences had to satisfy the prerequisite of having attended at least five conferences in the last five years. On hearing this, most prospective interviewees asked me how I defined a conference. Did workshops or trainings count? How about meetings over dinner with medical salespeople? Or one-day community forums? I told them they could decide what they considered to be a conference, and, as the interviews progressed, it became clear that the word *conference* means quite different things to different people.

> "Welcome to the Theater Parking Attendant Symposium."
>
> —*Title on a pamphlet being read by a woman sitting next to me while flying between Phoenix and Chicago on August 22, 2005.*

Thousands of books and articles have been written about conducting business meetings. In contrast, fewer than 50 books about conference organization are currently in print, and nearly all of these concentrate exclusively on *logistics*—the nuts and bolts of planning and running a conference—rather than what should actually happen during the event. Considering the massive expenditure of money and time spent attending conferences today, it's disconcerting to realize the lack of critical thought about the group processes used during them.

While it's true that any kind of conference can be improved by employing better logistics—a nicer location, tastier food, smarter organization—improving the logistics of a mediocre or downright poor conference will not make it great. This book is fundamentally about conference *process* rather than logistics.

What I know is how to create great conferences of a certain type. I call them "peer conferences." In order to understand what a peer conference is, it's first necessary to understand what it is not. Let's start by making some distinctions among the bewildering variety of present-day conferences.

How we got here

The word *conference* was first used around the middle of the 16th century as a verb that described the *act* of conferring with others in conversation, rather than a formal occasion where people met and discussed a topic. Over time, the word's meaning shifted to denoting the meeting itself. The neighboring quote is an early, perhaps the earliest, written English example that uses *conference* in the way we would today. Other words that are currently used for conference-like activities, listed with the century they acquired this meaning, are: *congress* and *convention* (17th), *symposium* (18th), and *colloquium* and *workshop* (20th).

In reality, conferences are arenas for many important activities not captured in these terms, such as maintaining and increasing professional status, making useful connections, conferring legitimacy, promoting issue activism, and building community.

> "These Conferences are held once in a Month by divers Able Masters making reflexions and observations upon the rarest pieces in the Cabinet of his Most Christian Majesty . . ."
>
> —*A Relation of the Conferences Held at Paris in the Academy Royal for the Improvement of the Arts of Painting and Sculpture, as 'tis Found in the Iournal Des Scavans, A. E. H. Love in Philosophical Transactions (1665–1678), Vol. 4, 1669*

Few of today's conferences provide substantive opportunities for consultation or discussion. They are instead primarily conduits for the one-to-many transfer of information on the conference topic. Predetermined presentations dominate these conference programs.

In this book I refer to these conference formats as *traditional* or *conventional* conferences: events built around pre-planned sessions where invited experts present to audiences of attendees. Attendee interaction and conference contributions are secondary to the main purpose of these events—imparting knowledge from those who hopefully have it to those who supposedly haven't. In general, traditional conferences provide little or no formal support for attendee interaction, which is expected to occur by default at meals and social events, during questions at the end of presentations, or via "birds-of-a-feather" sessions wedged into gaps in the conference schedule.

Although most people still think of conferences primarily as a vehicle for pre-planned content, the 1990s saw a rebellion against the rigid structure of traditional conferences, leading to the birth of a number of alternative designs. All shared an emphasis on the development of fruitful attendee interactions over the supply of predetermined material. Some of these approaches, such as World Café, the Art of Hosting, and Everyday Democracy, concentrate on building participant connections, conversations, and communities. Shared issues and concerns motivate these events, but their focus is on specific group processes that lead to group outcomes.

Three other conference variants—peer conferences, Open Space Technology, and unconferences—are also attendee-driven, but steer a middle ground between content-driven and group development process models. These conference formats, which I'll cover in more detail later, move the focus of the conference away from pre-planned sessions with fixed presenters and toward a more fluid program that is determined by the desires and interests of the conference attendees. Such attendee-driven approaches have arisen as a response to the rigid structure of traditional conferences.

Face-to-face versus online

I spent the summer of 1973 working for the Long-Range Studies Department of the British Post Office, a long-defunct group that attempted to predict the exciting future that new technologies would surely bring about. The Post Office had just built a few hideously expensive teleconferencing studios, connected by outrageously expensive telephone trunk lines, and one of our jobs was to find out what they could be used for. Could businesspeople be persuaded to stop traveling to meetings, to sit instead in comfortable local studios hundreds of miles apart, handsomely equipped with cameras, microphones, screens, and speakers that magically allowed them to meet as well as if they were all in the same room? Why yes, we concluded brightly in our final report. "A substantial number of business meetings which now occur face-to-face could be conducted effectively by some kind of group telemedia."

Thirty years later, my Macintosh laptop contains all the components of those glossy studios, and the Internet connects me, by both video and voice, to anyone who's similarly equipped. The technology is finally here for the masses, and video conferencing, web conferencing, and virtual worlds are starting to change the ways we have communicated, met, and done business for hundreds of years. And yet, face-to-face symposia, seminars, workshops, trainings, congresses, conventions, colloquia, and conferences still abound. In-person conferences, despite the significant expense and the explosion in other forms of communication, still apparently fulfill attendees' needs in ways that electronic alternatives do not.

Perhaps this will soon change; we may be at the beginning of a radical shift in the form and structure of conferences—a change that will relegate the face-to-face conference, little changed since its first blossoming over 400 years ago, to a quaint, old-fashioned technique, made obsolete by the advent of cheap, ubiquitous, high-bandwidth telecommunications available to every global citizen who wishes to connect with her peers.

It's true that online conferences offer a convenient and low-cost way to receive content, and they can provide limited interactivity. Yet you can also abandon one with the click of a mouse. Online conferences require little commitment, so it is harder to successfully engage participants when the cost of leaving is so low.

If you think of a conference primarily as a way of transferring content, then online conferences seem attractive, inexpensive alternatives to face-to-face events. If, however, you value conferences as opportunities to make meaningful connections with others, face-to-face conferences offer a number of advantages.

I expect that the unique benefits of face-to-face conferences will continue to be valued. The advantages of being physically present with other people, dining and socializing together, the serendipity of human contact, the opportunity to meet new people in person rather than hear a voice on the phone or see an image on a screen, the magic that can occur when a group of people coalesces; all these combine into more than the sum of their parts, building the potential to gain and grow long-term relationships and friendships. Anyone who has been to a good face-to-face conference knows that these things can happen, and that, either in the moment or in retrospect, they may even be seen as pivotal times in one's life.

Able Masters

We don't know much about the Able Masters of the Academy Royal who began holding their art conferences in 1666, but given that the mid-17th century was the dawn of formal art criticism, I don't think the Able Masters sat in rows listening to Abler Masters. Instead, I visualize a room of fledgling critics, magnificently gowned, standing around a Leonardo da Vinci drawing while arguing about the role of perspective in painting, creating a witty salon of a conference, full of arguments and opinions shared among peers.

This vision of mine is a fantasy—yet it illustrates an important point. When a new area of human knowledge or interest blossoms, *there are no experts*—only a vanguard struggling to see clearly, to understand more deeply, to learn. During this period a traditional conference format can only offer an uneasy fit—if there are no experts yet, who will present? Today's explosion of knowledge and, hence, associated conference topics, implies an increasing need for flexible conference approaches that can adapt to spontaneous, real-time discoveries of directions and themes that attendees want to explore.

So, why do most contemporary conferences follow the traditional, prescheduled model? There are several reasons.

Education as gardening

I was educated in England at a time when schools acted as master gardeners, with students their plants. Our teachers sprinkled a rain of knowledge on us and expected us to soak it up, with the successful students absorbing and growing the most. We were encouraged to compete with each other; individual test scores were announced in class, and a ranked list of each class's students, from best to worst, was publicly posted every school term. At the tender age of eleven, the infamous Eleven Plus exam weeded out the "second-rate" students; they went on to second-class comprehensive schools while their top-scoring classmates enjoyed superior opportunities available at prestigious grammar schools—just as gardeners weed less successful seedlings from their faster growing companions.

Not surprisingly, we grew up feeling dominated by our teachers' mastery of their subjects, and we believed that our role was to compliantly learn what they told us, as quickly as possible. In this environment, the idea that we students could contribute to each other's learning was as ridiculous as the idea that garden seedlings could help each other to grow.

Conference process = Elementary school process

In the main, traditional conferences have adopted this common and largely passive model of education, a mode that still permeates society today. Take a moment to think about how you were educated. How much of your time in school did you spend learning through interactions with your peers, compared to sitting in a room listening to a teacher? Probably very little.

There are, of course, important times and situations in which one-to-many classroom instruction is completely appropriate. Much vital learning of basic information and techniques is best imparted by teachers in the classroom. Elementary school students at the same level of achievement, for example, are not going to spontaneously learn from each other how to read and do arithmetic.

But conferences are for adults. By the time most of us reach adulthood, we are able to think critically, to learn from experience and from others, and to be creative in our work and our response to challenges. These abilities allow us to handle and contribute to much more complex and nuanced forms of learning and achieving personal and group goals. And yet, the traditional conferences we attend are still modeled on the classroom paradigm—sit still and soak it up—that we experienced when we were in school.

We have forgotten that we are no longer children and have, unthinkingly, chosen the old, comfortable classroom model for our conference process. As a result, our new adult abilities are restricted to the times during the conference when the classrooms are not in session.

Social events and meal breaks are the times assigned to peer interaction, just like when we were in school and had playground recess and lunch. Yes, traditional conferences continue to treat us as if we were still children.

Traditional conference = Training

One of my hopes for this book is that it will redefine your vision of the core function of conferences, which I see as providing structure and support for a group of people so they can effectively reflect, share, and learn about a common interest. Unfortunately, traditional conferences do not do this well.

Instead, many "conferences" nowadays are primarily *trainings*: events whose foremost aim is to transfer largely predetermined knowledge to the attendees via presentations and panels. This lack of distinction between conferences and trainings is a natural consequence of carrying over our early educational experience into adulthood—we instinctively fall back on the educational modalities we encountered in our youth. Because the word *training* sounds somewhat simplistic, such conferences are often promoted as "professional development"— around 15 percent of my interviewees reported being required to attend conferences for their "continuing education"—and in some professions, especially healthcare and primary and secondary education, such events are often the only kind of conferences that people attend.

Sponsorship distortion

Training-centric conferences can also suffer from an additional influence that further distorts their content away from what attendees really want. Commercial interests that inject their own self-promotion into the proceedings often financially underwrite these events. The effects of commercial sponsorship can be relatively benign—for example, displaying company logos on conference materials and in conference spaces. But sponsorship can also lead to serious distortion of the conference program. For example, sponsors may obtain prominent placement in the presentation schedule, amounting effectively to a paid promotional opportunity for the company, or they may be able to effectively censor the inclusion of subjects or sentiments that are at odds with their point of view.

> ". . . in several dozen symposiums during the weeklong meeting, companies paid the APA [American Psychiatric Association] about $50,000 per session to control which scientists and papers were presented and to help shape the presentations."
>
> —*"Industry Role in Medical Meeting Decried," Washington Post, May 25, 2002*

Conference form

Currently, traditional conferences make up the vast majority of conferences held. A traditional conference's format is determined by its program and schedule, which are planned by the conference organizers well in advance of the actual conference. The conference program announces who will speak, on what subjects, when, and for how long. Potential participants are so used to having this level of detail provided in advance that their decision to attend is based principally on the contents of the advance conference program.

In contrast, alternative conference process models support attendee input into what happens at the conference. This is usually done during the conference, though in some models participants suggest or offer topics of interest prior to the conference to provide a jumping-off place at the start of the conference. Although there are many similarities and overlaps, as we'll see, each alternative conference model implements an attendee-driven conference in its own unique way.

What Are Conferences For?

When I asked people why they went to conferences, the two most common answers were: (1) to network with others (80%) and (2) to learn (75%). Seventy percent of my interviewees mentioned both of these reasons. In addition, 15 percent told me that they were required to attend annual conferences to maintain their professional status.

I also asked people what factors make a conference better than average. Here are the 12 factors mentioned by 10 percent or more of my sample interviewees:

- Good presenters 40%
- Time to connect/interact with other attendees 40%
- Good content. 30%
- Sessions using modalities other than presentation 30%
- Ways to get to know more about other attendees 30%
- Good conference logistics 25%
- Group interaction during sessions 20%
- Good handouts and/or take-aways 20%
- Engaged attendees 15%
- Leadership responsive to what attendees want. 10%
- Detailed session descriptions 10%
- Field trips 10%

Interestingly, there are other reasons why people attend conferences that no one mentioned directly. They include: establishing and increasing professional status, conferring legitimacy, developing activism around issues, and community building. In this chapter I'll describe the multiple purposes that conferences serve—then we'll be in a position to explore how traditional conferences satisfy these needs.

Content

Although there are plenty of other reasons for going, people generally attend traditional conferences to experience well-delivered, useful content. "Useful" here means two things. The first is the acquisition of relevant knowledge. We expect to learn more about the conference subject, and we expect that the learning will be meaningful to us—whether that meaningfulness springs from a fundamental desire to learn more about the topic, or the required maintenance of professional status. The second way that a conference is useful is through the opportunity it provides for answers. Because conferences feature experts in the field, as well as peers with overlapping interests, they hold the promise of responding to attendee-specific questions.

In this section I'll briefly examine the changing nature of knowledge in our society and how well traditional conference structure handles answering attendee questions.

Acquiring knowledge

David Weinberger's perceptive book *Everything Is Miscellaneous*, quoted here, summarizes the traditional view of knowledge as passively acquired, "something done by individuals," and "something that happens inside your brain." According to this viewpoint, when we want knowledge, we ask experts to teach it to us, or look up answers in reference books.

> "Knowledge, we've thought, has four characteristics, two of them modeled on properties of reality and two on properties of political regimes.
>
> . . . the first characteristic of traditional knowledge is that just as there is one reality, there is one knowledge, the same for all.
>
> . . . Second, we've assumed that just as reality is not ambiguous, neither is knowledge.
>
> . . . Third, because knowledge is as big as reality, no one person can comprehend it. So we need people who will act as filters, using their education, experience, and clear thinking. We call them experts and we give them clipboards.
>
> . . . Fourth, experts achieve their position by working their way up through social institutions."
>
> —*David Weinberger. Everything Is Miscellaneous. Times Books, 2007*

Weinberger goes on to persuasively argue that, as we move from the physical to the digital world, important learning is increasingly *social*. We still test school learning by having students "sit by themselves and answer questions on a piece of paper" while these days our children learn together via social media and texting as they do their homework. Meanwhile, businesses are replacing static internal reports with collaborative software platforms, like wikis, to better share ever-shifting information and allow conversation that "improves expertise by exposing weaknesses, introducing new viewpoints, and pushing ideas into accessible form." "These diverse viewpoints," Weinberger continues, "help get us past the biases of individuals . . . we can not only listen, we can participate."

Weinberger concludes by positing that knowledge isn't in our heads but is social. "It is between us. It emerges from public and social thought and it stays there, because social knowing, like the global conversations that give rise to it, is never finished."

Traditional conferences, like traditional teaching, can be good tools for acquiring traditional kinds of knowledge. But how well do they work for the purpose of acquiring social knowledge? Unfortunately, conventional conference sessions simply don't fit the multiple-conversation, many-to-many approach that promotes socially generated learning. Only the informal breaks between sessions offer opportunities for attendees to build and share this kind of knowledge.

As a result, there is a growing mismatch between the structure of a conventional conference and the rising importance of social knowledge. As long as conferences are built around a one-to-many model of knowledge propagation, they will increasingly fail to supply what attendees need.

Getting answers

People come to conferences with questions.

- How do I do such-and-such?
- Has anyone else had this problem, and how are they dealing with it?
- When is the right time to start *XYZ*?
- Which one should I buy?
- What is *X*, and why should I care?
- Who can provide me with what I need, and whom should I avoid?
- What are the pros and cons of doing *Y*?
- Am I the only person struggling with this?
- OK, I did *Z*, now what should I do next?

What opportunities do traditional conferences offer to get questions answered? Conventional conferences provide schedules in advance that give us information about the available sessions: a title and the name(s) of the presenter(s), and perhaps a descriptive paragraph or two. If we're lucky, the content of one or more sessions will intersect with our questions and attending will answer some of them. If a presentation doesn't answer our questions, maybe there will be an opportunity to ask them during question time at the end of the session, although there is rarely sufficient time available to answer all attendee questions, especially if the audience is large.

Session breaks provide another opportunity to get our questions answered. If presenters stick around after their session, or if we discover other attendees who may have answers to our questions, we might buttonhole them outside the conference sessions and question them directly.

There are many caveats to the above traditional conference narrative. *Hopefully* there's a session that is billed as touching on our question, *hopefully* the session is actually about what the conference program advertised, *hopefully* the session content will answer our question, *hopefully* if it doesn't we'll be able to ask our question at the end of the session, *hopefully* if sessions don't answer our question there will be someone attending the conference who can, *hopefully* we can figure out who that is, and *hopefully* we'll get to talk to him or her during session breaks.

Clearly, conventional conferences are hit-and-miss affairs for getting answers to attendee questions. As you'll see, we can do better.

Conferring

If content is king at traditional conferences, conferring is queen. The word *confer* has gone out of fashion; most of my interviewees used the word *networking* to describe the most common response to my question about why they go to conferences. Given my desire to align conference process back toward its roots, conferring is the word I'll use here.

> "Confer: To converse, talk together; now always on an important subject, or on some stated question: to hold conference, take counsel, consult."
>
> —*Oxford English Dictionary, 2nd ed. 1989*

Conferring is different from one-to-many learning. Conferring doesn't happen at a presentation, except perhaps during a final question period, if there is one. At a traditional conference, conferring is largely an informal activity that occurs, through the efforts of attendees, during conference meals and breaks. Conferring is not part of the formal structure of traditional conferences. You only need to look at the feedback/evaluation forms they use; the criteria to be rated revolve almost entirely around the content and delivery of the presentations.

As we'll see, conferences can be designed to support appropriate and effective conferring, elevating its importance during the time attendees are together. Simply by providing this support, the conference reframes conferring as a natural, core ingredient of attendee interactions and experiences. For most attendees, this is a paradigm shift, but once they adjust to an environment where conferring is the primary activity, they find it surprisingly exhilarating and freeing.

In my experience, predetermined conference programs deter conferring. Even if all conference sessions use a discussion format, a predetermined program shuts out the possibility of spontaneous development, discovery, and subsequent discussion of unpredicted topics during the conference. Only if attendees are given the opportunity to discover and select both topics and format can the resulting sessions reflect what participants want. When attendees are in control of what happens at a conference, they take ownership of the event and become active participants—the essential ingredient for conferring to take place.

Meeting and connecting with peers

You would think that since networking (what I'm calling conferring) is such a high priority for many conference-goers, it would be a major focus of conference programs. But because traditional conferences rarely provide support for meeting people beyond meals and social events, you typically make new connections slowly, often by chance, throughout the conference. Noticing who else is at sessions you attend, overhearing nearby conversations, and glancing at name badges hoping to see familiar affiliations are the kinds of tactics most people resort to in the hope of meeting someone interesting.

Without support, meeting new people is difficult, especially if you know no one else at the conference. While some people are comfortable introducing themselves to strangers and good at striking up conversations, many are not. Sometimes a list of attendees is available at the

> "All we have to bring to our first meeting is our past experience. Our first experience of someone new is going to be an inner one, an experience with ourselves. What changes this and takes us beyond this point? We share. Taking our courage, we express something we are experiencing inside. We check out something with the other person."
>
> —*Virginia Satir et al. The Satir Model. Science and Behavior Books, 1991*

start of the conference, which attendees scan to look for people they have heard of or who have a colleague or an affiliation with which they have a connection. Whatever method is used, the attendee has to do all the work. Not surprisingly, at many conference openings it's common to see people hanging about trying to figure out how to connect with others.

Rarely used solutions

Given that there's no shortage of techniques—often called *icebreakers* or *openers*—available for getting people introduced and connected at the start of an event, it's surprising how infrequently they're used at conferences.

Icebreakers introduce people to each other. One example is *pair/triad interviews*, where attendees are divided up into pairs or triads, interview each other for a few minutes, and then introduce a group member to some or all of the other attendees. Another icebreaker divides attendees into small groups and asks each group to discover unusual things that group members all have in common. Then there are a host of physical activity icebreakers, such as having attendees stand in a circle, asking everyone to hold the hands of two other attendees (excluding those of the people next to them), and then challenging the resulting entangled mass to disentangle without letting go of any hands. Such techniques actively involve everyone, facilitate initial introductions, and increase trust and intimacy. They can also be extended into the body of the conference; for example, by scheduling time for conference pair buddies or triads to meet during the conference to debrief and share.

Openers are ice-breaking techniques that are related to the subject matter of the conference. The peer conference *roundtable* simultaneously introduces attendees to one another, while exposing topics and themes that attendees want to explore as well as expertise that others can draw on. Other openers include the regularly recomposed *café tables* of World Café and the *study circles* of Everyday Democracy. Well-integrated openers provide a powerful and intimate way to begin an interactive conference.

Although they are more common at small conferences, any conference can employ these techniques. Attendees at a large conference can't hope to get to know everyone; however, dividing them arbitrarily into small groups and using icebreakers or openers will ensure that everyone at the conference gets a chance to meet at least one other participant before the conference starts.

Humans share a universal longing for intimacy, closeness, community, and excitement. We are accustomed to suppressing this longing during our day-to-day work activities. A traditional conference offers an opportunity to meet new people, but in a format that de-emphasizes human connection, with attendees sitting facing the same direction listening to others speak. We have little opportunity to share in the way that Virginia Satir describes.

But when conference process is built around attendee interaction, when the very shape and content of a conference is created by the attendees themselves via their active involvement, the whole feeling of the conference changes, becoming energetic, even electric. Friendships develop, community grows, ideas germinate and some flourish. When such a conference acknowledges, allows, and supports the deep desire for human connection, amazing things happen.

In my experience, there are two prerequisites for this kind of connection to occur. The first is creating a conference environment that de-emphasizes potential hierarchical relationships between attendees. It's hard to create deep connections if some attendees are in awe of or dismissive of others. The second is creating a conference environment that feels safe and encourages attendees to take risks. Such an environment encourages participants to pose questions they've never asked because they worried others would see them as ignorant, and promotes outside-the-box ideas and activities that energize attendees in exciting and innovative ways.

Establishing and increasing professional status

Although you'll never see the phrase "Attending this conference is essential for establishing and increasing your professional status" in conference promotional materials, some conferences have a reputation for being must-attend events if you want to rise to the top of the associated profession or business. Such events are vehicles for publicly proclaiming and gaining status.

Presenters and panelists gain status, of course, simply from being chosen as presenters and panelists. But there are many other ways that professional standing can be promoted and telegraphed during a conference. At academic conferences, for example, ambitious graduate students buttonhole speakers in the corridors and ask smart questions at the end of talks, hoping to increase their visibility and future employment prospects. Similar schmoozing occurs at professional conferences. There can be public battles during presentation question times. How a colleague is greeted (or ignored) may signify volumes about professional pecking order, not only to the people involved but also those who witness the encounter.

> "Senior scientists make a habit of attending professional conferences. As a graduate student, postdoc, or assistant professor, you should also plan to attend such events. They are an important way to begin developing your professional reputation."
>
> —*Richard M. Reis. How to Get the Most Out of Scientific Conferences. Chronicle of Higher Education, February 4, 2000*

Traditional conferences, then, provide multiple opportunities for overtly promoting, adjusting, and reinforcing professional status. As we'll see, peer conferences, by providing ready access to anyone who has something meaningful to offer, de-emphasize the importance of professional status, replacing it with a more specific appreciation of an individual's skills, gifts, and learning.

Maintaining professional certification

Many conferences today exist for the sole purpose of maintaining professional certification. Continuing Education Units (CEUs), required to maintain professional licensure, are awarded at about 100,000 conferences each year in the United States alone. For many licensed professionals, these events are the only kind of conference they attend.

Few would argue against the regulation of professions requiring a high level of specialized skill, and continuing professional development opportunities help refresh and update such skills. Just about all of these events use a traditional conference format, which is effective for transferring predetermined information, but less useful for responding to specific attendee concerns and interests. Licensing authorities like to specify measurable learning outcomes ("by the end of this session you will have been taught the six critical ways to carry out *XYZ*"); alternative conference formats focus on satisfying attendee needs rather than licensor standards.

As a result, professionals who attend conferences oriented toward professional development certification do not get much opportunity to get their personal needs addressed or share their experiences. From my interviews, this is a frequent complaint from people who attend such conferences. The general practitioner who wants to find out how other doctors manage their practice, the teacher who is extraordinarily effective at helping her students to master algebra, and the social worker struggling to handle his multigenerational family caseload would enjoy and benefit from time conferring with their peers. This is rarely possible except informally and inefficiently, outside the regular conference sessions.

Unfortunately, when a conference is used to train, maintain competencies, or update skills, individual needs such as those described above take second place. How important is this? The answer is different from one person to the next, but from my interviews it's clear that many attendees would welcome a better way to connect and share with their peers while they are together. One of the core goals of peer conference process is satisfying these needs.

Conferring legitimacy

When a new profession, field of study, or specialty begins emerging, one of the first signs is the organization of a related conference. Interestingly, such initial conferences are generally small, informally organized, and exciting for the participants—they are often quite similar to peer conferences. Eventually the scope and intricacies of the conference subject becomes clarified, acknowledged experts in the field arise, and the conference form tends to move toward that of a traditional conference. Because they usually predate printed works on a subject, such as books, journals, and periodicals, conferences are a principal way in which their subject becomes legitimized as worthy of existing in its own right.

Issue activism

Examples of issue activism conferences are events that focus attention on a political or social issue, incentive and morale boosting conferences for salespeople, and organization or business planning events. What these conferences have in common is an emphasis on creating change around an issue; learning and sharing, though necessary, are usually secondary concerns.

Some organizers tightly script issue activism conferences to achieve a desired result. Only those who have bought into the dominant conference viewpoint are likely to enjoy such events. You're not going to see an unconventional format used here, as it would threaten the organizers' control over the event.

Conversely, if an issue is ill defined, or different viewpoints or approaches exist, an alternative conference format can be used to seek a way forward. Because each attendee has the power to contribute to and influence the conference's sessions, conclusions, and resulting planning, unconventional conference formats generally lead to better attendee buy-in to activism goals and plans that crystallize during the conference. If significant disagreements surface, perhaps it's best that they're brought into the open rather than simmering underneath, unvoiced and unresolved.

Building community

Some conferences are primarily about building community—finding new ways to work with others—rather than exploring a particular topic. The Art of Hosting exemplifies this approach by putting conversation and participation at the center of their meetings, and employing appropriate processes to maximize and harmonize meaningful human involvement.

Other conference designs recognize the importance of building community simultaneously as attendees work together on solving community specific or organization problems. Formats such as Future Search, which helps a group of people discover common ground and decide on appropriate responses, and World Café, which supports small and large group dialogue around central questions, use this approach.

Unfortunately, these conference processes are only used at a small percentage of conferences. At traditional conferences, community building is something that happens haphazardly; conference sessions focus on content rather than on discovering and strengthening connections between attendees. Any community that is built through such conferences occurs after multiple events, and is concentrated among the "old-timers," those who have been attending for many years.

Though peer conferences are not specifically designed to foster community building, they provide bountiful opportunities for people to meet, and to discover and build community in a meaningful way that works for each individual. The resulting community is organic, reflecting the true will and needs of the participants, rather than anyone's preconceived agenda.

What's Wrong with Traditional Conferences?

Four assumptions of a traditional conference

Four key assumptions lurk behind the traditional conference format—assumptions so deep-seated that they go unquestioned by most conference organizers. These assumptions embody, and consequently help perpetuate, a distorted and outdated way of thinking about conference purpose and structure, leading to a conference model that, as reported by a majority of my interviewees, does not well serve today's conference attendees.

Let's look at these assumptions.

Assumption #1. Conference session topics must be chosen and scheduled in advance.

During my conference experience interviews, I asked the following question:

> "Most conferences have a conference schedule and program decided in advance. How would you feel about a conference where, at the start, through a careful conference process, the attendees themselves determine what they want to discuss, based on what each person wants to learn and the experience each attendee has to share?"

Forty-five percent of my interviewees were unable to conceive of a conference that did not have a schedule of conference sessions decided on and circulated in advance.

The most common response was that the interviewee wasn't sure she'd want to go to such a conference without knowing what was going to happen there.

The next most common response was that the idea sounded great/interesting/intriguing, but the interviewee had no idea of how one would create a relevant conference program at the start of the conference.

Suspend disbelief for a moment, and assume that at the start of a conference it is somehow possible to use available resources to create a conference program that reflects actual attendee needs. Imagine attending such a conference yourself, a conference tailored to *your* needs. (You might want to reflect on how often this has happened for you.) Wouldn't it be great?

The peer conference model described in this book does indeed build a conference program that automatically adjusts to the actual needs of the people present—we'll see how later.

What is the origin of the assumption that a conference program must be pre-planned? Perhaps it arose from our experience of learning as children, from our teachers in school who knew or were told what we were supposed to learn following a pre-planned curriculum. Certainly, if one thinks of conferences as trainings by experts, a pre-planned schedule makes sense. But conferences are for adult learners, and adults with critical thinking skills and relevant experience can learn from each other if they are given the opportunity. We'll see that there are ways of putting conference attendees in charge of what they wish to learn and discuss. But this cannot be done effectively if a conference's program is frozen before attendees arrive.

Assumption #2. Conference sessions are primarily for transmitting pre-planned content.

The three communication modes used among a group of people are *one-to-one* (individual conversations), *one-to-many* or *broadcast* (presentations and panels), and *many-to-many* or *conferring* (discussions). Traditional conference sessions are predominantly one-to-many, with perhaps a dash of many-to-many at question time.

One-to-one conversations are infinitely flexible; both participants have power to lead the conversation along desired paths. Many-to-many conversations are powerful in a different way—they expose the participating group to a wide range of experience and opinions.

In contrast, one-to-many communication is mostly pre-planned, and thus relatively inflexible if the presentation involves a passive audience. At best, a presenter may ask questions of her audience and vary her presentation appropriately, but she is unlikely to get accurate representative feedback when her audience is large. Some presenters are skilled at creating interactive sessions with significant audience participation, but they are the exception.

Presentations and panels are appropriate when we are training, and have expert knowledge or information to impart to others. But with the rise of alternative methods for adults to receive training—reading books and articles, watching recordings of presentations, downloading answers on the Web—what can't be replicated at a face-to-face conference is the conversations and discussions that occur. So why do we still cling to conference sessions that employ the one communication mode for which a variety of alternatives can substitute?

Assumption #3. Supporting meaningful connections with other attendees is not the conference organizers' job; it's something that happens in the breaks between sessions.

People are impressed when I tell them that on arrival, peer conference attendees are immediately given a face book that includes photographs, names and contact data, and additional pertinent information about each participant. They tell me that it's rare to receive such a document at conferences. It's sad that conference organizers don't bother to provide this basic tool for learning about fellow attendees. (Perhaps it's not too surprising, since an attendee face book is not mentioned in any book on conference management I've read.) The absence speaks volumes about the lack of support for attendee interaction at traditional conferences.

Typically, support is limited to providing meals and social events where people can mingle. Attendees are left to their own devices to learn who else is at the conference, to seek out interesting people, and to introduce themselves to others. All these barriers must be surmounted before conversations and discussions can occur. Consequently, attendees who are new to a conference are disadvantaged compared to the old-timers who already know other participants, reinforcing the formation of cliques.

It doesn't have to be this way. Actively supporting useful attendee connections is an integral part of every peer conference. When the information, openings, and opportunities needed to meet like-minded attendees are provided, not only during session breaks but also as part of the formal conference structure, it becomes attendee-centered rather than session-centered, greatly increasing the intimacy and enjoyment of the event.

Assumption #4. Conferences are best ended with some event that will hopefully convince attendees to stay to the end.

How to end a conference? Trainings and conferences that professionals must attend to maintain certification can close with the triumphant presentation of certificates of completion or attendance, but other traditional conferences have no such obvious conclusion. All too often, the conference finale is manufactured: an awards ceremony, a closing keynote, a fancy dinner, a raffle, a celebrity speaker, or some combination thereof.

The reason for this artificiality is simple: Traditional conferences that are not training-oriented don't provide any kind of progression through their theme. The sequence of session topics is guided by logistical, political, and speaker availability considerations, rather than logical flow. One session doesn't follow from another. Such a conference doesn't have a beginning; how can we expect it to have an end?

> " 'We know that people will be strong in the beginning of the conference, so we anchor the keynote speaker at the end so attendees will stay,' says Karen Malone, Vice President of Meeting Services for the Chicago-based Healthcare Information and Management Systems Society."
>
> —*Jennifer Nicole Dienst. Meetings and Conventions Magazine, November 2007*

Some conferences dispense with the pretense of closure. This at least is honest, though the effect of "transmit content, go home" is somewhat blunt.

In contrast, peer conferences provide a progression, not through content, but through increased attendee connections as the conference proceeds. Two closing "spective" sessions build on the generated intimacy to provide a powerful and appropriate conference ending.

Predetermined content

Sometimes a trusted colleague will tell you about a conference you've never attended. *You really should go—it's a great fit for you. I've been the last five years and I wouldn't miss it.* Or, *I went once, never again. Badly organized, lousy location, sessions that weren't as advertised, and I didn't meet anyone who does what we do.* If you are lucky enough to get an evaluation from someone whose judgment you trust, this may be all you need to determine whether you should attend a conference.

Otherwise, how do you decide to attend a particular conference? Well, it seems obvious that you'd want to know in detail what the conference is about before you decide to spend valuable money and time on it. And what better way to find out than to obtain the pre-conference program and scan the lists of scheduled sessions. The more detail the better. *Aha, there's a presentation that sounds really appealing. And maybe I'll like that one. Hmm, nothing of interest on Monday afternoon, but perhaps I can do some sightseeing then.* Eventually you decide to go, or not. Simple. Reasonable. How else could you decide?

Access to this kind of information certainly makes sense when deciding whether you should attend a traditional conference. Since it's rare to find that dream conference where an appealing session is scheduled during every conference hour every day, perusing a pre-conference

Choice

For ten years I taught computer science at Marlboro College, a wonderful tiny liberal arts college in southern Vermont. Unlike most schools, Marlboro has almost no course requirements (a demonstrated ability to write with clarity being a notable exception), with students creating a "plan of concentration" for their last two years. Students' study culminates with an examination of their body of work by faculty members and an outside examiner expert in their chosen field, a process very similar to a master's level thesis defense. Because of the school's unusual learning format, students are essentially free to choose freshman and sophomore courses based on their interests rather than on degree requirements.

At the start of my seventh year of teaching, I thought I was finally becoming a half-decent teacher. So I was surprised and depressed by the atmosphere in my larger-than-usual fall semester introductory class. Students seemed distracted, homework was perfunctory, and getting classroom discussion going was like pulling teeth. Every class has its own personality, but I'd never experienced a class like this one. Was it me? Had I regressed to my early years of bumbling teaching? I didn't think so. Perhaps it was the students?

I soldiered on for a few weeks; the class environment stayed grim. So one day I summoned up my courage and asked my students about the class. I extracted the information that they thought the content was at the right level, but they just weren't that interested in it.

"So," I asked, "why did you sign up?" And finally the truth came out. The school had recently created a joint degree program with another local college. This joint degree program had requirements, one of which could be satisfied by taking my class. Unlike any class I'd previously taught at Marlboro, about two thirds of the students were in my class because they saw it as the easiest way to satisfy a degree requirement. The dead atmosphere I'd experienced was because a majority of my students didn't want to be there.

Unfortunately, this knowledge didn't make teaching the class any easier. But I did realize how lucky I was to have students in my college classes who, most of the time, were there because they wanted to be. And I came to appreciate the dedication of the vast majority of teachers who don't have this advantage.

During my interviews, it became clear that many traditional conferences are "have-to's" instead of "choose-to's." When people attend conferences to fulfill continuing education requirements or because the boss said so, all other things being equal, the conference atmosphere suffers, just as my class environment suffered when students had to attend. One of the reasons that peer conferences work well is that, with few exceptions, *attendees have chosen to be there*. And that can make a big difference.

schedule helps you figure out what proportion of the conference program is likely to be of interest. (Provided that the conference program doesn't mislead, which, as we've seen, is not uncommon.)

But behind this thinking hides a big assumption. To see it, let's first go over how a traditional conference program is developed. Usually, a program committee, representing (hopefully) the conference constituency, convenes long before the conference and decides on the conference structure and content. Formal academic conference program committees often issue a call for papers, with the conference content and presenters determined through who responds with what content, filtered through some kind of review process. Other program committees may decide on a list of hot topics and then go after big names who can present on them. Slowly a raft of sessions is assembled and scheduled, gaps filled, and the conference program takes shape.

Predicting what attendees want—and getting it wrong

For the last 15 years, I've been in a unique position to determine just how well the above process predicts and serves up the content that attendees want. Because what happens at a peer conference accurately reflects the participants' needs and wants, it has been possible for me to compare the pre-conference program predictions of the conference organizers with the actual programs that were developed by attendees.

The results of this comparison are sobering. Although, as you'd expect, some conference committees are better predictors than others, when I've compared program committee forecasts of hot topics with those that attendees actually chose, *I've found that even the best program committees predict less than half of the session topics chosen at the conference.*

This dismal showing may surprise you. I suspect that the majority of conference organizers will be dismayed by this finding, and will question its accuracy. After all, many traditional conferences receive highly favorable attendee evaluations—how can favorable reviews be reconciled with such a poor match between content offered and content desired?

One reason is that seasoned attendees' expectations for a conventional conference are, sadly, not very high. If they have never experienced getting more than half their concerns addressed, attendees will set the bar at that level, and define as successful a conference that meets this standard.

However, there are several other important reasons why peer conferences are so much more successful than program committees at generating the best conference topics.

Uncovering the unexpected

At every peer conference I've facilitated, attendees suggest unexpectedly popular topics during the conference roundtable that is the first step of the peer conference process. These are topics that were off just about everyone's radar, including the steering committee's. Usually these topics arise from expertise casually shared by an attendee, who often has no idea that others would be interested in her experience and want to discuss it further. I have seen these topics turn into informal presentations or panels attended by half or more of the attendees.

Although program committees sometimes make well-meaning attempts to poll attendees about potentially appealing topics to incorporate into a traditional program, I've found in practice that few attendees expend the time and energy to suggest subjects they'd like to see covered at an upcoming conference. Even if a popular topic is uncovered in advance, it may not be recognized as such by the program committee.

Timeliness

Conference programs developed in advance suffer from the curse of already being obsolete. Typically a multiday conference program will be fixed six months or more in advance. In some fields, a lot can happen in six months. I'm reminded of a conference-planning meeting held when legislation that affected our conference's target audience had just been passed. Everyone felt it was very important that we invite a legal expert to keynote the consequences for our attendees' organizations, so we found a suitable speaker and publicized our program. But by the time the conference was held, eight months later, a host of articles in related trade journals had thoroughly covered the issue, and our keynote covered what had now become familiar ground.

What can you do to ensure that fixed program topics are still relevant by the time your conference rolls around? Not much. I've noticed that sessions on structural issues, like the consequences of legal and accounting rule changes, are more likely to become dated than sessions that cover new approaches or research. But I've had little success over the years in predicting which topics will still be fresh and exciting when the presenter steps up on the stage.

A long lead time between the publication of a conference program and the conference itself also impacts presenters, who are required to turn in session descriptions and handouts months in advance without knowing yet either what their presentation will entail or what might prove pertinent in the intervening months.

Do conferences need to have keynotes?

It's sad that so many conference organizers think that a keynote is an essential part of a conference; that if there is no keynote then the conference is incomplete in some way. This is why keynotes are often unnaturally grafted onto a conference, creating a kind of Frankenstein mutant that roars around with great sound and fury, but is forgotten by all quickly soon after the conference is over.

I think that a conference keynote is appropriate when you can snag a dynamic, engaging, and knowledgeable speaker on a relevant topic that a clear majority of your attendees will find interesting. In my experience, if you start from the premise that you *must* have a keynote, there is a real danger of ending up with a speaker who does not fulfill these criteria.

Finally, if you engage a keynote speaker, have a backup plan. Recently, some conference organizers with whom I was working had a traditional conference keynote speaker cancel just one week before the event, because she was invited to the White House on the day she was scheduled to speak. The ensuing last-minute effort to find a substitute significantly increased the organizers' pre-conference stress.

Hot topics—that aren't

Besides worrying about scheduling topics that have passed their sell-by date by the time the conference is held, you also need to worry about choosing topics that, while seemingly "hot," draw little attendee interest come the day of the presentation. How can this happen? Well, sometimes a topic talked up as the "next big thing" just isn't—it's hype that attendees largely reject, either before the conference or when they get there and discover, outside the formal sessions, that no one else is really interested either.

Topics can also misfire at a conference when they're *too far ahead* of audience needs or interests. For example, this can happen at information technology conferences when new operating systems or software applications are first introduced. Sometimes these products are available well before attendees are interested in or able to purchase or roll out the software for their companies. The lead time required to put a program together further complicates the decision whether to feature such topics at a conference. While an experienced and knowledgeable program committee will help reduce this kind of audience-subject mismatch, it's nearly impossible to prevent entirely.

The case for predetermined content

Predetermined conference content has its place, and there are several situations in which it's entirely appropriate. For example, marketing of a conventional conference often is anchored around one or more big-name presenters. Their presentations, which are often complex multimedia affairs, require plenty of time to prepare—they can't be created on demand at a conference. Speakers with a proven reputation for visionary, dynamic keynotes are usually able to provide a relevant, up-to-the-minute, topical presentation, despite the delay between the time they were booked and the time they speak.

Similarly, conference sessions that provide a well-presented, comprehensive overview of a topic can be very valuable to attendees. Such sessions also need careful preparation, and must be solicited and scheduled in advance.

Some professional and amateur groups would not think of holding a conference where the acknowledged leaders in the field or topic were not given pride of place in the conference program. (Politics is one area that comes to mind; you can probably think of others.) A conference that lacked a program defined in advance is obviously not the best choice here.

Sometimes conferences are organized by a group with a strong agenda of conference activities and outcomes. Political and social activism conferences are obvious examples. In addition, company conferences are often tightly controlled affairs, focused on firing up a sales team or bringing employees up to speed on management's upcoming agenda. Events with such pre-planned, action-oriented goals require predetermined content.

Finally, conferences that are clearly marketed as trainings obviously need to provide a comprehensive description of the material to be covered in advance.

However, the fact that so much traditional conference time is taken up with content that is a poor fit to attendee desires is a depressing reality that program committees need to bear in mind. It's my hope that the approach to conference design described in this book will lessen our reliance on predetermined content, and encourage us to create conferences that are designed to respond to actual attendee needs rather than our best guesses as to what they might be.

The new kid on the block: making connections at a traditional conference

Just about everyone who's attended a conference has at one time or another walked into a room full of strangers. Unless you're an extreme extrovert, this can be a daunting experience. Think for a moment about how you like to meet new people. It's easier if you have some kind of opening to start up a conversation. The more people in the room you know, the more

Together, yet alone

In October 1984 I was one of 700 attendees at EDUCOM '84, a conference on information technology in higher education. I had recently started to teach computer science at Marlboro College, a tiny New England liberal arts college, and was looking for professional support and ideas.

Unfortunately, EDUCOM '84 turned out to be a depressing experience for me. The conference sessions focused on the needs of large institutions. Hundreds of people sat around me as we listened to talks on subjects that left me cold, or solutions requiring equipment and staff that I couldn't begin to afford. And there was a strong whiff of "look at all the cool stuff we're doing, bet you can't match this" that I didn't like.

I was sure that there were other attendees like me at EDUCOM '84. But how was I to find them? I tried talking to the people I sat next to at mealtimes. I struck up conversations with my seatmates as we were shuttled to campus tours and off-site demos. I scanned the directory of attendees for people from small schools like mine, and then scanned name badges, hoping to spot them. But I didn't meet a single kindred soul during the entire four-day conference.

Do I blame the folks at EDUCOM for my miserable experience? No. They organized a traditional conference that may have served many attendees well. However, it certainly didn't work for me.

But one good thing came out of my time at EDUCOM '84. I began to wonder whether I could create a conference that better met what I felt attendees needed. I wanted a conference that was responsive to the needs of attendees, encouraged positive attendee interactions, and fostered a spirit of community among those who came.

possibilities exist for you to meet others through your acquaintances' existing connections. When you know no one, you're completely cut off from the connections that already exist in the room.

It's even worse when no one in the room knows anyone else. Everyone then needs to build his or her connections from scratch.

A traditional conference lacks formal opportunities, opportunities that are part of the conference process, for these kinds of introductions to occur. It's hard to go up to a complete stranger and start talking to him. And, with many potential people to talk to, and not enough time to talk to them all, how do we pick whom we'll approach?

Because making connections at traditional conferences can be so inefficient, it's common for people to spend significant time preparing for upcoming potential conference interactions. As the quote at the start of this section recommends, people research in advance other attendees they want to meet, looking for the commonalities that they can use to engineer an introduction and subsequent conversation. Seasoned conference-goers advise new attendees to perfect their "elevator pitch," a 30-second introduction to their work and selves, so that when that all-important person is within range, they are ready to make their best attempt to create a connection.

This is all very well if you enjoy this kind of competitive behavior. In my experience, most attendees don't. Consequently, people make new connections at a traditional conference largely via the combination of chance and a slow increase in familiarity with other attendees. This is a pretty inefficient process.

Sadly, most of my interviewees seemed resigned to the session-centric format of conventional conferences. Although all indicated, one way or another, that making new, significant connections was important, expectations that this would happen were low. People saw making valuable connections as a relatively rare bonus, rather than expecting it as a matter of course.

So how can you find out about people at a conference? How can you discover attendees' backgrounds, interests, and personalities that provide points of connection for you? And how can you bring to light others' experiences that are valuable to you if shared? Read on, and you'll discover how peer conferences actively support all of these attendee needs!

Beginnings and endings

We have come to expect that stories we read will have well-crafted beginnings and endings. If the beginning is poor, we probably won't continue, and if the ending is unsatisfactory we feel profoundly let down. Given that attending conferences may require as much commitment of time and attention as reading a story, why do we accept token beginnings and endings at these events?

Beginnings

At a minimum, the welcome at a conference should cover the formalities of introducing one or more of the conference organizers or hosts, and sharing necessary logistical information

> "The reader is by no means obliged to read any story—is seduced, so to speak, into doing so; and, unless he can sense an entertaining half-hour within the first two or three paragraphs, then it is all over with the author . . .
> . . . the story ending should have just as critical and painstaking preparation as the introduction or the climax."
>
> —*Elinor Glyn. Beginning and Ending Your Story*

with attendees. Ideally, a welcome should also foster a comfortable atmosphere that reassures people that practical, conference-related needs can and will be taken care of. Once these items are out of the way, a traditional conference starts and sessions begin.

> "Once upon a time . . .
> . . . and they all lived happily ever after."
>
> —*Start and end of innumerable fairy tales*

Unfortunately, such a beginning does nothing to support forming connections among attendees. Consequently, people go to sessions not knowing other attendees, unless they knew them previously. Initially participants are isolated, at best slowly building a network of connections as the conference proceeds, but missing out on the benefits of finding simpatico peers early on.

It doesn't have to be this way. Later, we'll see how peer conferences use an initial *roundtable* to facilitate attendee connections in ways that minimize attendee isolation.

Endings

There will always be logistical reasons—like planes to catch, families to feed, or traffic to avoid—for people leaving events before their formal conclusion. However, a surprising finding from my interviews was the extent to which people either left or wanted to leave a traditional conference before it was over—not for practical reasons but because they had come to the conclusion that it wasn't worth their while to stay. Though personality certainly played a part in the variability of interviewees' responses—several people said that they were incapable of leaving before the end due to the way they had been brought up—the median answer to the interview question *"What is the percentage of the conferences you've attended where you either left before the end (for other than practical reasons) or wished you had?"* was 25 percent!

> "I usually leave when they have that canned stuff at the end."
>
> —*Interviewee*

Perhaps this high level of premature abandonment is not so surprising. First, traditional conferences are disjointed events; unless they are trainings or workshops, sessions tend to lurch from one topic to another with little coherence or progression. As a result, participants tend to decide whether to go to a session based purely on their interest in its subject, rather than considering its contribution to their experience of the conference as a whole. If they decide that the last session holds little interest, they may decide (or wish) to leave early. Second, a majority of my interviewees reported that the subject matter and/or perspective of traditional conferences are frequently misrepresented in conference marketing. This commonly leads to attendees chafing to abandon conferences that they belatedly find not meeting their expectations and needs.

Professional conference planners worry about keeping attendees until the end, and usually suggest scheduling some kind of climactic event to tempt people to stay. When the formal sessions of a conference fail to create an environment where people want to stay to the end, such manufactured closing events can be effective, but that they're used so often is a sad commentary on the level of event commitment generated by traditional conferences.

Read on to learn how peer conferences, by building an environment in which attendees actively participate, create a conference experience so compelling that attendees stay to the end because they don't want to miss a minute!

Passivity

As the home-schooling proponent John Holt pointed out, learning is not a passive process. And yet, the principal advertised activity at conventional conferences is largely passive—namely, sitting and listening to one or more speakers for the majority of each conference session. Even if we put aside attendees' needs for connection at conferences and concentrate on thinking of conferences as an event for learning, a traditional conference assumes this nonparticipative knowledge acquisition model.

> "The most important thing any teacher has to learn, not to be learned in any school of education I ever heard of, can be expressed in seven words: *Learning is not the product of teaching.* Learning is the product of the activity of learners."
>
> —*John Holt. Growing Without Schooling Magazine, No. 40, 1984*

Think about how you learned vocabulary as a child. It was primarily through active immersion in an environment where language was used (typically tens of thousands of words), rather than through vocabulary enrichment lessons at school (typically a few hundred words). In this case, active, interactive learning was far more effective than passive reception of a teacher's lessons. Like learning a living language, social knowledge acquisition requires active interaction with others, not passive reception of information.

> "Recent investigations of learning, however, challenge this separating of what is learned from how it is learned and used. The activity in which knowledge is developed and deployed, it is now argued, is not separable from or ancillary to learning and cognition. Nor is it neutral. Rather, it is an integral part of what is learned."
>
> —*John Seely Brown, Allan Collins, and Paul Duguid. Situated Cognition and the Culture of Learning. Educational Researcher, Vol. 18, No. 1, 1989*

Nothing is required from an attendee at a traditional conference beyond payment of the conference entrance fee. Even conferences created to maintain professional certification rarely require more from attendees than their physical presence. Conventional conference sessions, by tacitly endorsing passivity, drain energy from people who attend conferences with a desire for connection and social learning. We can't force anyone to actively engage at a conference, but I believe that it's possible to provide a structure that encourages and supports participation, and to offer an environment where active involvement is the norm, rather than something for attendees to attempt unaided outside conference sessions.

Size matters

Try this quick experiment. Think of an interesting short topic you'd like to share with other people.

Now imagine sharing your topic with someone and what that would be like. How might the sharing develop?

Next imagine sharing the same subject with 10 people simultaneously. What would that be like?

Finally, imagine the same sharing, but with 300 people simultaneously. What would that be like?

Notice any differences?

You probably found that changing the number of people involved in this simple thought experiment greatly affected your imagined experience. In all three cases you started the same way—with an audience. But as we all know, with another person or a small group, questions can be asked and conversations entered, conversations that can involve everyone present. In other words, the majority of conversations with another person or a small group are interactive, and any initial audience quickly dissolves into a discussion.

> "As the size of a group increases, the connectedness among members decreases, which can lead to increases in social loafing, bystander apathy, and even deindividuation. Larger groups also promote more conformity, since there are more peers to exert pressure on any individual to conform.
>
> On the other side of the coin, the effects of social facilitation increase with group size, and having more members means that there are more opportunities during group discussions to consider more perspectives and more knowledge. Thus, the real issue is not group size per se, but whether a group is managed well enough that its size is an asset rather than a liability."
>
> —*Linda K. Stroh, Gregory B. Northcraft, and Margaret A. Neale. Organizational Behavior: A Management Challenge. Lawrence Erlbaum Associates, 2001*

In contrast, sharing with a thousand people is, fundamentally, a one-way experience. There simply isn't the possibility of significant two-way interaction when a thousand people are listening to you—at best a few questions can supply interaction with a miniscule percentage of your audience. There is no possibility that your audience and you can have a discussion.

These scale-generated differences are large enough that we have separate words for these forms of communication. With a small group, we have a *conversation*. With a larger group, we call our sharing a *discussion*. And with a thousand people, we talk about a *lecture* or *presentation*.

So, how humans communicate varies radically with the size of the group involved. At a conventional conference, the emphasis is on the presentation sessions, where one or two people speak to many. Unless the conference is small, its sessions will be one-way—any conferring will be relegated to the hallways and social events.

How big is big?

How big is the average conference? It depends, of course, on your definition of "conference," but in 2007, according to *Meetings and Conventions Magazine*, an average of 1,440 people attended "association conventions," while "association meetings" had an average attendance of 146.

I am a confirmed small conference-goer, and my interviewees indicated a clear preference for small conferences too. Although I didn't ask specifically about conference size during my interviews, 35 percent of my interviewees indicated a preference for attending conferences with fewer than around 100 attendees.

As you might expect, interviewees who saw conferences primarily as training opportunities seemed unfazed by attending large conferences, while those who looked for connections with other attendees showed a clear preference for small events.

> "The downside of going for size and scale above all else is that the dense, interconnected pattern that drives group conversation and collaboration isn't supportable at any large scale. Less is different—small groups of people can engage in kinds of interaction that large groups can't. . . . You have to find a way to spare the group from scale. Scale alone kills conversations, because conversations require dense two-way conversations. . . . The fact that the amount of two-way connections you have to support goes up with the square of the users means that the density of conversation falls off very fast as the system scales even a little bit."
>
> —*Clay Shirky. A Group Is Its Own Worst Enemy. Speech at O'Reilly Emerging Technology Conference, April, 2003*

What's good about big?

What are the benefits of a big conference? Here are a few.

Big conferences can attract big-name presenters, people you wouldn't otherwise get to see.

Big conferences can include sessions on a wide range of topics, covering anything you might be interested in.

Big conferences, if you already know many of the attendees, give you the opportunity to get together with lots of colleagues or friends at one event.

Big conferences can conjure up big trade shows—all the exhibitors you might want to visit will be in one place.

The crucial question is whether these advantages compensate for the drawbacks of large conferences: the increased difficulty in making meaningful connections, the prevalence of one-to-many sessions with limited opportunities for interaction, and the de-emphasis on developing and transmitting social knowledge. If these deficits become increasingly important to attendees, we can perhaps expect a move toward smaller conferences in the future.

Meeting interesting people at conferences

When I attend a traditional conference, I'm fretting about who I'm missing. No, not my family at home; I'm fretting about missing meeting conference attendees who would be interesting for me to meet, who I'd love to get to know *if only I could figure out who they were*. Even if I can figure out who would be interesting to meet, I then have to find a time and place to meet them, and I also have to come up with a way to introduce myself.

Each of these concerns—who interests me, when can I meet them, where can I meet them, and how do I introduce myself—are obstacles to connecting with interesting people at a conference. Unfortunately, as the size of a conference increases, our ability to meet more people doesn't improve proportionately. As a result, trying to find new people who share specific interests at a large general conference is a daunting task.

Saving graces

Over time, many organizers have become aware of the limitations and frustrations of the traditional conference format, and have, to their credit, attempted to add ways for attendees to propose sessions and interact outside standard predetermined conference sessions. Three common formats are poster sessions, birds-of-a-feather sessions, and facilitated small group discussions. Although these approaches often appear to be uneasily grafted onto the conference, they are worth discussing for two reasons: First, they demonstrate the desire of participants for more control over their conference experience, and second, they show the limitations of attempting to provide what attendees want while clinging to traditional conference process. I've also added a description of the Gordon Research Conferences, which are designed to minimize some of the difficulties posed by the conventional conference format.

Poster sessions

Poster sessions originated at academic conferences as an opportunity for individual attendees to present their research to other attendees. Presenters stand next to a poster summarizing their work and present to any interested attendees. Nowadays, poster sessions are frequently used informally to display general information and invite viewers to ask more detailed questions of the person who created the poster. Because posters are prepared before the conference, poster sessions provide a somewhat makeshift method of broadening available content, following the usual teacher-to-student(s) model. Control over content can range from requiring preapproval for each session to an "anything goes" philosophy. The sessions are often held during meal breaks, though they sometimes merit their own conference time slot.

Adding a poster session to a conference program is a tacit acknowledgment that attendees possess potentially useful expertise and experience not available through the traditional conference sessions. A poster session offers participants a genuine opportunity to contribute, reducing the customary distinction between presenters and audience. Because the session supplies an intimate, usually one-to-one, interactive format, it provides useful feedback to the poster presenters: Are conference-goers interested in what I have to say, and, if so, what do they think about it? At a large conference, poster sessions may be the most practical method to expand the available content beyond the fixed program.

Unfortunately, poster sessions are a fairly crude way to democratize and extend a conference. They require would-be presenters to create session materials and dedicate conference time to standing by their display with no guarantee of interaction with other attendees. It can be disconcerting to make this commitment and receive limited attention. Even when like-minded souls appear, they may well arrive at different times, offering little opportunity for a group discussion on the topic. Given these limitations, it's not surprising that poster sessions have a reputation as second-class presentation opportunities for lower status attendees.

Birds-of-a-feather sessions

Birds-of-a-feather sessions, commonly known as BOFs, offer attendees an opportunity to create their own session on a topic of their choosing. Typically, the conference organizers supply a

Gordon Research Conferences

The Gordon Research Conferences (GRC) started in 1931 as a way to "bring together a group of scientists working at the frontier of research of a particular area and permit them to discuss in depth all aspects of the most recent advances in the field and to stimulate new directions for research." Currently the organization holds 150–200 conferences annually. The GRC model has several attractive aspects that minimize some of the unwelcome effects of traditional conference process that I've described in this chapter:

- Conferences are small (generally fewer than a hundred participants).
- Attendees are expected to participate actively and meaningfully in discussions.
- All information presented and discussed at the conference is considered private.
- Presentations are held in the mornings and evenings, with afternoons available for informal discussions.
- Presentations are short (15–20 minutes) with time scheduled for discussion, and discussant leaders provided.
- Invited speakers are encouraged to stay for discussions after their presentation. (They don't receive expense reimbursement unless they stay for at least 24 hours after their talk!)

These features promote active involvement by attendees, confidentiality (through the privacy requirement), and the flattening of hierarchy (by keeping speakers around and offering plenty of time for informal discussions).

Peer conferences, by contrast, provide a more flexible conference format, and are less narrowly focused and more tolerant of a wide range of attendee experience. Nevertheless, the GRC conferences, now in existence for over 75 years, provide an excellent strategy to address weaknesses of conventional conference process.

time or place for attendees to announce or post discussion subjects. The resulting sessions are usually scheduled during meals or evening free time.

BOFs are valuable additions to traditional conferences. Because they normally use a discussion format, they provide relevant, small group, interactive experiences. BOFs allow people to find and informally connect with others who share their interests, broadening their circle of conference acquaintances in the process.

Although BOFs appear to offer a conference format that is responsive to real-time attendee needs, like poster sessions they sometimes provide an inferior and frequently frustrating experience. Crucially, apart from providing a way for BOFs to self-announce, they are not otherwise supported by conference staff. As a result, it's hard to know how well attended a proposed BOF will be. Sign-up sheets are a useful but not reliable indicator of popularity.

More than once I've had to decide between attending an evening BOF or going out to dinner with a group of friends, chosen the BOF, and waited around only to have one other person turn up. Another consequence of keeping BOFs outside the traditional conference support structure is that any facilitation is strictly *ad hoc*. This can lead to BOFs being hijacked by a minority of vocal extroverts who may take over or steer the discussion in ways that a majority present don't want.

As we'll see later in Chapter 7, *the peer conference process optimizes the BOF experience*, providing time, space, and support for relevant, interactive conference sessions.

Small group discussions

My interviewees often cited the inclusion of small group discussions, usually called *discussant* or *breakout sessions*, as the saving grace or highlight of traditional conferences. It's clear that many participants hunger for small, focused group discussions of pertinent topics, and it's sad that most traditional conferences don't set aside time for such sessions. Small group discussions, usually run by a panel of experts or conference speakers, are *interactive* sessions where the central goal is to promote and support discussion between attendees. These sessions may be tightly focused around a set of papers or presentations, or loosely structured around one or more introductory themes.

For small group discussions to be successful, they must be well facilitated, and the topics and questions must excite and be pertinent to the people present. When these conditions occur, small group discussions are like peer sessions, the core of a peer conference. But when a small group discussion's predetermined topic or focus does not match attendees' needs, the resulting session disappoints. As we'll see, a peer conference avoids this outcome by generating the best topics to spark attendee interest and involvement.

Reengineering
the Conference

Why is reengineering a traditional conference hard?

Frankly, I find spreading the word about peer conferences to be a somewhat frustrating experience. That's one of the reasons I wrote this book! Despite hundreds of one-on-one conversations on this topic, I continue to need a significant amount of time—sometimes 10 minutes or more—to successfully convey the essence of the event and how a peer conference might work for the person I'm talking to. I've still not found a convincing 30-second "elevator pitch" for peer conferences, and each conversation brings up its own set of questions and concerns.

> "Things are the way they are because they got that way."
>
> —*Quip attributed to Kenneth Boulding*

Why is conveying the essence of a nontraditional conference so difficult? My work for over 20 years as an independent information technology consultant provides a clue. I occasionally encountered intermittent system failures that led to hours, sometimes days, of puzzled head scratching. Troubleshooting technical problems basically consists of cycles of brainstorming possible reasons and repeated testing: changing one thing at a time and trying to find the conditions that make the system fail. Invariably, the toughest problems to solve were those that had more than one underlying cause, where the system wouldn't fail until exactly the right combination of multiple changes was made for the test.

Reengineering a traditional conference is hard for a similar reason: Attendees need to make more than one significant change to their thinking about conferences in order to get to a model that makes sense. It's as if there is a complicated barrier between traditional and alternative approaches, a barrier consisting of multiple obstacles, all of which must be successfully jumped to arrive at a workable alternative. Getting people to make a single change in how they think about conferences is a challenge. Asking them to make multiple simultaneous changes to their perspective and expectations is a real stretch.

Here are some of the barriers that stand in the way of wide acceptance of nontraditional conference models:

- Acceptance of reframing a conference as an active event, where the expectation is that people can and will share their experience and expertise that is needed by others.
- Skepticism that it's possible to quickly and accurately determine what attendees really want to learn or talk about.
- Uncertainty whether the attendees as a group have the relevant expertise and experience that individual attendees want to tap.
- Reluctance to award Continuing Education Credits for a conference program that has not been specified and approved in advance.
- Concern that those with relevant expertise and experience will not be able to effectively share their knowledge without coming to the conference with a prepared presentation.
- Difficulty justifying to one's employer to pay for a conference with no pre-planned program.

I'm convinced that nontraditional conference formats, especially the peer conference model, offer some major advantages and improvements over traditional conferences. In this chapter, we'll investigate the factors that restrict traditional conference effectiveness, and we'll begin to see how the peer conference approach transcends these limits.

The program trap

Remember that 45 percent of my interviewees agreed with the first assumption of a traditional conference, "Conference session topics must be chosen and scheduled in advance"?

When both potential attendees and conference organizers believe this, everyone gets stuck in the *program trap*.

If potential attendees believe they need a detailed predetermined conference program and schedule in order to decide whether they will attend, then they will only attend pre-planned conferences. If conference organizers believe that people will only attend conferences with a predetermined program, they will only organize pre-planned conferences.

These two beliefs reinforce each other, making it difficult to successfully market an alternative. Both beliefs need to be challenged simultaneously in order to hold a successful non-traditional conference.

Because most people have never experienced an attendee-driven conference, it's hard for them to imagine or understand how such an approach could work. Usually, people imagine the generation of attendee-driven conference sessions as an idealistic, unwieldy, and interminable process of obtaining consensus among all conference participants. When I explain how they can not only learn about other attendees but also determine and schedule a conference program that truly reflects participants' needs within the first two hours of a peer conference, their skepticism evaporates and they become excited.

Who's in charge?

Every conference needs logistics leadership. The conference must have a location and a time frame. It must be adequately publicized and financially viable. Appropriate meals and lodging must be provided, together with all the other items and services needed when a group of people come together to meet for some period of time. Logistical needs are common to every group event, and how they are addressed doesn't vary significantly between conference formats.

When we consider the *process needs* of a conference, however, the leadership models used for traditional and untraditional conferences are quite different.

At a conventional conference, a clear group of leaders is defined and publicized up front, in advance. The conference organizers are leaders who define the conference structure, determine content and choose additional leaders, session presenters who will deliver the content. Other conferees merely need to show up; their power is limited to choosing which sessions they attend.

> "Just as our culture is moving from the printed book to the computer, it is also in the final stages of the transition from a hierarchical social order to what we might call a 'network culture.'"
>
> —*Jay David Boulter. Writing Space: The Computer, Hypertext, and the History of Writing. Lawrence Erlbaum Associates, 1991*

Conventional conference structure is an example of top-down organization. The power to define the event's structure, content, and content providers resides in the hands of the conference organizers. These are the people who are clearly in charge. They must be trusted to provide a conference that is worthwhile for attendees.

Top-down power offers multiple benefits to the organizers. Because attendees have little input into the traditional conference planning process, it's clear that the organizers are doing the work needed to pull off the event, making it uncontroversial that they get paid, often handsomely. Because the organizers define the rules for the conference planning process, they control how the event is developed, and can easily shut out rival perspectives on content or presenters. Finally, because the organizers have clear control of what happens at the conference, they obtain status and influence in the field of the conference topic.

In contrast, at a nontraditional conference, the organizers' role is restricted to designing, communicating, and supporting a conference framework that provides openings and encouragement for any participant to be a leader. At such a conference, attendees are given a process to choose session topics, together with appropriate leaders (who may not even be content experts if the session merely requires facilitation). Leadership here has two distinct components: (1) facilitation of conference process and (2) as-needed contributions to the creation and implementation of attendee-chosen sessions.

> "I'm still keen on the untapped potential of emergent bottom-up systems. But . . . the bottom is not enough . . . to get to the best we need some top down intelligence, too. . . . The systems we keep will be hybrid creations. They will have a strong rootstock of peer-to-peer generation, grafted below highly refined strains of controlling functions. Sturdy, robust foundations of user-made content and crowd-sourced innovation will feed very small slivers of leadership agility."
>
> —*Kevin Kelly. The Bottom is Not Enough. The Technium*

In an attendee-centered conference, power devolves to the attendees. Rather than being the source of power, conference organizers are supporters, facilitators, and servants of participants. The philosophy of attendee-centered conferences is that attendees themselves, given just the right amount of structure and support, can be trusted to create an event that works for the individuals involved.

Nontraditional conferences use a mixture of bottom-up and top-down organization. The attendees themselves determine most of what happens at the conference; relevant content and how it is shared emerges bottom-up from the offerings and choices of the entire body of people present. Any facilitation of this process is top-down. Some formats include one or more additional top-down closing sessions that give attendees the opportunity to integrate and reflect on their conference experience. The function of top-down organization at a nontraditional conference, then, is to provide a minimal but sufficient structure that enables attendees to effectively determine what they want to do, do it, and, perhaps, reflect on their experience.

At their core, traditional and nontraditional conference organizing philosophies are diametrically opposed. Traditional conferences adhere to a top-down process model, with control firmly in the hands of the conference organizers. Nontraditional conferences are driven from the bottom-up desire that every attendee contributes to what happens, creating an experience that is meaningful and useful, for individual participants, for the group, or for both. As with Kevin Kelly's quote about achieving a balance between top-down and bottom-up strategies, nontraditional conferences add just enough top-down process to support the fundamental drive for bottom-up.

Ultimately, the kind of value that attendees expect to derive from their conference experience should determine the appropriate power structure. If the conference is framed as a training—"by the end of this conference you will know how to do X, Y, and Z"—then power should reside in the session presenters. However, if the conference goals are exploration and understanding of an issue or idea, effective networking, and the acquisition of social knowledge, attendees must be given the power to shape the conference in a way that works for their desires and needs of the moment.

How many attendees?

Most professional conference planners want to be responsible for large conferences—the bigger the conference the more lucrative and the greater the resulting professional status. Traditional conference organizers have a vested interest, therefore, in creating the biggest conference possible, a motivation that is not necessarily aligned with the best interests of attendees.

If, instead, we focus on attendees' best interests and are planning an attendee-driven conference, a question then arises: How big should it be? We've seen that competing size-sensitive factors drive participant interactions. As the number of attendees increases, potential group knowledge and perspectives increase, but interactivity between participants decreases. If we are looking for the maximum amount of useful interactivity, then, ideally, we'll want to have just enough attendees to provide a useful amount of group expertise and experience.

Obviously, there isn't a single optimal size for all attendee-driven conferences. All other things being equal, a conference of relative novices would need to be larger than a gathering of

> "This all leads me to hypothesize that the optimal size for active group members for creative and technical groups—as opposed to exclusively survival-oriented groups, such as villages—hovers somewhere between 25–80, but is best around 45–50. Anything more than this and the group has to spend too much time 'grooming' to keep group cohesion, rather then focusing on why the people want to spend the effort on that group in the first place . . ."
>
> —Christopher Allen. The Dunbar Number as a
>   Limit to Group Sizes.

experts, while a topic that attracts participants with varied experience can get away with a smaller attendance than one where conferees come from similar backgrounds.

So, perhaps the best we can do is to come up with a workable range of attendee-driven conference sizes. I think it's significant that, without prompting, 35 percent of my interviewees said that they preferred small conferences, and when I asked them what they meant by small, they invariably gave me the figure of under a hundred attendees. This response is consistent with the thoughtful musings of social software consultant Christopher Allen, quoted above, and with my own experience. As far as the latter is concerned, I've been surprised and pleased by how well a flexible conference format adjusts to the people present, whether there are 20 or 80. And so have the attendees.

Satisfying the desire for connection with others

How can we best satisfy the desire for connecting with others during a conference?

The answer in principle is simple: rather than consign networking to an afterthought, something that happens outside the formal conference sessions, we need to move it to center stage—not as a replacement for sharing of content but as an essential, supportive tool for effective learning. And this needs to happen formally at the start of the conference, as an integral part of the format, so that the knowledge and relationships gained can be built on fruitfully throughout the event.

What this means in practice is the addition, right after the opening welcome and housekeeping, of a new kind of session. This kickoff session first sets up a conference environment where sharing is acceptable and safe, and then provides time for participants to introduce themselves while simultaneously exposing topics and themes that people want to explore and expertise that others can draw upon. Such a session, the *roundtable,* is held at every peer conference, where it sets the stage for everything that follows.

Safety

Traditional conferences have no overt ground rules. Attendees don't get together at the start and agree on guidelines. I think that this is an unfortunate oversight, but luckily, one that is easily remedied.

Crucially, a conventional conference offers no expectation of or agreement to privacy for anything that is said. As a result, only the most confident or highest status attendee is likely to be comfortable revealing a lack of knowledge in some area, sharing a problem that he has, or asking a "stupid" question. Without a public group commitment to confidentiality, participants fear that what they say at the conference may make its way to their superiors or colleagues in their organization. This leads people to censor themselves on many topics.

I have been amazed at what occurs at a conference when attendees agree to keep confidential what is shared. Giving people permission, encouragement, and a safe environment in which to express themselves and take risks makes a huge difference. It becomes easy and natural to ask important questions, reveal oneself, and be vulnerable, exploring beyond one's habitual boundaries. Many participants find that taking risks can be rewarding, less scary than they'd imagined, and even fun.

Opening to possibilities

Unfortunately, a prepared conference agenda normally eliminates, or at best reduces, the likelihood of unexpected, impromptu sessions—of "messiness." Most people don't possess the necessary mixture of on-the-spot chutzpah and charisma to successfully modify a conference program that has been carefully prepared and scheduled. Unless a conference reserves specific time blocks for attendee-nominated sessions and provides a workable mechanism for attendees to propose and choose topics, the event is very unlikely to depart significantly from its pre-planned course.

> ". . . messiness isn't a flaw. It's a strength."
>
> —*David Weinberger.*
> *Everything Is Miscellaneous.*
> *Times Books, 2007*

Remember that I've found that half or more of attendee-desired conference topics are missed with a pre-planned conference schedule. Not only fruitful session topics but also optimum session modalities, such as tours, discussion groups, or impromptu workshops, get overlooked.

Giving attendees the power and responsibility to drive what happens within a truly supportive, safe, and confidential process creates an environment so different from a pre-planned event that it has to be experienced to be fully appreciated. Treating conference participants as adults, able to ask for what they want and to offer their own wisdom and curiosity, frees people to be creative and take risks. In the process, the event expands to encompass the full range of possibilities asked for and offered by participants.

De-emphasizing status

At any conference, participants come with varying degrees of expertise in and experience of the conference topic. A conventional conference makes distinctions between attendees based on pre-conference decisions about who has useful expertise and experience to convey. In contrast, a peer conference does not prejudge attendee knowledge and potential contributions, and does not even attempt to decide in advance what subjects should be covered.

Naturally, people have different levels of experience, expertise, and ability to communicate. But when these characteristics are not prejudged, where a person's overt status—presenter or audience member—is not predetermined by a small group and frozen into a static conference structure, we have the freedom to create an environment where relevant expertise, experience, and ability to communicate can be chosen by attendees in a way that optimizes value for each person present.

There is another way in which de-emphasizing status at the start of a conference can be helpful. When attendees are not intimidated by the perceived or proclaimed higher status of others, they are more likely to share their genuine wants, rather than self-censoring for fear of appearing ignorant. They are also more likely to let others know about their own expertise and experience, which frequently turns out to be of significant interest to their peers.

Reducing the consequences of perceived or proclaimed conference status leads to a flattening of the conference hierarchy, supporting a conference environment where relevant contributions are more important than the external status of the contributors. When conference hierarchy is flattened, the roles in any interaction become more fluid, allowing conferring attendees to switch more easily, moment to moment, between learning and teaching, which in turn enhances the level of valuable two-way communication at the event.

Increasing transparency

At a conventional conference, the conference planners are the only people who know how the form and content of the conference was determined. The conference program is presented as a given to attendees, a mysterious construct that cannot be easily questioned or changed.

This lack of transparency imbues a traditional conference with a paternalistic hue—someone somewhere has figured out that this structure and content is good for you and worthy of your time and energy. Paternalism leads to passivity—just sit back and listen to the experts. "If you should have any questions, or something to contribute, don't worry, we've left a few minutes at the end of each session for you to stick your hand up and, possibly, be heard" is typical of the extent of interaction that is provided for between presenters and attendees.

Conversely, when attendees help determine what will happen at their conference and when the procedures used to do this are transparent—open to inspection and participation by all—participants become involved at a deeper level than does a traditional conference audience, leading to increased group engagement and intimacy.

Ensuring timeliness and relevance

A number of years ago I was working with a program committee on a blended peer/traditional education conference—a peer conference with a sprinkling of fixed presentations. As they began conference planning, the program committee noted that concerns were emerging about a new phenomenon engaging the nation's youth—the social networking website MySpace. Questions abounded about the consequences of allowing children access to a place where potentially intimate information could be easily exchanged with other users who could invent identities; how kids could be taught to stay safe in cyberspace; what kind of security precautions the site offered; and so on.

The subject seemed to offer plenty of material for a traditional conference session, so we found educators who were grappling with these issues and scheduled a panel. Fancy color brochures were printed, including the session description, and mailed out to potential attendees.

You've probably guessed what happened. Right after our planning meeting, MySpace fell under heavy media scrutiny; the issues the session was designed to address were extensively debated publicly for months. By the time the conference rolled around, the original issues were common knowledge, and plenty of good advice was available on how parents and schools might respond. We had little choice but to hold the session, and, as we expected, it did not get good ratings.

Although many issues withstand the test of time (at least the time between the dates a conference program topic is chosen and presented), some will not, and it's usually impossible to predict whether a topic will be obsolete or still fresh when the presenter strides to the podium.

A few years later, when Microsoft released its new operating system, Vista, the same program committee discussed whether we should hold a pre-planned session on switching to Vista. It became clear we had no idea whether this would be a popular topic, though we presumed that some attendees would be interested. We decided to leave the choice to the peer conference process. At the conference, to our surprise, no one was interested in discussing the topic. We were glad we had let attendees decide, rather than scheduling a traditional session that no one wanted.

Unfortunately, pre-planned conference sessions that turn out to be of little or no interest to attendees are all too common. A majority of my conference experience interviewees told me that their highest satisfaction conferences were those where most or all sessions were relevant to their particular needs, and how rarely this occurred. In fact, most people seemed to be resigned to attending conferences where significant portions of the scheduled sessions held minimal attraction.

The obvious solution to the problems of timeliness and relevance incurred by the traditional conference model is to reduce or eliminate pre-planned sessions. All alternative conference formats make this change by providing various mechanisms for sessions to be proposed and held at the conference.

Breaking down barriers between attendees

Well before a traditional conference begins, the publication of the conference program confers status on the keynote speakers, presenters, and panelists. By the time the conference starts, attendees have already received the message that there are two classes of people present, those who will speak at the front of the room and everyone else, the listeners and receivers of the first group's knowledge. During the conference, other class distinctions develop in the conference's public arena: the people who ask questions at sessions, or who socialize with presenters outside the conference sessions.

Predetermined conference programs send a message to attendees about their status in the conference community. The message is not explicit; it is fashioned indirectly by the program and the social groupings that emerge during public events, and it subtly affects the range of conference opportunities available to every attendee.

The conference program effectively says: "These are the people who are worth listening to, these are the people that attendees will spend their official conference time with, these people are the conduit to the knowledge for which you have come." The program bestows a familiar role on conference presenters, the role of classroom teacher. Everyone else, unnamed in the conference schedule, becomes the students. There's an analogous role available for attendees who ask lots of questions at sessions or who hang out with presenters; they become the teachers' favorite students—"teachers' pets."

Implied roles have great power. Imagine you're driving down the road and up ahead you see a man you've never laid eyes on before, dressed in the uniform of a police officer. As you approach, he puts up a hand, palm facing you, while the other signals for you to slow down. If you're a law-abiding citizen, you'll stop your car before you reach him. The visual cues of this stranger's uniform and hand motions, coupled with your socially conditioned response to symbols of authority, significantly affect your behavior. In the same way, a conference program's implicit assignment of roles affects attendee behavior.

Once conference roles have been introduced, they tend to be self-reinforcing. Presenters may spend time with each other, boosting each other's status via their mutual association, while attendees congregate with their fellow attendees, discussing sessions from the perspective of a learner rather than a peer. The resulting barrier between the two groups, built by these predetermined roles, is surmounted only by attendees who are confident and extroverted enough to approach a presenter, or by those presenters interested in engaging with attendees outside of their sessions.

Conferences with no specific sessions arranged in advance significantly reduce this barrier. The open space, unconference, and peer conference formats avoid the use of predetermined sessions in slightly different ways. Later we'll see how these different conference designs affect the overall conference environment, but for now let's concentrate on how these formats flatten the conference hierarchy.

The classic open space approach to conference session formation is a free-for-all. (Numerous variants of the original open space approach are in use, all labeled "open space," so your experience may differ.) At the start of the conference, anyone can suggest and schedule session topics. What happens subsequently depends on who shows up. Attendees announce sessions they want, leave sessions that don't meet their needs, and move to sessions that do. The proposed session schedule is displayed in a central area and usually changes during the conference. Attendees vote with their feet in open space, providing a somewhat chaotic session environment that responds to their needs. Since anyone can propose a session and participate however they want, open space abolishes the presenter/audience dichotomy present at a traditional conference.

"Unconferences" often use open space to develop conference sessions. Sometimes they are invitation-only events, where every attendee is expected or required to make a presentation at the conference. This approach gives every attendee a voice, but at the cost of excluding those who have just entered the field, have recently become interested in the conference topic, or are simply not welcome by the people doing the inviting. The conference hierarchy is flattened, compared to that of a conference where anyone can attend, by restricting the conference to experts. It's tempting for people who have significant expertise, experience, or renown to hold conferences that are invitation only, where participants get to mingle with only the people they choose and where they don't have to bother with novices asking them "dumb" questions. There's nothing wrong with this, of course, and such people, because their companionship is valued, find it relatively easy to get together with their expert buddies when they feel the need. In contrast, a peer conference welcomes everyone who has an interest in the conference subject.

A peer conference supplies a more structured process for determining conference sessions, while still eliminating distinctions between presenters and audience. First, a roundtable process exposes individual attendee needs and expertise, providing detailed information on the interest, energy, and resources associated with attendees' desired topics. Then, a process called peer session sign-up provides clear indications of the sessions that people want to attend, resources for facilitation and expertise, and the information needed to optimally schedule sessions. These processes allow peer conferences to match participants' needs seamlessly to available expertise session by session, avoiding predefined roles for attendees.

Publish-then-filter, not filter-then-publish

For most of human history, teaching pedagogy has emphasized a *filter-then-publish* philosophy, in which what is to be taught is first chosen/filtered by the teacher and then transmitted/published to the students. Traditional media still uses this model, with news and opinions filtered by publishers and editors and then printed or broadcast to an audience. Filter-then-publish is a top-down approach to communicating information, in which content flows in one direction, from the filtering publisher to the passive receivers. Similarly, traditional conferences use a filter-then-publish model, where potential conference program topics are chosen by organizers and then published in a conference schedule of events.

Times are changing. The Internet and associated technologies have lowered barriers to publishing. People now have new ways not only to access the ever-increasing amounts of information human society is generating, but also to generate and publish any information they wish. When everyone with an Internet connection can both search for and retrieve information on almost any subject, and create content that's easily accessible by others, is filter-then-publish still an appropriate model for obtaining content?

Writer Clay Shirky thinks otherwise. "Filter-then-publish," he says, "whatever its advantages, rested on a scarcity of media that is a thing of the past. The expansion of social media means that the only working system is *publish-then-filter*." Shirky argues that traditional media is transitioning from an expensive, limited outlet, one-to-many, broadcast model to an inexpensive many-to-many communication model.

Publish-then-filter is not a recent development. A hundred and fifty years ago, the philosopher John Stuart Mill argued in his radical book *On Liberty* that society should "give the freest scope possible to uncustomary things, in order that it may in time appear which of these are fit to be converted into customs." Another example is group decision making, which combines the popular technique of brainstorming, first marketed in the 1930s by advertising manager Alex Osborn, with a process that winnows the ideas produced.

Filter-then-publish is a purely convergent process, where experts or gatekeepers choose what will be taught, published, or occur at an event, by filtering their known or imagined possibilities through their knowledge, beliefs, experience, and expertise. In contrast, publish-then-filter is a two-phase process that first encourages divergent thinking to generate a wide range of ideas, followed by some kind of convergent process (such as voting on high priority items) that whittles down possible choices to a manageable set.

Attendee-driven conferences all embrace a publish-then-filter model, though they realize it in different ways. An unconference might begin with an attendee list of potential topics posted on a pre-conference wiki, an open space event with a parade of attendees announcing sessions they would like to see occur, while peer conferences use a suggestion and sign-up process that implements publish-and-filter using sign-up sheets on walls or tables.

Providing relevant content

Perhaps at this point you're saying to yourself something like this:

> "Yes, all this sounds good in principle, but what is actually going to happen at a peer conference? And, more important, how do I know that what happens is going to be something that's useful and meaningful to *me*? Without a conference program and schedule, without some idea of what's going to take place during the conference, you're asking me to commit my time to an event that may not address my needs. I'm not sure this is going to work for me."

Such concerns are extremely common, and perhaps the hardest obstacle to overcome when convincing people to attend a peer conference. The concept that a group of people with a common interest can come together and rapidly and accurately determine what they actually want to talk about is hard to believe. Until you've experienced it.

Of course, traditional conferences don't offer any guarantees either. As we've seen, dissatisfaction with traditional conferences is high, and a mismatch between desired and received content is one of the most frequently mentioned reasons. (Forty-five percent of my interviewees reported that they had attended conferences where the pre-conference program seriously misrepresented conference content.) Government-sponsored events are major culprits, with conferences being used to inform attendees about changes in policy or to justify actions already taken, rather than to provide a genuine opportunity for discussion among and input from a constituency.

Yes, it's possible that your needs will be out of sync with the needs of the other participants at a peer conference. However, it's very unlikely. In 20 years, I don't remember receiving a single conference evaluation that panned even a majority of the sessions attended.

In other words, provided the conference marketing materials clearly and accurately portray the theme and the interest or professional specialty shared by potential attendees, the odds are very high, *far higher than for a traditional conference*, that peer conference participants will be very happy with the content that is covered.

I find it fascinating how the attendee-determined program for an annual peer conference changes from year to year. For example, I have been facilitating the annual peer conference for edACCESS, an association of information technology staff at small schools and colleges, since 1992. You might expect the conference to encompass mainly technical issues arising in an educational environment. Indeed, for the first few years, conferences were almost entirely devoted to technical topics. And then, for no discernible reason, at the next conference half the program switched to covering "people issues": staffing, management, consulting, and leadership.

Since then, a wide variety of people issues and technical topics have been favored, but what's surprising is not just the scope of the subjects chosen, but their utter unpredictability. Often, unexpected topics suggested during the roundtable have proved popular, while subjects that committee members were sure would be attractive evoked little interest. As a result, the conference steering committee gave up long ago trying to divine the future; now the members trust the process and are totally relaxed with the subjects that the process uncovers.

Comparisons with other nontraditional conference formats

There is general agreement that what defines a nontraditional conference is that what happens at the event is attendee-driven, rather than being largely prescribed by traditional conference organizers. Each variety of unconventional conference builds on this fundamental contrast in its own unique way—here are some differences.

Comparing Open Space events with peer conferences

Open Space is an exhilarating approach to self-organizing conferences, first described by Harrison Owen in his 1997 book *Open Space Technology*. Attendees are given a minimal structure and left pretty much to themselves to figure out what should happen. Anyone can suggest and schedule any topic. Because there is little or no information initially available about the context or content of a session, the Open Space process needs its "Law of Two Feet," which encourages attendees to leave sessions where they are neither learning nor contributing and go somewhere more productive.

Peer conferences provide a more structured approach than Open Space. They use an initial roundtable that allows attendees to get to know each other and that reveals popular topics for the conference's subsequent sessions. In contrast, Open Space, once the process has been explained, starts immediately with attendees proposing and scheduling sessions. Because there is less information available about Open Space sessions, these events can be less efficient with attendees' time than peer conferences, as people have to expend a certain proportion of their time discovering and leaving nonproductive topics and finding the right sessions to attend. Proposing an Open Space session and having no one turn up, or watching everybody leave after a few minutes can be upsetting. As we'll see, peer conferences avoid such situations by scheduling the most popular sessions.

In its original formulation, Open Space was designed to work on group outcomes, for example, helping a corporation work on plans for the future, or resolve a conflict between groups. Over time, Open Space's scope has been generalized to encompass attendee-driven conferences without specific outcome goals. In contrast, peer conferences were designed from the start to concentrate on individual learning, sharing, and growth, while allowing group initiatives to rise naturally out of the peer conference process.

Open Space works well for people who are, at the start, confident and clear about what they want to do with an open format. Extroverts flourish, but introverts often just stay quiet. Peer conferences provide, via a roundtable where everyone speaks, an inclusive, deliberate, and nurturing beginning. In my experience, this leads to a more comfortable and ultimately more useful and meaningful conference for most attendees.

Another bonus provided by a peer conference roundtable is that each attendee publicly discovers when he has experience that others value. These attendees are then empowered to participate actively in the conference. Other conference formats, such as Open Space conferences, have no place to provide this information and resulting opportunity to participants.

The original formulation of Open Space included a closing ceremony, the *Talking Stick Ceremony*, where each attendee has the opportunity to speak to the group. It's not clear how often it's used today—most reports I've seen of Open Space conferences don't mention it. To end a peer conference, I use a "group spective," which can employ a range of approaches, including discussion of initiatives that energize the group. Rather than using a fixed closing session format, I tailor a group spective to the expressed needs of the group.

Comparing unconferences with peer conferences

Wikipedia's definition of unconference is broad enough to encompass every kind of unconventional conference—indeed it's not uncommon to see an event described as an "unconference" that uses Open Space or other conference process models. If the popularity of peer conferences continues to grow, I'm sure it won't be long before we see people being invited to "an unconference that uses the peer conference model."

In practice, unconferences that don't use the unconventional models I've enumerated often tend to assume that attendees will come prepared to offer one or more presentations. (Some unconferences go so far to imply that if you haven't got something to present you shouldn't attend.) This brings up the subject of conference preparation.

At a conventional conference, conference organizers tell you in advance whether you will be presenting or not. If you're presenting, you know to prepare for your presentation.

At an unconventional conference, the scope and quantity of your contribution is unknown in advance. Once you're there, you may find that you have much of value to share; perhaps on topics that you had no idea would be of interest. Under these circumstances, preparation is difficult or impossible.

> "An unconference is a facilitated, participant-driven conference centered around a theme or purpose."
>
> —*Wikipedia*

Many unconferences offer pre-conference wikis or websites where attendees can suggest topics that they think will be of interest. The idea is that attendees can be given a heads up about popular topics, which they can then use to prepare interesting talks or sessions.

Although there's nothing wrong with attempting this kind of pre-conference polling, in my experience, it doesn't work very well. Usually only a smattering of participants respond, and the topics suggested make up a minority of those that attendees want. I've found that participants don't spend much time thinking in advance about what might happen at the conference unless the stakes are high—unless they know they will be presenting and there's something significant riding on how well they perform.

In addition, I have a couple of concerns about the effects of expecting prepared presentations at unconferences. First, there is the risk that extrovert participants will skew the conference sessions toward their interests at the expense of other attendees. Second, it becomes less likely that unknown common interests will be discovered and explored. Without an equivalent to the peer conference roundtable, where everyone has an equal opportunity to share their needs and expertise, it's easy for such topics to be overlooked, or, at best, be given less conference attention than they deserve.

At peer conferences, I try to steer between the conflicting concerns described above. Attendees are encouraged to bring potentially useful materials—existing presentations and associated resources—to the conference, but with no guarantee of whether or how they will be shared.

Comparing community-building conference models with peer conferences

Unconventional conference formats like peer conference, Open Space, and unconference allow participants to completely define session content, while community building approaches, like World Café, Future Search, and Everyday Democracy begin the conference with a set of questions that lead to subsequent dialogue. In my experience, these questions fundamentally shape subsequent events and create boundaries to what will and will not be discussed.

When a conference's defining statement or questions accurately capture the scope of participants' concerns and desires, community-building models offer powerful methods to engage participants in discovering and exploring their interests and priorities. The pertinence and quality of the seed questions, then, is of paramount importance, and conference organizers must devote sufficient time and care in crafting them. If they do not, the conference may start off in a direction that doesn't match participants' expectations, at best wasting time while realigning with actual needs, or, at worst, permanently weakening future community involvement.

Another concern with community-building models arises from a potential lack of flexibility around the application of the model process to a particular conference topic. For example, I recently took part in a Future Search conference working on addressing racism and prejudice in our community. Future Search uses an eight-step methodology, where the last three steps are: "Identify Common Ground," where small groups post themes they believe are common ground for everyone; "Confirm Common Ground," where the whole group dialogues to agree on common ground; and "Action Planning," where volunteers sign up to implement action plans around the agreed commonalities. Perhaps because the conference facilitators did not explain all the remaining steps in advance, some small groups came up with many broad themes that, while desirable, were clearly outside the direct control of people in our region. As a result, much time and energy was spent on "confirming common ground," a process requiring 100 percent consensus, and the attendees grew noticeably testy and impatient while waiting to get to the final action planning step.

While it's true that slavish adherence to any conference process can take away from the conference experience, community-building process is especially vulnerable, as it involves a chain of steps, any of which, if poorly executed, can compromise the event's success. Because peer conferences do not promise specific group outcomes, they are essentially immune from such negative outcomes.

Avoiding session conflicts

Even if you can somehow choose relevant content using a traditional conference model, you're not off the hook regarding *access* to that content at your conference. Another common content-related attendee problem is finding two interesting sessions—and then discovering that they're scheduled at the same time. What could be more frustrating than a conference offering an exciting session that you can't attend?

Most conferences with simultaneous sessions try to minimize conflicts by scheduling sessions in conference tracks, with each track designed for a different kind of attendee, topic, or specialty. *If* the program committee can devise and predict accurate attendee groupings, program tracks can minimize scheduling conflicts. When program tracks do not reflect attendee needs, however, disappointment is likely.

Practically speaking, it's impossible to schedule conference content to eliminate conflicting sessions for all attendees. So how can a peer conference minimize conflicts? It turns out that peer conference scheduling has a big advantage over traditional conference program scheduling. As you'll see in Part 3, by the time we are ready to schedule peer sessions to time slots, *we know who is interested in attending every proposed session*! This makes it easy to see the potential conflicts for *any* desired simultaneous scheduling of *any* particular group of sessions, which allows us to determine an optimum schedule. Unless preregistration is mandatory for every session before the conference schedule is created, this kind of information is simply unavailable at a traditional conference.

Delivering relevant, accessible content with a peer conference

Combining highly relevant content with effective scheduling that maximizes access to sessions leads to a *conference program that works* for the vast majority of attendees. The end result seems like magic. Attendees don't have to know the details of the process, but they are invariably happy with the program that is developed. And, surely you'd agree, that the relevance and accessibility of a conference program is key to that conference's success. That's what a peer conference delivers! Every time.

The Peer Conference Alternative

So far in this book I've supplied a steady stream of tantalizing hints and imputed claims about this thing I call a peer conference. In this chapter I'll explain in general terms how peer conferences overcome the deficiencies of traditional conferences that I've previously cataloged. The following three chapters cover peer conference process in more detail.

Definition, assumptions, end goals, and process goals

Let's start with the definition and basic premises of peer conferences.

Definition

A peer conference is a set of process tools used by a group of people with a common interest who want the experience of a conference that's intimate, meaningful, and useful to each person who attends.

Assumptions

We attendees collectively:

- Possess a tremendous variety of experience and expertise;
- Create the conference during the conference;
- Own the conference; and
- Value reflecting as a group on our conference experience.

Each of us:

- Affects what happens at our conference, for ourselves and for others;
- Is responsible for our own conference experience;
- Needs to share why we came and what we want to have happen;
- May have experience or expertise that is valuable to other attendees;
- Has something to learn from other attendees;
- Longs to invest our energy in things that matter; and
- Values reflecting personally on our conference experience.

Sharing our experience, expertise, and stories with our peers feels good.

When the right process is provided, the right content and the right way to share it will emerge.

End goals

The primary goal of a peer conference is to create the best possible conference for each individual attendee.

A peer conference maximizes participant interaction and connectedness.

Community-building and future group initiatives are not primary goals of a peer conference; rather, they are welcome potential outcomes.

Process goals

We create the best possible conference for each individual attendee by:

- Creating an environment:
  - where attendees get introduced to one another;
  - where it is safe for attendees to share experience, expertise, and stories;
  - that encourages interaction, despite differences in individuals' experience and expertise;
  - that encourages attendees to stretch and grow; and
  - that encourages and supports fun.
- Providing flexible structure that allows:
  - learning about other attendees;
  - uncovering individual attendee needs;
  - uncovering available experience and expertise; and
  - matching discovered needs with discovered experience and expertise.

- Offering appropriately sized sessions to support conferring as well as presenting.
- Providing facilities, time, a schedule, and facilitation for the sessions that attendees want.
- Holding our conference in enjoyable surroundings.
- Providing supported opportunities for individual and group reflection, introspection, and looking forward.
- Supporting group growth and the appropriate creation of new activities and events.

A peer conference provides just the right amount of process, structure, and support, and then gets out of the way.

What subject and how long?

Here are some broad answers to basic questions about the scope of peer conferences.

A peer conference can be about anything—a specific subject, a broad topic, an issue—that captures the interest of a group of people. Many peer conferences focus on professional themes, but peer conference process works just as well with community-based issues or personal interests. Here are a few examples of peer conference topics:

- Municipality facilities maintenance
- Building sustainability in our community
- Beer brewing
- Pharmacy management
- Providing childcare services
- Credit counseling using volunteers
- Amateur photography
- Working to reduce discrimination and prejudice in *XYZ* county

While some go to traditional conferences because it's expected of them or required, peer conferences are for people with a personal interest in the conference topic. Peer conference process encourages and supports engagement, guiding formerly passive attendees into active participation. As with any conference, an attendee who is disengaged or distracted may receive little benefit from the event, but a peer conference has a much higher likelihood of capturing the interest of even the most jaded conferee.

Peer conferences are small by traditional standards, with between 20 and 100 attendees. The initial roundtable process is practicable with up to 60 participants per roundtable session. When necessary, two simultaneous roundtables can be used without significantly impacting the intimacy and interactivity that exists at the center of a successful peer conference.

Developing the necessary trust, knowledge of other participants, and resulting connectedness, as well as supplying adequate opportunities for introspection and reflection at a conference takes time. Although I have held peer conferences in a single day, such events invariably feel rushed. Using a schedule that starts in the afternoon and lasts at least until the end of the following day provides the right amount of time for a short conference. At the upper end, peer conferences can run as long as three and a half days, providing ample time for attendees to explore multiple issues around the central topic.

An introduction to peer conference process

While peer conference process is certainly not infallible, I've found it offers a much better chance than a traditional conference of turning a conference *attendee* into a conference *participant*. Here's the big picture.

Think of a peer conference as a process, not an event—the *how* of a peer conference generates the *what*. Out of the process comes relevant learning, meaningful connections and interactions, and, sometimes, the creation or strengthening of a community.

A peer conference is a way for people to connect with each other around a common topic, face to face, in ways that are maximally useful and meaningful for each person. Peer conference process facilitates participants' connections by providing a supportive framework in which they can occur, leaving the nature and details of the connections to the people involved.

Providing a supportive framework without encroaching on the specifics of the interactions is important because people have such a wide variety of reasons for wanting connection. They may want to:

- Learn
- Meet other people who share their interests
- Get answers to questions
- Share useful or important information with others
- Build a community of people with whom they have something in common
- Build community around social or political action
- Grow
- Have fun
- Reflect on what they have learned and shared

By focusing on process that facilitates these reasons for connections, rather than a prescribed set of content-driven sessions, peer conferences free participants to ask for and get what they want from the event.

Peer conference process components

Peer conference process is divided into three phases, which I've imaginatively labeled "*Beginnings*," "*Middles*," and "*Endings*."

Beginnings

The beginnings of a peer conference are rooted in its opening session, the roundtable, which early on establishes a common framework for a safe and intimate conference environment, and then provides equal time for each attendee in turn to share his answers to three questions: how he came to the conference, what he wants to have happen during the event, and what experience or expertise he has that others might find useful.

Feeling safe is a prerequisite for attendees to be open to intimate sharing and making connections. So a peer conference starts by supplying a set of ground rules that define a supportive and safe environment. After these rules are explained, attendees commit to them, establishing a secure and comfortable environment for what is to come.

The roundtable is the only time when each attendee is asked and expected to share publicly. Roundtable sharing sets up the necessary conditions for subsequent interactions and connections between participants, and is important for many reasons. It makes a clean break with the convention that at conferences most people listen and few speak, setting up an alternative paradigm for the rest of the conference. It gives everyone the experience of speaking to the group, allowing people who might rarely or never open their mouths discover that it's not as bad as they feared (hey, they think, at least *everyone* has to share). It provides participants with the rich stew of ideas, themes, desires, and questions that is bubbling in peoples' minds. And it exposes the collective resources of the group—the expertise and experience that may be brought to bear on the concerns and issues that have been expressed.

As you might expect, during the sharing at a roundtable, participants pick up a great deal of useful information about other attendees, as well as the range and intensity of topics and questions on peoples' minds. What is less obvious is what happens as attendees experience and practice sharing while supported by the framework of the conference ground rules—the intimacy, respect, comfort, and excitement that develops as they begin to make meaningful connections with the people they are with.

Middles

Most of the time that attendees are together is spent in the Middles of a peer conference. The Middles include a set of short processes that turn the information and connections gleaned from the roundtable into a schedule of appropriate conference sessions, which are followed by the sessions themselves.

Peer conferences use a publish-and-filter model to determine conference sessions. First, attendees suggest session topics, posting them on blank sign-up sheets displayed in a common area. Second, people sign their names under titles of sessions they are interested in attending. They also indicate whether they could potentially help with a session, perhaps as a facilitator, presenter, or scribe.

Finally, a group of volunteers uses the sign-up sheets to determine the most popular viable topics and the appropriate session form. The chosen sessions are then scheduled, and the resulting conference program circulated to attendees.

Unlike traditional conference sessions, peer conference sessions are informal. Because session topics are determined at the conference, subsequent presentations or panels are nearly always *ad hoc* events. But informal doesn't mean disorganized. To support good process at peer conference sessions, all attendees receive a concise handout that explains how sessions work, and every session is assigned a facilitator.

Endings

Traditional conferences rarely provide useful closure, at best offering a symbolic dinner or a hopeful-incentive-to-stay-to-the-end keynote speaker. In contrast, peer conferences offer two closing sessions that build seamlessly on what happened during the conference.

The *personal introspective* closing session has two parts, the first private, the second public. To start, attendees answer five questions that encourage individual reflection on their conference experience and the development of plans for consequent action. Then, attendees are given the option to share some or all of their realizations and plans with the other attendees. An introspective's personal work fashions a natural bridge between attendees' conference experiences and their post-conference life and work, while the subsequent public sharing further enriches and deepens group bonds.

The second closing section, the *group spective*, gives participants an opportunity to discuss the conference and explore appropriate options for future group activities. Because every group of people has unique needs, desires, and energy, group spectives vary between events more than any other peer conference session, requiring careful facilitation using a toolbox of group process techniques described in detail in Part III of this book. Group spectives offer participants the chance to create their own collective future, extending the reach of the conference beyond the moment when people leave.

Unlike the close of a traditional conference, these two sessions provide support for building a coherent transition from the formal end of the peer conference to individual and collective future actions and events.

Graduate student story

I've been a teacher at various times in my life, including a 10-year spell teaching college-level computer science. I've never had any teacher training. I was a poor teacher when I started; I've gotten better over the years, though there's still plenty of room for improvement.

Conferences are one of the principal conduits for adult continuing education and learning. I'm talking about teaching in this chapter because, not surprisingly, there's significant carryover between the way we've been taught in school and the way we expect to receive knowledge at traditional conferences.

Sitting on a bookshelf in my office is a large blue cloth hardcover book. I wrote every word in it, and painstakingly hand-lettered every mathematical equation it contains with a Rapidograph pen. On the basis of this book, and a two-hour thesis defense, at the age of 25 I was considered fit to be awarded a Ph.D. in elementary particle physics.

I have a confession to make.

When I wrote that book I didn't understand everything I wrote.

How did this happen?

During my first two years as a postgraduate student I attended various particle physics courses. These classes were small, with fewer than 10 students, even though they included graduates from several London universities. Because I had transferred from another school, I didn't know any of the other students, and didn't socialize with them much. We sat in tiny classrooms, while a harried professor took us through what we were supposed to know in order to be awarded an advanced degree.

We've all had the experience of listening to a teacher in class and not understanding something he has said. Perhaps the teacher asks if there are any questions. At the moment you have to decide—do you admit that you're lost and ask the teacher to explain again, or do you say nothing? If you say nothing, is it because you are convinced that you will never understand what is going on, or are you hoping that all will become clear shortly, when the lesson continues?

In those days it was rare for me to give up on anything I was being taught. On the other hand, I was reluctant to display my apparent ignorance when I couldn't understand something during a class. In my experience, I would either "get it" later on, or nobody would understand and the teacher would eventually discover this and assume he hadn't been clear himself. For over 20 years this approach had worked for me. But toward the end of my second year I was understanding less and less of a mathematics course I was taking. The professor seemed to be going through the motions—he asked few questions, and there was no homework. Elementary particle physicists are either mathematicians or experimentalists, and I was the latter, working on a large-scale neutrino experiment at CERN, the European laboratory for particle physics, so my lack of mathematical understanding was not affecting my research work. But the experience was disconcerting. And, as the semester went on, the percentage of class material I understood gradually declined.

One day, our teacher announced that we would be studying Green's Functions, a technique used to solve certain kinds of equations. After the first 20 minutes of the class I realized that I understood nothing of what was being said, and that I was at a crucial turning point. If I kept quiet, it would be too late to claim ignorance later, and it was likely I would not understand anything taught for the remainder of the semester. If I spoke up, however, I was likely to display my weak comprehension of everything that had been covered so far.

Looking around, I noticed that the other students seemed to be having a similar experience. Everyone looked worried. No one said a word.

The class ended and the professor left. I plucked up my courage and asked my classmates if they were having trouble. We quickly discovered, to our general relief, that none of us understood the class. What should we do? Somehow, without much discussion, we decided to say nothing to the teacher.

The class only ran a few more weeks, and the remaining time became a pro forma *ritual. Did our teacher know he had lost us? I think he probably did. I think he remained quiet for his own reasons, perhaps uncaring about his success at educating us, perhaps ashamed that he had lost us.*

When I didn't speak up, I chose to enter a world where I hid my lack of understanding from others, a world where I was faking it.

For the next two years I analyzed experimental results and compared our findings with theoretical physicists' predictions. I understood the experiments, but not all the mathematics. And that's why I didn't understand some of those laboriously scribed equations in my thesis.

This confession of mine doesn't affect the scientific significance of the work I did. The mathematicians who supplied me the equations understood them, and I was comparing their predictions to experimental results that I understood. What is significant is that I chose to sit through meaningless classes rather than admitting my ignorance. That

(continued on following page)

> *mathematics course failed to provide me with a workable learning environment, not because it didn't contain useful content, but because its structure and context made it easier and safer for me to be silent.*
>
> *Probably you've had a similar experience; a sinking feeling as you realize that you don't understand something that you're apparently expected to understand, in a context, perhaps a traditional conference, where nonresponsiveness is the norm. It's a brave soul indeed who will speak out, who is prepared to admit to her classmates, teacher, or conference presenter that she doesn't get what's going on. Did you? Do you?*

A community of learners

At a well-planned traditional conference, conference planners invest significant time and effort before the conference attempting to determine who can potentially provide an "above average" contribution on the conference subject. These people are asked to be presenters and panelists. Everyone else who attends becomes the audience. By the time the conference starts, this distinction between the knowledge "haves" and the "have-nots" has been locked into the conference program.

In contrast, peer conferences make no such *a priori* assumptions about who is a teacher and who is a learner. Rather, they promote an environment in which teaching and learning are ever-fluid activities; the teacher at one moment is a learner the next. Sometimes, everyone in an interaction is learning simultaneously as social knowledge is discovered, constructed, and shared.

> "Communities of practice are groups of people who share a concern or a passion for something they do and learn how to do it better as they interact regularly."
>
> —*Etienne Wenger*

Peer conferences aren't built on the expectation that every attendee will significantly contribute to the event. There are always participants who have much to offer, intermingled with those who, for whatever reason, add little to the communal pool of relevant knowledge and experience. Rather, peer conference process provides the opportunity for anyone to contribute, perhaps unexpectedly, but ultimately, usefully.

Peer conferences are tools for what educational theorist Etienne Wenger calls *communities of practice*, as defined by three key elements: a shared domain of interest; a group whose members interact and learn together; and the development of a shared body of practice, knowledge, and resources. Such entities can take many forms: artists who rent a communal space to work and grow together, programmers linked online for the purpose of creating or improving public domain software, or a group of people with a common professional interest meeting regularly over lunch to swap ideas and experiences.

In my experience, peer conferences are high-quality incubators for communities of practice—they provide a wonderful way for a group of people to explore the potential for creating an ongoing community. The majority of peer conferences that I have facilitated have turned into regular events, but, even when this does not happen, a conference inevitably leads to new long-term relationships and communal projects of one kind or another. Conversely, communities of practice can use regular peer conferences to effectively explore and deepen their collective learning and intragroup relationships.

An environment for taking risks

Think of the last time you were with a group of people and made a stretch to learn something. Perhaps you admitted you didn't understand something someone said, wondering as you did whether it was obvious to the others present. Perhaps you challenged a viewpoint held by a majority of the people present. Perhaps you proposed a tentative solution to a problem, laying yourself open to potentially making a mistake in front of others. These are all examples of what I call *risky learning*.

> "Only those who will risk going too far can possibly find out how far one can go."
>
> —*T. S. Eliot. Preface to Transit of Venus: Poems by Harry Crosby. Black Sun Press, 1931*

Whatever happened, was the learning opportunity greater compared to *safe learning*—the passive absorption of presented information?

Traditional conferences discourage risky learning. Who but a supremely confident person (or that rare iconoclast) stands up at the end of a presentation to several hundred people and says they don't understand or disagree with something that was said? Who will ask a controversial question, share a problem, or state a controversial point of view, fearing it may affect their professional status, job prospects, or current employment with others in the audience? People who brave these concerns are more likely to be exhibiting risky behavior than practicing risky learning.

Peer conferences provide a safe and supportive environment for risky learning in several ways.

First, and perhaps most important, is the commitment attendees make at the very beginning of the conference to keep confidential what is shared. This simple communal promise generates a level of group intimacy and revelation seldom experienced at a conventional conference. As a result, participants are comfortable speaking what's on their minds, unencumbered by worries that their sharing may be made public outside the event.

Second, because peer conferences are small, there is an increased chance that attendees will be the sole representatives of their organizations and will feel comfortable fruitfully sharing sensitive personal information to their peers, knowing that what is revealed won't filter back to coworkers. Even when others are present from the same institution, the intimacy of a peer conference usually helps to develop amity and increased understanding between them.

Third, peer conference process makes no presuppositions about who will act in traditional teacher or student roles during the event, leading to fluid roles and learning driven by group and individual desires and abilities to satisfy real attendee needs and wishes. In an environment where it's expected that anyone may be a teacher or learner from moment to moment, participants overcome inhibitions about asking naive questions or sharing controversial opinions.

> "Learning is also a risk-taking business since as we learn we question our past knowledge and even our previous attitudes, beliefs, values and emotions so that teachers need to provide a safe environment for risks to be taken. It is crucial to all adult learners that they feel safe and supported as they launch out into the deep and learn new things."
>
> —Peter Jarvis. *Adult Education and Lifelong Learning: Theory and Practice.* Routledge, 2004

Finally, peer conference facilitators model peer conference behavior. When they don't know the answer to a question they say "I don't know." When they need help they ask for it. When they make mistakes they are accountable rather than defensive. Consistently modeling appropriate conduct fosters a conference environment conducive to engaged, risky learning.

Ultimately, each attendee decides whether to stretch. But peer conferences, by supplying optimum conditions for risky learning, make it easier for participants to learn effectively.

Ask, don't tell

Right before each one of my early peer conferences, the same disturbing thought ran through my mind. What if everyone came expecting a traditional conference program to be given to them, just like every other conference they'd ever attended, and no one volunteered topics they wanted to talk or hear about? I was concerned enough about this embarrassing possibility to ask steering committee members to think of presentations they could give if attendees failed to have any ideas of their own.

After a few years I stopped worrying. No one showed difficulty coming up with a list of topics they'd like to learn about or discuss. In fact, just about everybody seemed to be surprised and pleased to be asked. And what's more, even when their desires were not fulfilled at the subsequent conference (no, you really can't please everyone), their disappointment was clearly mollified by the information they received about why their coveted session(s) didn't take place.

It's not surprising that giving attendees the opportunity to ask for what they want to have happen is an option conspicuously absent from traditional conferences, which have no way to follow up on the suggestions and requests that would be made. Sadly, instead, conference organizers tell attendees what they will be getting. In

> "Many times people do not voice their expectations."
>
> —*Virginia Satir et al. The Satir Model. Science and Behavior Books, 1991*

contrast, a peer conference encourages attendees to share what they want to have happen, and then provides a supportive process that generates appropriate sessions on the popular topics.

In my experience, Virginia Satir was right—people often don't express their expectations. But we needn't make it any harder for them by not even asking what they want.

Rich interpersonal process

Here's what happens interpersonally *officially* at a peer conference: Participants discover and share the interests, needs, and knowledge of each attendee; the conference supplies tools for people to determine via a shared public space what will happen during the conference; attendees generate, staff, and participate in the resulting sessions; and finally, the conference provides group sessions for private and public individual and group reflection and future initiatives.

Imagine what happens *unofficially*!

I am fascinated with how much interactive richness evolves out of the right amount of structure. Business visionary David Weinberger, in his thought-provoking book *Everything Is Miscellaneous*, describes Wikipedia

> "Conversation is king. Content is just something to talk about."
>
> —*Cory Doctorow. boingboing.*

as a "pragmatic utopian community that begins with a minimum of structure, out of which emerge social structures as needed." Like Wikipedia, where a majority of edits are done by less than two percent of the contributors, but most of the content is created by unregistered occasional contributors, a peer conference is not pure bottom-up, but contains a mixture of top-down structure, and bottom-up attendee-driven content.

Similarly, too much structure at a conference leads to excessive formality that gets in the way of conversations, while too little structure fails to generate the necessary level of personal information that attendees need to quickly engage in meaningful interactions. I've worked on observing and tuning this balance at peer conferences for years. Getting the mix right, sustaining it throughout the conference, and ending with sessions that integrate and enrich individual and group understanding creates a rich, productive stew of interaction and discovery that is largely absent from traditional conferences.

Flattening hierarchy

In the previous chapter, I described the benefits of de-emphasizing attendee status at the start of a conference. Following this intent, a peer conference works to flatten perceived and proclaimed hierarchy throughout the event. Ground rules, roundtable process, methods for determining session topics, even the closing sessions formats are all designed to minimize overt and covert preconceptions about whether some attendees are more important than others.

Peer conference ground rules fashion a confidential environment where freedom to ask questions, be they specific or fundamental, is made clear and agreed to by all participants. Confidentiality removes the fear of extra-conference repercussions, making it easier for the unconfident attendee to ask questions. Specifically agreeing that everyone has the freedom to talk about what they want to talk about, including feelings, and that everyone can ask about anything puzzling, lowers self-imposed barriers to bringing up "stupid" questions and topics (which, it frequently turns out, many of the attendees want to ask or discuss).

The roundtable reinforces this initial message. By allocating the same amount of time for each attendee to speak to everyone present, and by having people speak in no particular order, the roundtable implies that everybody's needs, desires, experience, and expertise are important, and that the conference is about learning and sharing, things of which we are all capable, whether newcomers to or 30-year veterans of the conference's subject.

When it comes to suggesting session topics at a peer conference, everyone has an equal opportunity to publish their ideas for all to see. Democratic voting, tempered only by feasibility, drives the selection of sessions. Anyone can volunteer to help analyze the votes and organize and schedule the resulting peer sessions.

Peer conference sessions are rarely large, and are invariably informal, with questions welcomed. Small sessions do much to reduce conversational barriers between attendees with different levels of knowledge and understanding.

Finally, sharing at the personal introspective provides a surprisingly intimate window on attendees' realizations, conclusions, and plans. When, in a single session, a seasoned CEO states that he hasn't been treating his staff well and needs to change his behavior in some areas; an industry veteran announces that the conference has helped her decide to take a whole new direction in her professional life; and a novice communicates his touching new-found excitement about the conference, attendees are drawn closer and status is the last thing on anyone's mind.

Creating community

Creating community is not a primary goal of peer conferences, but rather a delightful bonus outcome. Peer conferences usually evoke intimate communities-of-the-moment, but they also often lead to the formation of long-term associations. While there's no guarantee that a peer conference will be the initial seed that blossoms into a lasting community, about half of the peer conferences I've facilitated have led to some kind of repeat engagements for a significant percentage of the original group.

Because peer conferences de-emphasize attendee status, the nature of any resulting community is likely to be more inclusive and less cliquish than communities that form around traditional conferences. The peer conference atmosphere permeates attendee interactions outside the conference, making it easier for people to ask other participants for advice and support.

The key to getting important questions asked— answering attendee meta-questions

For a conference to be able to answer attendee questions effectively, attendees must feel comfortable asking questions in the first place. There are a couple of conditions that, if satisfied, will greatly increase the likelihood of this occurring.

First, the conference has to create an environment that encourages attendee questions and supplies ample opportunity for asking them. The opening session of a peer conference, the roundtable, explicitly gives attendees permission to ask any questions they have and offers a safe environment that encourages them to do so.

Second, we can help attendees overcome one of the biggest obstacles to making meaningful connections with others—getting started. To make it easy to strike up conversations with the right people, we can supply attendees with the answers to *meta-questions* about the other participants and the conference environment. Here are some examples of early conference meta-questions:

- Who else is here?
- Who might I be interested in talking to?
- How can I start a conversation with them?
- Who here may be able to answer my questions?
- What are other people interested in talking about?

TABLE 5.1 • Meta-questions and the Corresponding Peer Conference Session(s)

META-QUESTION	PEER CONFERENCE SESSION
Who else is here?	Roundtable
Who might I be interested in talking to?	Roundtable and peer sessions
How can I start a conversation with them?	Roundtable
Who here may be able to answer my questions?	Roundtable and peer sessions
What are other people interested in talking about?	Roundtable and peer session sign-up
Where can I talk about what I want to talk about?	Peer sessions
What have I learned?	Personal introspective
What might I want to change in the future?	Personal introspective
What might we want to do in the future?	Group spective

Unlike traditional conferences, peer conferences offer unique opportunities for attendees to get these questions answered. Table 5.1 lists attendee meta-questions, paired with the peer conference session or sessions that provide corresponding meta-answers.

Answers to these meta-questions give attendees the information they need—the right people to talk to, interests in common, and conversational openers—for asking their specific, topic-related questions during the peer sessions. At every peer conference I've run, attendees have commented on the ease of getting to know the participants they find interesting and rewarding to meet.

Synergy

It's difficult to convey the cumulative effect of the peer conference components. A safe and welcoming environment, introductions to the other attendees, discovering what people want to talk about and what they know about, the ability to create a conference that fits personal needs, and the opportunities to reflect on what happened individually and as a group—the combination of all these factors creates the conditions where wonderful things happen for attendees.

> "They speak only of such a Synergie, or cooperation, as makes men differ from a sensless stock . . ."
>
> —*Peter Heylin. Historia quinqu-articularis. London, 1660*

A peer conference is synergistic; greater than the sum of its parts. In the same way that a good book's plot, characters, and writing draw in and engage readers, a peer conference contains just the right ingredients to draw in and engage attendees. When people are given the permission, tools, and support to fashion a conference that is just right for them, they quickly become immersed in a flow of ideas, learning, and connection that builds on itself, creating not only fruitful personal experience but also an infectious group energy. Such is the power of synergy that permeates a peer conference—my wish for you is that you get to experience it for yourself.

Combining peer and traditional conference sessions

I'm pragmatic, not a purist. Including peer and traditional sessions can combine the best features of both conference models into one event. The trick is to restrict your traditional sessions to presenters and topics that you are confident will be dynamite for your conference.

This requires a willingness to scrutinize proposed conventional presentations or keynotes for excellence, and avoiding any quota for conventional sessions. If you can get a fantastic keynote speaker who can address a hot topic at your conference, book her. If no choices for a keynote excite you, don't have one. Similarly, review proposals for traditional presentations or panels, and don't worry about not having enough fixed sessions. A peer conference will soak up the time available—more time means there's time for another round of peer sessions.

The advantages of this approach are twofold: First, advertising specific speakers and presentations will attract attendees who prefer to know in advance that at least some of the conference program will be of interest, and, second, taking comfort in knowing that the fixed sessions you offer are of high quality and likely to be enjoyed by participants.

Novelty

I have been scared of doing new things for most of my life. When I first started college teaching, I was a nervous wreck, preparing every lesson meticulously for hours. I was scared I would not know the answer to some question, scared that I would get confused and look like an idiot, scared that my students would discover that I didn't know everything about my subject. It took about five years before I started to relax, discovering that I could make mistakes and not know all the answers, and still feel okay about myself.

The same thing happened when I first started facilitating conferences. I was anxious in front of the assembled attendees—would I be able to explain the conference process clearly and facilitate effectively, or would people be baffled and frustrated, and leave?

These days I'm relaxed about teaching and conference facilitation. It's not because I have mastered my subject and approach—on the contrary, I learn every time I teach, train, or facilitate. Rather, time has built familiarity with my self-knowledge and self-confidence. I know, more or less, my strengths and weaknesses and am comfortable with them.

But this has taken me years.

When you go to a conference that you haven't attended before, you'll usually feel anxious on arrival. It's normal to feel somewhat awkward or embarrassed to be among a bunch of strangers, some of whom are gaily chatting away with each other while you, knowing no one, wonder how to strike up a conversation. People suppress these feelings at conventional conferences, because they believe they should project a "professional" appearance that avoids the display of emotions considered negative, like fear or anger.

People come to conferences with questions. A traditional conference provides, primarily, a framework for answering attendees' questions about content, the topics covered at the conference. By reading the published conference program, people can get some idea of what topics are, ostensibly, going to be covered. But, as we've seen, attendees have many other kinds of questions, and a traditional conference has no direct means to provide the answers they need.

A peer conference allows novelty, in both structure and content. If attendees want to hold a session with an unusual format—a performance, say, or an impromptu simulation, or a three-hour presentation—then conference organizers will make every effort to "make it so." Creating such a conference schedule is challenging, but the work is made easier by the knowledge that *this is what attendees want.*

The culture of a peer conference embodies flexibility, which in turn makes it easy for attendees to suggest and carry out novel ideas. Sometimes, one year's amusing novelty turns into a quirky and beloved annual tradition—the annual softball game or the midnight swim in the nearest available body of water. I like it when that happens.

CHAPTER
6 Beginnings

Connections

Since 1978 I have lived in Marlboro, Vermont, a town of sixty square miles and about a thousand residents. Today I drove eight miles to downtown Brattleboro to help run a raffle booth for the local United Way during the monthly Gallery Walk, an evening for artists to display their work. Standing at the intersection of Main and High Streets, I saw a continual stream of acquaintances. As they passed by we exchanged smiles, nods, sometimes a hand raised in greeting or a few words exchanged. Some people stopped and we talked for a while. The weather was warm and pleasant, and no one seemed in any kind of hurry. Much of my enjoyment came from the serendipity of whom I might next see.

> "Of all the domains in which I have traced the consequences of social capital, in none is the importance of social connectedness so well established as in the case of health and well-being."
>
> —*Robert Putnam. Bowling Alone. Simon & Schuster, 2000*

When I moved to Marlboro 30 years ago I knew no one in this part of Vermont. My connections with the people I greeted today spring from many different facets of my life. Some live in Marlboro, where I met them over the years through town functions, or because their kids went to school with mine. Others I ran into through my consulting work, or via community events my family attended or helped to organize. A few I knew through parties at friends' houses, or perhaps a chance conversation at the local food coop. These days it's unusual for me to go anywhere locally and *not* bump into people I know.

My experience of community is very important to me. Meeting other people nourishes an essential need I have, the need for human connection. My existing connections, the commonalities we have already discovered, give me an opening, an introduction to possibilities that may follow. I am comfortable being alone; in fact I need regular solitude for thinking, working, learning, and relaxation. But I am rejuvenated, stretched, and sparked by the people connections, whether casual or deep, that I have made and that I continue to delightedly explore.

Most of us have chance encounters with others every day, especially in a big city where you're perpetually surrounded by hundreds of people whenever you're in a public space. But in a city it's rare to ever meet again the stranger whose eyes met yours yesterday in a crowded bookstore. One of the reasons I love living in a rural community is that it's very likely I'll run into acquaintances when I go into town, pick up my mail at the local post office, or join a yoga class.

I believe that the great majority of people, like me, hunger for connection with others. Without it, our lives suffer. Indeed, Robert Putnam in *Bowling Alone,* his sobering opus on social change in America, states that about half the observed decline in life satisfaction among adult Americans over the last 50 years "is associated with declines in social capital: lower marriage rates and decreasing connectedness to friends and community." And the sociologist James House tells us that "the magnitude of risk associated with social isolation is comparable with that of cigarette smoking and other major biomedical and psychosocial risk factors."

Traditional conferences—content over connection

So, why, when we hold a conference in our culture—an occasion when we bring together people with a common interest in a subject—do we place such little emphasis on the potential for connection with our fellow conferees? After all, we have the ideal requisite for enjoying each other's company—we all share a common interest! Why, then, are traditional conference sessions structured to fill us with content from the few, limiting interaction with our peers? Why are the opportunities for developing connections relegated to the gaps in the conference schedule, the "informal" time when we are not in sessions together?

I can think of a couple of reasons for this sad state of affairs, and I'm sure there are others. First, as Jerry Weinberg reminds us: "Things are the way they are because they got that way." It's my observation that conferences mirror the structure of their professional origins. As organizations or professions develop hierarchies of power and status—consultants/practitioners/ interns in medicine, or professors/lecturers/postdocs/postgrads in academia, or president/ vice-president/manager/staff in business, for example—conferences for these groups tend to reflect these hierarchies. How do we publicly display the status of a profession's heads? By singling them out as presenters at the profession's conferences.

I am not making a value judgment about the worth of publicly recognizing or taking advantage of anyone's mastery of a topic or field. Clearly, attendees benefit when they are presented with cutting-edge information, unavailable elsewhere, from leading experts. But when conference sessions are used to announce or confirm status of individuals in the profession, this leads to session formats—predetermined keynotes, presentations, or panels—designed to emphasize the contributions of the folks at the top. Such formats highlight what a few have to say at the expense of session formats that can strengthen connections between *all* attendees.

There's another reason why we cling to one-to-many session formats at traditional conferences. Unless you've been attending the same annual conference for years, you probably won't know much, if anything, about most of the other attendees. Unfortunately, a traditional conference gives you little if any opportunity to readily discover kindred spirits. So when a conventional conference attempts to use more inclusive session formats, like discussion groups where people have opportunities to make individual connections, participants don't have the information they need—either to decide whether it's worth joining a particular discussion group or to easily make connections with attendees at the session. This makes such sessions difficult to carry off successfully.

Building meaningful connections into the conference process

Unlike traditional conferences, creating an environment that encourages and supports the building of meaningful connections between attendees is a key goal of every peer conference. How can we do this?

Think about the conditions I needed to build my web of local connections over the past 30 years. There were two fundamental requirements. *I needed opportunities to discover and meet like-minded people, and I needed reasons or excuses to fall into conversation with them.*

We don't have 30 years to build connections at a conference. We have, at most, a few days together, perhaps a few minutes of potential interaction with each attendee. So how can we best build the above requirements into our conference process?

Whatever we do, it should happen quickly, and at the beginning of the conference. No waiting to try to meet people during session breaks. If we're going to be proactive about fostering connection, let's start right at the beginning of the conference to maximize the opportunity.

How do we discover like-minded people? We need an opportunity to ask them what we want to know and hear their answers. Their answers inform us about interests and experiences we share, commonalities that will provide openings for us to engage with them.

Suppose we could create an initial conference session where we could ask everyone present what we wanted to know about them. What kind of questions should we ask?

We need open-ended questions, questions that are appropriate for any attendee to answer.

We need questions that can be answered safely by an anxious participant, questions for which there are no wrong answers.

We need questions that cover the past, the present, and the future. Hearing where someone is coming from tells us about their context and their experience; it gives us baseline information. Hearing about what they want to do now, at the conference, and in the future, their wishes for their professional or personal life, tells us about the interests we may share and where their energy is focused. All of this is valuable information.

We also need to ask about people's experience or expertise that might be useful to other attendees. There's no guarantee that what people tell us will be useful, but if we don't ask, how will we know?

It turns out that we can satisfy all of the above requirements with just three questions. These are the questions we ask every attendee to answer publicly at the first session of a peer conference—the roundtable, which is the next topic of this book.

The roundtable

By now, you're probably curious about what happens at a roundtable and why. This chapter will answer your questions!

Roundtable overview

To introduce you to what happens at a roundtable, let's start with an overview of the roundtable process, as shown in Figure 6.1.

Before the actual roundtable starts, the roundtable facilitator:

> "How did I get here?"
>
> "What do I want to have happen?"
>
> "What experience do I have that others might find useful?"
>
> *—The three questions that each attendee answers publicly at a peer conference*

- Explains the conference ground rules and asks attendees to commit to them.
- Describes how the roundtable works.
- Explains the three questions listed on a card given to each attendee.

The conference ground rules consist of the Four Freedoms, described below, and rules about safety and staying on time. Attendees are asked to display their commitment to these ground rules by standing.

FIGURE 6.1 • Roundtable Process

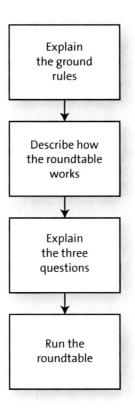

Each attendee is given a card printed with the following three questions:

"How did I get here?"

"What do I want to have happen?"

"What experience do I have that others might find useful?"

The roundtable facilitator explains that each attendee in turn will have the opportunity to answer these questions, gives some examples of answers attendees might provide, and explains that everyone will get an equal amount of time to share. Attendees are then given a few minutes to think about their answers.

After the facilitator provides the guidelines, sharing begins. A timekeeper provides an audible warning before each person's time is about to expire, and a second warning when time is up. As topics and themes emerge, two scribes record them on flip charts or whiteboards.

History

The first time I used a roundtable at a conference was in 1992 at the first ACCESS (later edACCESS) conference, held at Marlboro College. I remember that we sat around a solid block of rectangular tables, in the room the school used for faculty meetings. Hardly anyone present knew anybody else, so it seemed natural to go around the room and have everyone introduce themselves, say a little about why they had come, and describe what they were interested in talking about at the conference. There were only 23 attendees, and we didn't really have anywhere else to meet, so we ended up running the conference as a series of whole-group discussions that were based on the popular topics brought up during the initial roundtable.

For a number of years, my conference roundtables continued to be structured as a relatively informal way for attendees to introduce themselves to each other as they saw fit. I let people take as much or little time as they wanted; this occasionally proved annoying when some people spoke too long. So I added a fixed time duration for each attendee, using a roundtable timekeeper who gave an audible signal when an attendee's time was up. Later, I found it was helpful to have the timekeeper provide a second warning signal 30 seconds before an attendee's time expired.

In 1995, I came up with the idea of providing questions for each attendee to answer during the roundtable; questions that would both elicit the kind of information needed to build connections as well as uncover the topics and themes that participants wanted to explore. I'll say more about these questions later in this chapter. Initially, I used two questions— "How did I get here?" and "What do I want to have happen?"—adding a third question, "What experience do I have that others might find useful?" in 1999.

The value of a roundtable

The first session of a peer conference, the roundtable, serves three broad purposes. First, it defines and models an active, interactive, and safe conference environment. Second, the roundtable provides a structured forum for attendees to meet and learn about each other's affiliations, interests, experience, and expertise. And third, the session uncovers the topics that people want to discuss and share, as well as indicating the level of interest in each topic.

A roundtable always begins with a description and explanation of conference ground rules and then asks attendees to commit to them. I began providing explicit ground rules at the start of a peer conference when I discovered it led to increased sharing, intimacy, and sense of connection among participants. These ground rules, which are detailed later in this chapter, send participants the following powerful messages:

> "While you are here, you have *the right and opportunity to be heard.*"

> "*Your* individual needs and desires are important here."

"*You* will help to determine what happens at this conference."

"At this conference, *you can create, together with others, opportunities to learn and to share.*"

"What happens here will be *kept confidential.* You can *feel safe* here."

Roundtables provide a structured, nonthreatening way for attendees to learn about each other early in the conference. During the session, people discover topics that interest others. They get a sense of the depth of interest in these topics, and they find out who has experiences that they want to connect with and explore further.

At a conventional conference, people meet and learn about each other slowly, mostly outside the programmed sessions. A peer conference roundtable introduces every attendee to every other participant, right at the start of the event. Hearing a little about each person makes it much easier to introduce yourself to anyone with whom you share a particular interest.

At a roundtable, every person has the same amount of time to share with other attendees. This flattens the initial conference hierarchy: Any attendee may possess something of value for her peers, allowing the conference process itself to uncover what experiences are of value to the people present.

By not making assumptions, either about what content is of value or about who has valuable content to share, a peer conference roundtable provides a safe environment for participants to express and explore what is truly of value to them. The practical result of this approach is remarkable: *Valuable topics are uncovered and valuable participants are discovered that were simply unknown to the conference organizers.* This occurs at every roundtable I have facilitated.

Finally, I've found that the simple act of starting a conference with structured group sharing has a profound effect. It provides a powerful, infectious model of interaction and creates an intimate atmosphere that attendees rarely experience at a traditional conference.

These are some of the benefits of a peer conference roundtable. Let's go over the details now, so you can see how a roundtable works, and understand how these benefits arise.

The shape of a roundtable

When I started with roundtables, I didn't especially care where people sat. As long as we were all roughly facing each other the setup seemed good to me. Sometimes people came in late, took a chair and formed a second row around the assembled group. I recall one conference where people arranged themselves in an irregular shape several rows deep, principally because the room was too small to hold everyone in a single closed loop of chairs.

Roundtables where people were arranged haphazardly seemed less intense, less focused, than those where people sat in a more regular fashion. Where people couldn't see each other, the sense of intimacy in the group was reduced. People were more likely to fidget, side talk with their neighbors, and simply be less involved in the process.

Eventually I began to insist on using a circle of chairs for the peer conference roundtable. In a circle, everyone can see everyone else—people are more exposed—which creates a group tension that encourages alertness and concentration on what the speaker in the circle is saying at each moment. The circle of chairs provides a ritual space, a space in which each person in the group can meet, however briefly, every other person present.

Ground rules

Facilitators of a group that plans to work together for an extended period of time will normally have the group establish its own ground rules, not only because group-developed ground rules will handle the specific needs of the group, but also because the process of development creates buy-in for the rules that are chosen. Unfortunately, it takes up too much time to brainstorm and negotiate ground rules for a single conference. Consequently, I've chosen to use the following rules, developed over many years, at peer conferences. I've found they work extremely well.

I provide the peer conference ground rules in a handout to attendees describing the *Four Freedoms*, a rule about *confidentiality*, and a rule about *staying on time*. The facilitator explains the rules at the start of the roundtable, and attendees are asked to commit to them for the duration of the conference.

Four Freedoms

All of us have a comfort zone for our interactions with others, a social space inside which we feel comfortable. The boundaries of this zone vary, depending on who we are interacting with, our context (home, professional, social, etc.), and the level of safety we feel in a specific situation.

The Four Freedoms are important ground rules, derived from the work of family therapist Virginia Satir and further refined by Gerald Weinberg and Donald Gause and Norman Kerth. I provide a copy, printed on a card, for each attendee. Here they are:

- You have the freedom to talk about the way you see things, rather than the way others want you to see.
- You have the freedom to ask about anything puzzling.
- You have the freedom to talk about whatever is coming up for you, especially your own reactions.

- You have the freedom to say that you don't really feel you have one or more of the preceding three freedoms.

The Four Freedoms invite attendees to be fully present with each other.

The first offers the gift of talking freely about what a person sees and understands, despite what others may think or say.

The second offers the gift of asking freely about what a person does not understand.

The third offers the gift of freely expressing feelings in response to what is happening.

The fourth offers the gift of freely discussing the lack of any of the other three freedoms.

In my early peer conferences I did not offer Four Freedoms to attendees. Since I started including them, my roundtables have felt more intimate and empowering. The Four Freedoms create a supportive, safe environment for people to take risks and speak about subjects, beliefs, questions, and feelings that they would not normally share. This environment encourages attendees to commit to and engage in the conference experience, rather than remaining passive observers and occasional contributors.

I end my introduction to the Four Freedoms by asking each attendee to help all of us by exercising their four freedoms while we are together.

In my experience, *offering these Four Freedoms at the start of a conference encourages attendees to interact beyond their normal comfort zone.* This is a heady experience for many attendees who have never before felt empowered to be either proactive or revelatory at a conference.

There are three conditions that enable these freedoms to become an integral part of the conference culture.

1. The Four Freedoms have to be clearly communicated. Participants must understand up front that they are free to express their point of view, it's okay to ask any question, it's fine to talk about how they're feeling, and they can speak up at any time they feel these freedoms aren't available to them.
2. The conference facilitator(s) and organizers must model using the Four Freedoms during the conference. (I frequently invoke the second freedom: "I'm sorry, I don't understand *XYZ*.") If you don't do this, attendees will rightly conclude that the Four Freedoms are empty words, and the conference environment will suffer greatly.
3. Attendees must actively commit to the Four Freedoms (and the two other ground rules.) How this is done is described below.

Confidentiality

The confidentiality ground rule further enhances attendee safety:

> *What we discuss at this conference will remain confidential. What we share here, stays here.*

When attendees adopt this rule, it frees them to talk about many intimate topics. Difficult situations and associated feelings, relationships at work, questions unasked for fear of revealing incompetence, even the simple enjoyment in meeting kindred souls are common examples of what may be shared at peer conferences.

It surprises and saddens me how rare it is for such a ground rule to be adopted at conferences. Providing and committing to confidentiality encourages much more sharing among attendees. Being able to safely share and be heard is often of the greatest importance to attendees, sometimes far more important than even conference content. This ground rule provides an environment for attendees who may have no other avenue to communicate confidentially and safely with their peers.

Staying on time

How many conferences have you been to where sessions started late or ran late, wasting the time of the people who were punctual, and cutting into later sessions? Too many, according to a majority of my interviewees. Breaking the tacit agreements promised by a published schedule irritates attendees, and reduces their trust in the value of the conference. When schedule times prove unreliable, people are more likely to arrive late or leave early. This causes further problems—arriving late at a session is disruptive in itself, and latecomers may want to ask time-wasting questions about content they missed.

We can't prevent people from arriving late to a session. But we can publicly request that sessions start and end on time, and ask the people who are organizing sessions to honor this desire. (A conference can also *support* staying on time by having someone available to remind session organizers, if necessary, to begin and end at the times when their sessions are scheduled to start and end.) I've found that simply providing the following ground rule:

> *We ask that you start and end all sessions on time.*

together with appropriate reminders during the conference, ensures a punctual conference.

Committing to ground rules

Imposing ground rules on attendees, no matter how well chosen, is an empty gesture unless there is attendee buy-in. Providing a list of ground rules, asking whether anyone has any objections, taking silence as assent, and hastily rushing on to the next agenda item implies that the rules are just a formality and needn't be taken seriously. But, given that we have little time to spare, how can we get some kind of commitment from participants?

I like to use a brief ritual requiring active attendee participation. (Don't worry, no animal sacrifice is involved.) I say:

> *"I would like all of you who commit to using Four Freedoms, maintaining confidentiality, and staying on time to stand."*

(People who have difficulty standing can raise their hand instead.) Simply asking attendees to change their physical stance to demonstrate their commitment to the conference ground rules may not seem like a big deal, but it's an unusual enough request to get everyone to think, if only for a moment, about what they are committing to and to help cement the ground rules in their minds. (If anyone didn't stand, I'd say "Everyone standing sit, everyone sitting stand," ask those standing to explain what they feel they can't commit to, and, if necessary, work on an agreement as to how to proceed. It hasn't happened yet.)

The Three Questions

Each attendee receives a copy of the Three Questions, printed on a card. Having each attendee publicly answer these questions comprises the core activity of the roundtable. Everything up to this point has laid the groundwork for the novel concept of everyone participating actively in the conference, a participation that will lead to rich dividends for all attendees.

This point in the conference is the only time when every attendee is expected to speak publicly. Some people have a hard time speaking to a group. By providing a supportive environment and requiring each attendee to speak, however briefly, a peer conference gives reluctant attendees a relatively safe opportunity to discover that sharing a little about themselves in public may not be as scary an ordeal as they thought. Expecting each attendee to say something at the roundtable gently reinforces the notion that the conference's culture embraces active participation, and once they've had this experience, they are more likely to contribute during the conference.

Before sharing starts, the roundtable facilitator points out that *there are no wrong answers* to the three questions. This helps attendees who are nervous about sharing in public to relax, and gives people permission to share as much or as little as they wish, depending on their comfort level. The facilitator then explains the three questions to everyone and gives a few minutes for attendees to reflect on what they want to say.

Let's look at each question in turn.

How Did I Get Here?

Most group introductions, when they occur, are of the form "My name is John Smith and I work at MegaCorp." In contrast, the question *How did I get here?* provides a safe way to uncover whatever each attendee chooses to reveal about his connections to the other participants. An attendee might say "I drove from Springfield on I-89" or "Fred, who I work with and who came last year, told me this was a great conference" or "When I came to this conference two years ago, I discovered I was not alone." Often, attendees say a great deal more. This question allows participants to learn more about their fellow attendees, and, in the process, begin to form ideas about who they may want to spend time with during the rest of the conference.

What Do I Want to Have Happen?

This question invites attendees to share what they would like to experience at the conference. What do they want to learn more about, what questions do they want answered, and what topics do they want to discuss? The facilitator encourages attendees to answer this question as if the conference could provide everything attendees asks for—as long as they ask! Attendees are told they can ask for general topics, the answers to highly specific questions, technical issues, "people" issues; *what's important is that attendees ask for what they want.* Some examples:

- "I want to talk about marketing with anyone who has experience with community supported agriculture."
- "I need to find out how to configure X widgets so they will frambolize successfully."
- "How has your organization decided on Acceptable Use Policies?"
- "My division head often rejects my professional opinion—I'd like to know how I can be more credible with her."

Two roundtable scribes record topics mentioned by attendees onto flip charts or whiteboards. The resulting lists are displayed at peer session sign-up; they also serve the purpose of reassuring each attendee that his concerns and interests have been heard and captured for the group.

What Experience Do I Have That Others May Find Useful?

When I added this question in 1999, I had no inkling how valuable it would turn out to be. In every conference I've facilitated since, the responses have uncovered experiences or expertise unknown to the conference organizers, experience that has been of great worth to attendees.

I have seen casually mentioned topics evolve into rave conference sessions (in one case, a session that everyone at the conference attended). And at a more intimate level, I have seen someone discover the one other person at the conference who understands *exactly* what she is talking about, with the resulting blooming of a fast friendship. The only thing that's predictable about this question is that the responses will uncover unexpected topics and unanticipated interest in some of these topics.

There is another benefit from this question that I did not expect. *Often, the people who describe their experience have no idea that others would find it valuable!* What has been warming for me is to see how this discovery empowers these individuals. To discover that your peers value and admire your work in an area validates you professionally and personally. What a gift to receive! At a peer conference, such gifts are easily and frequently given.

Sharing answers

Before sharing begins, the roundtable facilitator provides four guidelines to attendees.

1. The facilitator encourages people to share what they want to have happen, even if others have already mentioned the same topics. This helps reveal to everyone present the degree of interest in specific subjects.
2. The facilitator tells attendees that if they hear a request for help on a specific issue and they can help, they can stick up their hand, say their name and a brief "I can help with that." This connects attendees on specific issues right at the start of the conference, issues that might be too specialized to attract enough interest for a conference session.
3. The facilitator asks those who can't stay for the entire conference to mention when they're leaving. This helps avoid scheduling a session involving someone's expertise after they have left.
4. The facilitator recommends that attendees use the draft copy of the conference *face book* to record information of interest that is shared during the roundtable. The face book is a printed list of attendees with their affiliations and other pertinent information, including attendee photographs, which is provided to each attendee before the roundtable begins.

The facilitator's final task is to explain how timekeeping works. Each attendee receives the same amount of time, though no one has to use all of it. The amount assigned, normally between 90 and 150 seconds, depends on the number of attendees and the conference duration, as explained in the third part of this book. The timekeeper demonstrates the signals, playing the warning sound heard when an attendee has 30 seconds left, and then the "time's up" sound.

Finally, it's time to share! The facilitator can start with a prearranged volunteer, perhaps one of the conference organizers who can model good answers for attendees to follow, or ask for a volunteer to start, or go alphabetically, using the face book order as a guide. By not employing any special expertise-based order for sharing, the roundtable reinforces the message that everyone's sharing is equally important.

The roundtable as speed dating

Motives aside, trying to find a date for Friday night and trying to meet interesting people at a conference are pursuits with some common features. Both activities necessitate finding people who interest you from a larger pool, and both require you to figure out how to introduce yourself to potential candidates.

While every modern culture has developed socially acceptable ways for meeting potential dating partners, some methods don't lend themselves to quickly meeting someone new. (Not that that's necessarily a bad thing, when thinking about finding someone with whom you might spend the rest of your life.) Traditional matchmaking, for example, requires introductions via professional matchmakers, family members, or close acquaintances. If you're looking for a date without matrimony immediately in mind, such formal methods can be frustrating, as apparent in most Bollywood movies.

Western culture has recently come up with a variety of alternatives for casual dating, such as online dating, singles events, and speed dating. I'm going to talk about speed dating here, because it turns out to have a number of things in common with a peer conference roundtable.

Successful traditional dating requires solving a number of problems. How do you meet someone you're interested in going out with? If you do meet someone interesting, how do you know whether this person is even looking for a date? Since traditional dating typically implies a minimum com-

> "Speed dating has some obvious advantages over most other venues for meeting people, such as bars, discotheques, etc. in that everybody is purportedly there to meet someone, they are grouped into compatible age ranges, it is time-efficient, and the structured interaction eliminates the need to introduce oneself. And unlike many bars a speed dating event will, by necessity, be quiet enough for people to talk comfortably."
>
> —*Wikipedia, March 22, 2008*

mitment—at least a first date—are you willing to spend time with and/or money on someone when you may quickly find that the requisite chemistry isn't there?

Speed dating potentially solves these problems. Interestingly, despite matchmaking's long history, speed dating was invented very recently, in 1998. People gather in a large group, and are then organized to meet in pairs over a series of short "dates," usually lasting a few minutes each at an arranged location in the room. At the end of each date, the organizer signals the participants to move on to their next date. At the end of the event, attendees give the organizers a list of the people they would like to meet again. If there is a match, contact information is forwarded to both parties.

So, how is speed dating like a peer conference roundtable?

First, a roundtable and speed dating provide a structure that enables you to meet a large number of new people in a short amount of time. All things being equal, the more people you meet, the more interesting folks you'll identify.

Second, speed dating and the roundtable both avoid the need to commit a significant amount of time meeting each person. Traditional dating generally involves at least an hour spent on the first date, while meeting people at a conventional conference usually occurs via chance, during meals or social events, resulting in

conversations from which it can be hard to disengage quickly.

Finally, both activities provide the information you need to introduce yourself to the interesting people you've identified. Unlike a traditional date, or a conference lunch meeting, you won't need to manufacture an opening gambit to begin conversing. You already know things about each person at the event, mutualities you can use to take things further.

To summarize: Roundtables and speed dating allow you to meet more people, spend less time with each person figuring out whether you want to get to know them better, and obtain the information you need to deepen the relationship. What's not to like?!

What happens during roundtable sharing

As you might expect, some people are anxious about sharing at a roundtable. Most discover, when their turn comes, that speaking to everyone else isn't so bad (especially when they remember that *everyone* gets to do it).

Many interesting things happen during attendee sharing.

Obviously, you get to hear intriguing tidbits about and from people you haven't met before. I especially appreciate that I get to experience even those I already know in a fresh context through the roundtable. Sharing allows me to check in with old friends and hear what's currently on their minds.

The roundtable provides explicit feedback about the level of interest in topics. Hot subjects become evident through repetition, murmurs, and body language. Unexpected subjects come up, and are incorporated into subsequent sharing. And sometimes, it becomes clear by default that there's little interest in a topic that was expected to be popular with attendees.

But what I find to be most interesting and wonderful about roundtable sharing is how the atmosphere invariably changes as people speak; from a subdued nervousness about talking in front of strangers to an intimacy that grows as people start to hear about topics that engage them, discover kindred spirits, and learn of unique experiences and expertise available from their peers. When sharing is over, both a sense of comfort and excitement prevail: comfort arising from the knowledge attendees have of their commonalities with others, and excitement at the thought that they now have the rest of the conference to explore the connections and possibilities that the roundtable has introduced.

The peer conference roundtable is a gift to attendees, a gift to be taken and used as each person wishes, a gift that keeps on giving during the conference. Surprisingly, the roundtable is ultimately a catalyst—supplying nothing, save perhaps permission, to the interactions that participants create—a gift that people give of and to themselves.

Observations on roundtable size

There is a practical limit to the number of participants for a successful roundtable. This limit comes from the maximum amount of time that people can be expected to sit in one place and concentrate on what is being said. The roundtable is held at the start of the peer conference when attendees' energy and power of concentration is generally highest. But even so, sitting and listening to people speak, one after the other, will eventually lead to overload.

The maximum time I'd inflict on a group to sit and listen to each other is two and a half hours. Any longer moves into the realm of cruel and unusual punishment. Introducing the roundtable takes 15 minutes, leaving 135 minutes for sharing. I've found that 120–150 seconds is an adequate amount of time for each person to speak for conferences longer than a day. This leads us to a maximum roundtable size of 55–65 attendees before attendees' eyes start to glaze over.

Although a one-day conference can get away with a shorter sharing time, perhaps 90 seconds per attendee, I have found it difficult to create an intimate one-day conference with more than 50 attendees. Putting these considerations together, *we end up with a maximum roundtable size of around 60 people.*

So what can you do if you have over 60 attendees? My solution is to hold two simultaneous roundtables. At first glance that might seem to remove one of the most important benefits of the roundtable—the ability to be introduced to everyone else at the start of the conference. Well, it's true that you have to give up a *direct* connection to everyone, but it's possible for everyone to learn the important stuff that happens in the other roundtable by using a "buddy system." The details are laid out in the third part of this book, but, briefly, the process involves the following steps:

- Divide attendees into two roundtable groups;
- Create attendee pairs with one person from each group;

- Have each pair share their answers to the three questions with each other;
- Run the two roundtables separately, during which each attendee adds a brief summary of their pair buddy's answers to the roundtable questions; and
- Have each pair member summarize for their buddy their roundtable's responses, especially those relevant to their buddy's interests and experiences, and share any topics of special interest.

There are two reasons why I have not tried to increase the maximum size for a peer conference by running three or more simultaneous roundtables. First, the buddy system described above for communicating information between the two roundtables becomes unwieldy and impractical if the buddy groups contain more than two people. And second, it's my belief that above a hundred people, the communal environment of a peer conference fragments into mostly non-intersecting groups.

The end of the beginning

The roundtable is normally the longest single session at a peer conference, calling for a high degree of sustained concentration by participants. When it ends, the immediate participant response tends to be one of relief at being able to relax after processing an intense flood of information from everyone present.

Once participants have had an opportunity to absorb what's happened, however, a new dynamic sets in. They find that they have received both permission and opportunity to act in a way that is new for anyone who hasn't attended a peer conference before, a way that not only leads to meaningful interactions between people but also gives them the power and responsibility to determine what will happen next.

> "Now this is not the end. It is not even the beginning of the end. But it is, perhaps, the end of the beginning."
>
> —*Winston Churchill. Speech given on November 10, 1942*

In my experience, people love the fresh and energizing start that a roundtable provides to a conference. You hear a loud hum of conversation as they seek out and engage the other participants they've discovered who share their interests and experience. It's clear to me, both from direct observation as well as attendee post-conference evaluations, that the roundtable alone offers a major improvement on traditional conference process.

But wait, there's more! In the next phase of the peer conference, peer session sign-up, attendees discover how their wishes and collective expertise transform into matching conference sessions. Read on to see how this works.

CHAPTER 7

Middles—the "Meat" of the Peer Conference

Preparing for peer sessions

After the roundtable and a break, I like to schedule a social event, usually one involving food. This is a time for people, primed with information about the other participants, to start connecting with each other. At this point, the roundtable has uncovered both the topics that attendees are interested in, as well as the expertise and experience the group possesses. Now it's time to see what people want to do with this knowledge and to give them the means to do it.

I call the conference sessions that are developed during this time *peer sessions*. The most popular formats are discussions, presentations, and panels, but I've also seen workshops, tours, and simulations proposed.

Sharing at the roundtable gives an indication of the level of interest in topics that people mention, but, in my experience, the roundtable is a crude instrument for reliably gauging the appeal of a topic. If, for example, the last person who speaks at the roundtable reveals that she knows about something important to other attendees, there's no opportunity for anyone to express interest at the roundtable. People often think of topics they want to discuss after the roundtable is over, and sometimes these topics turn out to be surprisingly popular.

So, in order to determine a peer conference program that truly reflects what attendees want, it's necessary to go through three short but crucial activities—(1) *topic suggestion*, (2) *peer session sign-up*, and (3) *peer session determination and scheduling*. The first two activities embody Clay Shirky's "publish, then filter" model for communities of practice that I discussed

Examples of peer session flexibility

Yes, most peer sessions consist of two to four simultaneous presentations, panels, or discussions. But peer session sign-up sometimes uncovers other appropriate formats . . .

- At a peer conference held at Hildene, Robert Todd Lincoln's family home in Vermont, participants took advantage of three naturalists in their midst to create a "Walk in the Woods" peer session where they enjoyed and learned much about the estate's spectacular four hundred acres.

- At another peer session sign-up, it became clear that everyone was interested in a presentation that an attendee had given elsewhere a few months earlier. The attendee was happy to repeat the presentation as the sole activity scheduled during a peer session timeslot.
- Some attendees at a third peer conference were fascinated by the technology available at the conference site. A technical tour of the facilities was quickly arranged and hosted by site personnel.

in Chapter 4. Attendees get to publish anything they want to have happen (topic suggestion), and then vote for the topics that interest them (peer session sign-up), thereby transparently filtering the most popular topics for the group. Finally, a volunteer subset of conference attendees reviews the sign-up sheets, chooses the most popular viable topics, and schedules them into the conference program (peer session determination and scheduling). The whole process usually takes less than an hour, and can be done while people are socializing. Here's how it's done.

Topic suggestion

Now that many potential conference topics have been aired during the roundtable, we need to bring the divergent phase of conference topic selection to a close. We do this by asking attendees to *visually document* their wishes for the upcoming conference sessions. I call this process "topic suggestion," and it takes less than fifteen minutes.

By creating a visual record of all attendee session suggestions, each attendee can be sure that their desires have been included in the group's pool of topics, and the entire spectrum of possible choices is made available for all to see.

The procedure is very simple. I set out, either taped or pinned on walls or laid on tables, multiple sign-up sheets like the one in Figure 7.1 and Appendix 2.

FIGURE 7.1 • Peer Session Sign-up Sheet

Peer Session Topic: _____

_____

_____

_____	_____
_____	_____
_____	_____
_____	_____
_____	_____
_____	_____
_____	_____
_____	_____
_____	_____
_____	_____
_____	_____
_____	_____

Please . . .

. . . place an (**F**) next to your name to indicate you'd be willing to *facilitate* the group.

. . . place an (**E**) next to your name to indicate you have some *experience* or *expertise* in the peer session's topic.

. . . place a (**P**) next to your name to indicate you'd be prepared to be a *presenter* or *panelist* for the group.

. . . place an (**S**) next to your name to indicate you'd be prepared to *scribe* for the group.

Also, indicate your level of interest in the topic by placing the number **1**—*low*, **2**—*medium*, or **3**—*high* next to your name.

I ask everyone to write descriptive titles of session topics that they'd like to attend and/or present on the sign-up sheets. Only potential peer session topics are entered on the sheet at this stage. People can suggest as many sessions as they'd like, writing each one at the top of a separate sheet. They are encouraged to ask for anything they'd like to have happen, irrespective of whether they think it will be popular or not. Attendees are also told that they don't need to duplicate a topic that someone has already suggested, but, if they have a slightly different idea for the session, they should write their own version on a separate sheet.

At the end of peer session sign-up, attendees have a wall or tables full of session topics to review. Now we move to the convergent phase of peer session selection—winnowing down the complete list of suggestions to a manageable number of topics—peer session sign-up.

Peer session sign-up

With a full array of topics of interest displayed for all to see, it's time to determine the peer session topics that will make it into the peer conference program. We now need to discover which topics are popular, and to find attendee resources that will enable us to create feasible sessions on the subjects people want.

To determine which topics are popular, peer session sign-up uses a simple voting scheme. Attendees are asked to review all the topic sheets on display and sign their names under the topic titles they are interested in. I explain that signing their name doesn't obligate them to attend any session; it simply will be used to indicate the degree of interest in each topic.

I also use peer session sign-up to find out who can help make sessions happen, and to gauge individual interest in each topic. As people sign their names, they indicate whether they could potentially help with the session—as a facilitator, as someone with experience or expertise in the subject, as a presenter or panelist, or as a volunteer scribe who will create a record of the session. They do this by placing an "F" (facilitator), "E" (experience/expertise), "P" (presenter/panelist), or "S" (scribe) next to their name. In addition, they are asked to add the number 1—low, 2—medium, or 3—high, indicating their level of interest in the topic.

Discovering available resources for proposed peer sessions allows us not only to find people to lead sessions, but also to avoid scheduling sessions on popular topics that no one at the conference knows much about.

Once peer session sign-up is over we have almost all the information we need to choose and schedule sessions that meet attendees' expressed needs and wants. The whole process generally takes no more than fifteen minutes. At the end of sign-up, I ask for a small group of volunteers to work on the final step in creating the conference program—peer session determination.

Peer session determination and scheduling

Peer session determination and scheduling is one of those processes that can take more time to explain than it takes to do. I've provided a detailed guide to the process in Chapter 25, and will give a brief outline here.

While peer session sign-up is going on, I assemble a small group of volunteers to create and schedule the peer sessions. I include people who are subject matter experts on the conference theme, so we can evaluate topics that people have proposed. Once sign-up is over, the volunteers retreat to a quiet location with plenty of table space where the sign-up sheets can be easily viewed, shuffled, and clustered.

Before the conference begins, I draw up a preliminary schedule for the time allocated for peer sessions. Over the years, I've found that assigning time slots of 45–60 minutes works well for most peer conferences. Occasionally you may want to revise this schedule if a compelling session opportunity turns up, for example, someone offers a long presentation that other attendees are eager to hear.

Normally you'll want to have more than one peer session scheduled during each time slot. An exception would be if a suggested topic is so popular that just about everyone wants to attend the session, though this rarely happens. A very small conference might have as few as two simultaneous sessions, a larger conference as many as four. Once you've decided on the maximum number of sessions, you can start selecting the most popular topics that are also viable (meaning that there are people signed up to facilitate and/or provide the requisite expertise).

Figure 7.2 shows the steps needed to determine which peer sessions will be held, and to schedule the resulting sessions. First, topics are scanned for overlap, low interest topics are removed from consideration, and the most popular topics (based on the number of signatures) are chosen.

After a final decision as to whether similar topics should be merged, the remaining topic sheets are checked to see whether the session is viable—are there attendees who are able and willing to facilitate and/or provide appropriate expertise? Expertise is not always needed, as discussion-oriented peer sessions often just require a competent facilitator. If a particular peer session requires specific attendees to be present, this is the time to ask them whether they will commit to being there. Most people are flattered to be asked, and happy to agree.

If expertise is needed for a group but not available, then the topic is not scheduled. This rarely happens, but it's important not to schedule a session that can't be supported by peer experience. I usually announce this to attendees, so they understand why a popular session isn't on the program. If the conference is a repeated event, the organizing committee may want to consider inviting an appropriate outside expert to a future conference.

FIGURE 7.2 • Peer Session Determination and Scheduling

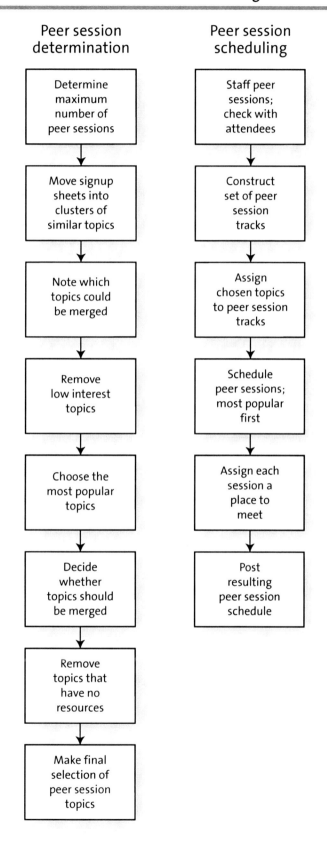

Once a final set of peer session topics has been chosen, scheduling them for specific time slots in the program is done essentially in the same way as a conventional conference. The topics are sorted into tracks, and each topic in a track is scheduled to a different time slot. One advantage over scheduling sessions at a traditional conference is that we have the sign-up sheets for each topic. By comparing the names signed up for each topic, we can schedule peer sessions to minimize conflicts between simultaneous sessions.

The last task is to assign each group a place to meet. This involves matching the popularity of the group and any resources it may need, like whiteboards or digital projection, to the size and capabilities of the available locations.

After the selected peer sessions have been scheduled in time and space, the schedule is printed and given to each attendee. I also post copies of the schedule around the conference site, including the places where attendees socialize and where peer sessions are held.

Running peer sessions

So, which is it? Actually, Merlin and Chris are both right. At traditional conferences, the juicy stuff often happens away from the sessions, in the hallways, while at peer conferences or the Open Space events that Chris facilitates, the rooms where the sessions are held are the loci for the conference energy. In this section I'll describe the heart of every peer conference: *peer sessions*, the sessions generated by the roundtable and peer session sign-up processes.

> "It's all about the hallways."
>
> —*Merlin Mann. Comment about traditional conferences, MacBreak Weekly podcast #78, 2/20/08*

> "It's all in the room."
>
> —*Chris Corrigan. The Tao of holding space.*

During peer session determination and scheduling, the format for each chosen peer session—presentation, panel, discussion, workshop, simulation, tour, or excursion—becomes clear. Sometimes the actual session strays a little from what was originally proposed, for example, when a presenter discovers that there are two people present who have valuable experience to contribute, or an attendee clearly knows considerably more than her fellow panelists. Peer sessions handle such developments on the fly, with the help of a short printed *Peer Session Primer* (see Appendix 4) that provides attendees the information they need to participate in a peer session. Take a moment to review this handout now—it answers the majority of questions people ask.

Although the mix of session formats varies from conference to conference, I have noticed that peer conferences tend to have a much higher proportion of discussion-based sessions than traditional conferences.

A peer session, whatever its form or subject, is informal. The number of attendees at any session is small, usually less than fifteen, encouraging a casual atmosphere. As a result, peer session presentations or panels are very different from traditional conference presentations or panels. Because topics are determined at short notice, no one attending a session expects polished speeches, thus providing an unthreatening environment for attendees who have discovered that they have something of value to share. In general, questions during the session are welcomed.

Every peer session has an attendee facilitator assigned before the session takes place. (For a presentation, the presenter *is* the facilitator.) The handout *Peer Session Facilitation* (see Appendix 5) gives session facilitators appropriate guidance.

It's important to capture what happens during conference peer sessions by creating a record of each session's activities and content. This record is often of great interest to people who couldn't be present, and the inclusion of participants' names provides the opportunity of follow-up by non-attendees. I recommend that a peer session scribe be found for each session. The scribe is responsible for recording the names of people present (using a circulated attendance sheet) and creating notes on peer session content. The scribes' work is then posted on a conference website or wiki, together with links to any other resources mentioned during the session, for the benefit of all attendees.

CHAPTER 8 Endings

How to end a conference?

At a traditional conference, where the emphasis is on transferring information via fixed presentations, it's hard to provide a meaningful closing event—there's nothing to close. Because the conference doesn't develop around its theme, or around attendees' individual journeys, it lacks logical progression from one session to the next. As a result, once there are no interesting sessions left, an attendee has no reason to stay. From this viewpoint, providing lavish banquets, award ceremonies, or celebrity speakers for a closing session are artificial attempts by traditional conference organizers to prop up attendance until the conference is officially over.

At a peer conference we have an easier task. The peer conference process encourages the flow of each attendee's journey through the conference. First, conferees meet at the roundtable and get to know each other through discovering shared themes and topics. Later, peer session sign-up exposes significant interests; attendees then explore these interests through the peer sessions that follow. As the conference proceeds, attendees share and learn in ways that are individually meaningful, and their connections with each other grow. By the time that the last peer session ends, attendees have had significant opportunities to build individual and group relationships, leading to the creation of a *conference community*, a group of people who are bound together by their recent experiences together.

Traditional conference planners worry about keeping people there until the end of the conference. They may feel that a significant number of early departures gives the impression that the

98

conference was not successful, or they may be concerned that defections from an expensive closing banquet or other high-profile event will lead to waste or monetary loss.

Whatever you do, some people are going to leave before a conference is over. However wonderful a conference may be, it is not the primary focus of attendees' lives, and the constraints of work, family, and travel arrangements can conflict with the demands of a conference schedule.

Rather than trying to reduce attendee early defection by supplying inducements to stay until the end, we should be working to make our conference so valuable, so relevant, that attendees don't want to miss a thing. They will take an inconvenient late-night flight, put up with a shortened weekend home with the family, and make every effort to stay at your conference simply because it's such a great experience and they don't want to leave.

So, how should we end a peer conference? Attendees have spent time learning and sharing about important and meaningful topics, and they've made connections with each other. What could we offer that would build on their experience up to this point?

> "If an association planner's worst fear is miniscule attendance, then the second biggest fear is attendees scooting out before the final night banquet."
>
> —*Jennifer Nicole Dienst. Getting attendees to stay for the final night bash. Meetings and Conventions Magazine, November 2007*

I believe that effective closure for a group of people who have spent time together requires opportunities to personally integrate what has happened; share conclusions, realizations, and plans with others; and discuss and decide collectively about the group's future activities. To address these needs, I have developed two closing peer conference sessions that complement and enhance what has happened at the conference for each attendee.

Making learning stick

Remember the conversation between the two women on the San Francisco Airport shuttle bus? One of them announced she didn't remember anything about the conference she attended last year, and probably wouldn't remember anything from her current conference either. At how many of the conferences you've attended do you remember specific learning that was valuable to you?

If your answer is along the lines of "not many," you're in good company. Sadly, most people are unable to recall significant conference experience from the majority of their conference attendance. Many an attendee has left a conference on a Friday fired up with ideas and resolutions, only to have their plans fade once they become re-immersed in their busy work life the following Monday.

So, how can we make our conference learning and generated passion stick?

One flaw of traditional conferences is the lack of formal time to integrate and reflect on personal learning acquired during the conference. After attending a conference that gave me this opportunity (as described in the next section) I became convinced that such a session would be valuable, and added a guided *personal introspective* to my longer peer conferences. The session was immediately popular, occasionally life-changing for some participants.

A personal introspective has two parts. The first gives each attendee the gift of conference time to review and evaluate what she has learned, tools to determine consequent life and work changes she might make, and a framework for a workable and measurable plan for making the changes. Providing specific conference time for the review sends the message that an attendee's individual conference experience, what she learns from it, and any resulting plan or life changes are of value. Just the act of reviewing her conference experience while it is fresh reinforces her memory of what took place, increasing the chance that she will actually carry out any plans she has come up with. Providing tools to decide on specific changes and a plan to carry them out supports attendees in making the first important steps toward appropriate, empowered change.

The second part provides an opportunity for all conference attendees to share their conclusions with the group. This sharing turns out to be very powerful, invariably creating a heightened sense of connection and intimacy among the group members. I'll say more about this later on.

Looking backward and forward

The Roman god Janus, the god of beginnings and ends, is usually depicted with two heads looking in opposite directions, representing his ability to see both the future and the past.

When I first began organizing conferences, it seemed natural to me to include a closing session where the entire conference group could act like Janus—we would get together to look backward and forward, discuss what we had learned, what we had gained, and what we might want to do next. I called it a wrap-up session, and ran it as an informal discussion, letting it ramble the way people wanted.

Over time I began to see different ways in which groups used this time. Groups that

hadn't met before, for example, wanted to talk about whether and/or how they might meet again, or changes that they might make in the conference format or defining theme. Repeated conference groups often concentrated on refining the conference process or schedule. Sometimes group initiatives were proposed and discussed, and, if they were found to have substantial support, people wanted to use the session to explore how they could be implemented.

These varied, and usually unpredictable, needs make this final session the most challenging peer conference session to facilitate.

Eventually I learned about facilitation activities that support the various kinds of group process and interaction that groups want. I experimented using these approaches. I continue to experiment today, but by now I have a handful of time-tested ways to facilitate what I call a *group spective*. You can read more about the group spective later in this chapter.

The personal introspective

History

In 2003 I attended Amplifying Your Effectiveness, an innovative annual conference in Phoenix designed around experiential learning. Software and team management consultant Esther Derby facilitated the last session: "Reflection Leading to Action." Esther had us reflect about our experience at the conference, about what we might want to happen in our lives as a result, about how we might go about making changes, about how we would know we were successful, and about how we would get support. Her questions helped us to focus on what we had learned at the conference and what we could commit to changing in our lives as a result.

I found Esther's session valuable, and adapted it into what I now call a *personal introspective*, a session I include near the end of all but the shortest of the peer conferences I facilitate.

What happens at a personal introspective?

A personal introspective is a peer conference session where, to start, attendees privately answer in writing the five questions listed at the start of this section. These questions offer attendees an invitation to think about their conference experience, how it may impact their life in the future, and what changes they may want to make as a result. After five to ten minutes of reflection, each attendee, in turn, is given the option to share her answers with the entire group.

Purpose

The fundamental purpose of a personal introspective is to give attendees a chance to explore changes they may want to make in their life and work as a result of their conference experiences.

Each attendee is free to respond at whatever level he finds appropriate and comfortable at the time. Some people come up with ideas for small changes in their lives, while others come to profound realizations that have significant consequences. At first glance, the space and time provided for answering these questions is another peer conference tool that attendees can use as they see fit. Practically, at the personal level, the personal introspective is a significant process and opportunity that a peer conference offers to each attendee.

If this service were all that a personal introspective provided, then, in the words of the Jewish Passover song "Dayenu"—*It would have been enough*. But the subsequent sharing by attendees adds more to the personal introspective, creating a vehicle for a heightened sense of connection and intimacy among group members. It can feel risky to share with others what are often personal aspects of the changes one wishes to make, and to then share the decisions one has made to start work on such changes. Taking such risks is an integral step on the path of building intimacy—not only the increased intimacy that the sharer feels, but also the group's connectedness as more and more people share. In a safe environment, the outcome is increased trust, which further builds safety.

By sharing with the group, attendees deepen their commitment to carrying out the goals and actions that they share.

The five questions

The personal introspective questions I use are based on Derby's, which in turn derive from the concept of SMART goals outlined in management consultant Peter Drucker's 1954 classic, *The Practice of Management*. SMART is a mnemonic that is most commonly described as standing for Specific, Measurable, Attainable, Relevant, and Timely goal characteristics. Stressing these qualities when fashioning personal goals helps attendees avoid impractical plans and activities.

The first question, *"What do I want to have happen?"* helps attendees focus on future plans and actions, as shaped by their conference experience. It makes explicit the start of attendees' transition away from the intensity of the conference back to their normal work or life routine. The question suggests others: "What has struck me during my conference experience?" or "What new ideas do I want to take back, to foster and nurture after the conference is over?" or "What changes might I want to make in my life and work?" This question is asked first to encourage an open-ended big-picture approach to change.

The second question, *"What is the current situation?"* brings attendees' attention back from their future goals to the present, inviting them to summarize where they are now. This is an important question, one that grounds people in their current reality.

The first two questions define the starting and potential ending points of each attendee's future journey. The third question, *"What am I willing to do?"* invites attendees to plan the practical actions that will take them from where they are now to where they want to go. The inclusion of "willing" in the question guides attendees toward a response to which they can commit.

> • What do I want to have happen?
> • What is the current situation?
> • What am I willing to do?
> • How will I know when it happens?
> • Where and how will I get support?
>
> —*The five personal introspective questions*

The fourth question, *"How will you know when it happens?"* checks whether what attendees want to happen is measurable in a way that has meaning for them. The emphasis here is on the *process* individuals use to choose what to measure rather than *what* they decide to measure. Without measurable actions and outcomes, how will attendees know how to manage the process of change, gauge progress toward their goals, or know when they've succeeded—a sure recipe for frustration.

The fifth question, *"Where and how will I get support?"* encourages attendees to create a list of potential resources they can use to support their plans for change. If these resources include people at the conference, they can touch base with them before the conference ends.

The value of a personal introspective

I continue to be surprised by the power of a personal introspective. At every session I have run, a number of people have, emotionally, publicly announced how important the exercise was for them. In peer conference evaluations, typically about 60 percent of attendees rate personal introspectives "high," 35 percent "moderate," and 5 percent "low." Giving people the opportunity to come together, process, and then share their experiences and realizations generates a sense of connection and intimacy among attendees that needs to be experienced to be believed.

The group spective

The personal introspective and the group spective encourage attendees to take stock, reflect on where they started, the path traveled, and the journey yet to come. The *personal introspective* enables attendees to make this assessment personally, while the *group spective*, the last session of a peer conference, provides a time and place to make this assessment collectively.

The group spective is an exciting session because it holds great potential—it offers the possibility to determine and manifest an explicit future for the group, allowing the gathering to create something lasting, something more than an intense, one-time experience for attendees.

During the session, attendees begin exploring their future together. They may decide to hold another peer conference, and/or they may decide to plan meetings or activities that are targeted to specific needs and interests. Every group spective I've facilitated has led to future collective activity by conference attendees.

The group spective is a *consensus-building* session. I define *consensus* in this context as an understanding or agreement that allows the group to move forward; a consensus does not mean that everyone agrees one hundred percent, or will be involved in a specific initiative. Consensus is not determined by win-lose voting, or by selling a course of action to reluctant attendees. Rather, reaching consensus requires a collective process involving the development of group understanding, and the discovery of the necessary energy and commitment for future action.

There is a temptation for personal agendas to emerge early in a group spective. Some attendees may see the gathering as a way to further their own ideas of what participants should be doing. Careful facilitation can help avoid the proceedings being biased by the strong opinions of a few.

Every group responds to the challenge of a group spective differently, and, as a result, I find it to be the most difficult session to facilitate. And yet, as a session defining the future of the group, a spective promises great rewards that are well worth the work and concentration invested in facilitating the process.

Why a group spective?

Influenced by consultant Norman Kerth's book, *Project Retrospectives: A Handbook For Team Reviews,* I used to call the final peer conference session a group *retrospective*. Halfway through a 2007 conference, information technology director J. T. Amirault, reviewing the upcoming schedule, remarked to me that calling our final session a group retrospective implied that it was about looking back on the past conference experience, rather than moving forward, toward what might be possible, what we might do in the future. This was a good point, and when the group retrospective started, I repeated his comment to the attendees. I then attempted to justify my use of the word *retrospective*, saying that *we need to know where we are now, and how we got there, before we can figure out both where we want to go, and our path for the journey.* Once we have explored and shared our common understanding of our current position and inclinations, I said, we can start to examine and plan our potential futures together.

Although that got me through the conference, I subsequently felt dissatisfied with the term *retrospective.* I wanted to give the session a name that didn't contain a reference solely to the past, a way for attendees to examine and absorb the group lessons that the conference had provided, in order to foster group and individual understanding that informed attendees in their discussion and planning for the future.

While searching for a better word, I discovered that Chaucer's *Squire's Tale*, written around 1395, employs the wonderful noun *prospective* to describe a glass or mirror that allows one to see objects or events not immediately present. Wanting a word that combined looking back *and* looking forward, I decided to discard both prefixes and simply call the group session a *spective*, reflecting the Latin root *spicere*, to look at or see.

Describing the group spective as a process encompassing the past, present, and future, a process that creates a coherent view of where we have come from, where we are now, and our choices and plans for the future, helps me and attendees understand the role the group spective fills.

Choices

The goal of a spective is to provide a place and time for people to productively reflect, share, discuss, and perhaps decide on future projects and activities. The peer conference up to this point has already developed an environment where attendees are open for such work. What makes facilitating a spective difficult is that it's hard to predict how people want to use their time together. Clues appear—sometimes rapidly, sometimes subtly—during the session. This means that a facilitator must pay close attention and continually provide structure and guidance that's appropriate to the changing needs of the group.

Facilitating a group is challenging work that grows increasingly difficult as the group gets larger, and I don't know of any substitute for experience. Often, the group itself will have plenty of ideas about what should happen, and the facilitator's job involves hanging on for the ride and providing what direction and support she can. Fortunately, there are a number of established methods for facilitating healthy group process. The ones I use—*informal discussion, plus/delta, go-around, affinity grouping,* and *focused discussion*—are described in the third section of this book.

Group spective outcomes

Ultimately, the group spective exposes attendees' responses to the currents and themes evoked by the conference. Their reactions, in turn, generate energy and ideas about the group's future. Thus the spective provides an arena for group reflection and action, once attendees have connected over the course of the conference. A good group spective's energy and ideas honestly represent the outcomes of the group's time together. While a peer conference concentrates on and supports each attendee's individual journey, that journey would go nowhere without the contributions from the other people present. This is the paradox and beauty of the peer conference process, the blending of individual and group work into a single, complex, and fascinating event.

CHAPTER
9 Wishes

The other day I was sitting in my favorite chair, checking my email, when a message arrived from a good friend, telling me about an upcoming conference on a subject dear to my heart. At that very moment, there was a pop and a puff of smoke and a beaming, elderly woman appeared beside me.

"Who are you?" I blurted out.

"Why, I am your fairy godmother my dear. Hmm," she continued, reading over my shoulder, "that looks like something you'd like to go to. Tell you what. I'm going to grant you three wishes about this conference. Sorry, but they can't include winning the closing raffle, avoiding all flight delays, or anything like that. Our powers are limited these days, but I *can* change what happens there so it's more to your liking. So, what do you wish? No rush."

OK, this didn't happen to me. Yet. But here's my list:

1. The conference will be about what I want it to be about, and will answer my pressing questions.
2. I'll get to know and hang out with all the attendees I'd most like to meet.
3. I'll have lots of fun.

What would your list be like? Would it be like mine?

I believe that the peer conference model provides the best opportunity for each attendee to get what he or she wants and needs out of a conference. In the next two sections of this book, you'll find out in detail how to plan and prepare a peer conference, and how to run one. My wish is that you find peer conferences valuable and rewarding for you.

PART II

Planning and Preparing for Your Peer Conference

CHAPTER 10 Overview

P rior to the creation of any new conference, there's always someone with a vision:

"Wouldn't it be great if the people in the different social service agencies in town had an opportunity to talk to one another?"

"I really want to meet quality control professionals who are struggling with some of the same problems I have."

"Credit counselors in the area need to get together and discuss the new trends and challenges facing them, and our organization is going to make this happen."

"This specialty didn't exist anywhere five years ago—how can we get together with other people who do what we do?"

"How can the county primary school teachers meet and productively talk about what *they* want to talk about, rather than the school district's agenda?"

Somehow, the vision gets shared with a few other people. They respond enthusiastically, and—excitement is kindled! We want to bring people together in a meeting! But how?

If I'm describing you right now, and you've read this far, perhaps you've decided to take the plunge and hold a peer conference. Or maybe you want to find out what's involved before you make a commitment to begin. Either way, this part of the book is for you!

You've got plenty to do—but don't worry about missing anything important. In this section I'll guide you through all the necessary steps to prepare for and plan the details of your conference. From how to get started, how to form a conference steering committee, choosing and scoping out a conference site, right through site setup, all the way to preparing conference evaluations, I'll show you how to make your conference a practical reality. Read on for all the details!

CHAPTER 11

How to Start Making Your Conference a Reality

I've never *organized* a peer conference by myself. I've run a small one-day conference by myself (and that was tough), but I'd never dream of doing the pre-conference design, planning, and marketing work solo. Here's why.

First of all, organizing a conference is a *lot* of work. Unless you're working full time at it, you're going to need and appreciate some help. But there's another important reason not to go it alone.

In my experience, a successful conference flows from a *diverse steering committee* that represents the variety of individuals, organizations, and viewpoints that are the target audience. A steering committee is a group of people who take responsibility for making a conference happen; they organize and run the conference. Although other people may do significant tasks, the steering committee is ultimately responsible for ensuring that the conference takes place and is successful.

Besides the benefit of sharing the workload, a well-chosen steering committee will supply multiple viewpoints on the conference design, and a variety of personalities and skill sets for the various conference tasks. One person happily handles conference registrations and conference fee deposits, another enjoys creating marketing materials, while a third is skilled at updating the conference website. You'll also have more resources for the external contacts you may need to develop any conventional parts of your program. And, perhaps most important, is the pleasure and excitement of sharing with your committee in creating an event that can meaningfully touch attendees' lives.

How do you start? Looking back at the conferences I've helped organize, there's always been an existing group that formed a starting point for the conference steering committee. It doesn't need to be a large group, maybe just three or four people. Typically, someone in the group suggests the idea of a conference and the others respond enthusiastically. You're on your way!

I'm not saying it's impossible for a single charismatic individual to inspire a conference and persuade volunteers to help, but I haven't seen it done, and I'd be wary of a peer conference that was largely the product of a single person's vision.

If you can't easily find people who will volunteer to help you, that's a strong indication that you need to think twice about creating the conference in the first place. There needs to be a certain level of energy for the conference to happen and for people to attend, and ease in finding people willing to serve on the steering committee is a good predictor of your readiness to organize a successful conference.

So, you and some members of an existing group decide you want to hold a conference. Perhaps there are three of you. What do you do next?

Forming a steering committee

I have organized peer conferences with steering committees as small as three and as many as a dozen people. In my experience, 5 to 10 volunteers is a good size for a conference steering committee. With fewer than five, the workload starts to become excessive for a typical volunteer. Committees with more than 10 people tend to become unwieldy and decision making slows down, but I would not reject a couple of extra members if everyone has useful skills and enthusiasm for the work.

Try to form your conference steering committee from the members of an existing group. Suggest the idea of a conference to the group and, if there's sufficient interest, explore the time commitment and work involved and ask for volunteers to help organize and run the conference.

Even if there isn't an existing group to approach, it's often possible to create a conference steering committee by contacting appropriate individuals who you expect may be interested and who have the energy and time to commit.

When you're talking to potential committee members, have in mind the variety of work you'll need to make your conference a reality. Use the list of jobs in Table 12.1 as a guide. Provide this list of conference tasks to the people you approach, so they can think about how they might best contribute and make a preliminary commitment to one or more areas. As people volunteer to help out, keep track of what remains as you assemble a committee that can, collectively, take responsibility for everything that needs to be done.

Group culture, leadership, and your steering committee

The quality of your peer conference and your pleasure, or lack of it, while you are planning and running the event can be greatly affected by how well your steering committee members work together. Over 100,000 books have been written about group dynamics, management, and leadership, and I doubt I have anything new to say on these subjects. Even so, I hope that the following comments provide some useful advice on the many subtleties of working with a group of people toward a common goal.

There are many models of how people behave in groups, and each of them is useful in certain contexts. In the context of organizing and running a peer conference, I tend to employ an *organic* model, in which group members are seen in terms of their uniqueness, rather than categorized by their roles. An organic point of view allows and encourages people to find ways to work together in a variety of complex situations, and leads toward problem-solving that benefits everyone.

For example a steering committee I coordinated was offered the option of engaging a well-known, desired keynote speaker for a conference to be held in six months. Initially, his appearance fee was more than our budget could

> "I believe organizations are successful when they have shared values, a clear vision of success, motivation to succeed together, and respect for the various roles required to succeed. Shared values help avoid irreconcilable differences. . . . While the vision must be clear, the leadership needs to be flexible. The world changes, and successful organizations need leaders who can guide them through those changes. Every member of the team must be motivated to participate in the team's success, although different people may have different motivations. One of a leader's roles is to understand those motivations and address the needs of the people on the team. One critical shared value is recognition of the importance of every person's role on the team. When people don't feel valued, they lose motivation to support the success of the team."
>
> —*Ken Flowers*

handle, but at the last minute he suggested appearing virtually, giving his presentation on a large video screen, at an affordable fee. We needed to quickly find out whether the conference site could support a virtual presentation.

If we had been using a linear approach to group organization, we would have already chosen the steering committee member responsible for technical issues and it would be her job to resolve this issue. If she were busy or sick, I'd have had to poll the other committee members for help and ask someone to take on additional work. In this case, our committee was comfortable with an organic approach, so I sent a request for help to all the steering committee members, most of whom had some technical expertise.

Because the committee culture was one of staying flexible in the face of unexpected circumstances, cooperatively working together to solve problems, and respecting each member's unique constraints and contributions, I didn't worry about treading on anyone's toes by sending out a general request for help. The outcome: One of the committee members had some free time and immediately offered his expertise, while another, the speaker liaison, told us he thought the speaker would have the information we needed and would check with him.

How do you build this kind of culture for your steering committee? This brings us to the question of what *leadership* means in the context of organizing and running a peer conference. Every book on leadership has a different approach; here's what fits for me.

Author and polymath Jerry Weinberg describes organic leadership as leading the *process* rather than *people*. "Leading people requires that they relinquish control over their lives. Leading the process is responsive to people, giving them choices and leaving them in control." Jerry's resulting definition of leadership is "the process of creating an environment in which people become empowered." This is what I try to elicit when working with a peer conference steering committee.

I also find Dale Emery's definition of leadership helpful. Dale describes leadership as "the art of influencing people to freely serve shared purposes." Bear this definition in mind as you work with steering committee members. It ties your interactions with them to your shared goal of realizing a vision, in this case organizing and running of a conference.

Who on the steering committee leads in this way? Unlike the traditional, role-based version of leadership, any member can help build a committee atmosphere that supports this kind of leadership. Once the seeds of this culture are established, I've found that it tends to become self-perpetuating. People like working together in this way. Experiencing a steering committee coming together, with the members enjoying their interactions while creating a great conference, is one of the most satisfying aspects of my work.

Although the impetus for an organic approach can come from any committee member, the conference coordinator is the natural initiator of these flavors of leadership. She is responsible for keeping the conference planning on track and avoiding planning and execution snafus. She does this, not by ordering people around, but through a respectful flow of timely reminders, check-ins, questions, requests for assistance, and appropriate redirections.

Some people have little experience working organically. They may join your committee with the expectation that their responsibilities will be determined by others, that a committee leader will give them well-defined jobs to do. Often, given a relaxed and open environment where their ideas are encouraged, they will grow into a more active role as they become more confident in their ability to contribute creatively and flexibly to the needs of organizing and running the conference.

Jerry Weinberg suggests you assume that everyone you're working with wants to feel useful and make a contribution. He quotes Stan Gross's device for dealing with his feelings that people are not trying to contribute: "They're all doing the best they can, under the circumstances. If I don't think they are doing the best they can, then I don't understand the circumstances."

Such a mindset will help you focus on finding solutions to people problems that inevitably arise in any group working together on something they care about.

Working with volunteers

Some peer conference steering committee members are paid by their organizations, but the majority, in my experience, are volunteers. When peer conference organization goes well, there's no significant distinction between these two groups. All organizers get paid in intangible ways. Volunteer motivations, usually shared by those receiving a paycheck, are numerous—altruism, the joy of service, giving back to a community that has benefited the volunteer, social opportunities, and many other reasons.

But the flip side of working with volunteers is the very lack of that paycheck. Interests and enthusiasm change with time, for both internal and external reasons, and there's no financial cost to bailing out from a committee if a volunteer's child or parent falls sick, he discovers a new passion, or finds that organizing the vendor exhibit takes more time than he thought it would.

As a result, volunteers sometimes are unable to follow through on their commitments. When this happens, don't take it personally. The reasons probably have nothing to do with you. Find out, with respect, what's going on, renegotiate responsibilities if possible, and ask committee members for help with any unassigned tasks.

Treating steering committee volunteers as individuals with unique motivations, and understanding and respecting these motivations, whatever they may be, is key to creating an environment for committee members to be effective and enjoy their work, thereby contributing to a positive and rewarding conference planning effort for all involved.

CHAPTER 12

The Steering Committee in Action

Your conference steering committee is responsible for planning and performing, either directly or by delegation, the work needed to create a successful conference. Now that you've pulled together a promising group of people, the next step is to figure out how you're going to meet, and what to discuss when you do.

How to meet?

Unless steering committee members have previous experience organizing a peer conference, I strongly suggest that you arrange for the first steering committee meeting to be face-to-face. Committee members are going to be working closely with each other organizing and running the conference, and you just can't duplicate the intimacy and exposure to other members' personalities and working styles that a face-to-face initial meeting provides. Becoming aware of and overcoming people's natural skepticism about the peer conference process is hard enough to do when you are meeting in person. Using a conference call for your first meeting makes it too easy to gloss over this skepticism, leading to a disappointing lack of buy-in by committee members.

If steering committee members are geographically separated, think about how you know each other. Perhaps you can meet during a traditional conference that you all attend.

I make an effort to have everyone present at the first steering committee meeting, as there are invariably questions about the peer conference approach. It helps to have steering committee members who have attended a peer conference before, as they can vouch for the effectiveness of the peer conference format. You should be prepared to spend some time explaining how a peer conference works, and reassuring skeptics that people will attend a conference where some or all of the sessions are not pre-planned.

If this isn't the first time your steering committee has organized an event, you may be able to meet solely via conference call or Internet conferencing. Even if you have one or two new members, they can usually be brought up to speed by another member.

Subsequent meetings can be face-to-face, or via conference call or Internet conferencing. Email is also often an appropriate way to get a lot discussed, but, compared to a real-time meeting, it can slow decision making.

Set aside at least a couple of hours for your first steering committee meeting—you've got plenty to talk about! If you're running a local conference and have a strong candidate for a site, try to meet there if possible. Make sure that someone takes minutes and distributes them to the committee afterwards, so that it's clear what has been decided and how the conference preparation work has been assigned.

The first steering committee meeting

Once you've figured out the when and where of your first steering committee meeting, it's time to prepare for the meeting itself.

What do you need to cover at the first meeting? Every conference is different, so use common sense to adapt what follows to your circumstances. Here's a typical agenda that you can use as a guide:

1. Introductions
2. Explain peer conferences
3. Determine conference theme, target audience, and possible traditional program elements
4. Discuss conference length, dates, and site possibilities
5. Brainstorm marketing strategies
6. Present conference tasks and roles
7. Agree on conference tasks and roles
8. Schedule future meetings

Let's look at these agenda items in more detail.

1. Introductions
If steering committee members don't know each other, have them introduce themselves. Ask them to tell everyone "how I got here."

2. Explain peer conferences
If committee members haven't attended a peer conference, it's natural for them to be skeptical about the feasibility of a conference where session content is undetermined until the conference is underway. (Distributing copies of this book before the meeting can help!)

Getting committee members comfortable with a conference with no predetermined agenda can take a while, but it's a critical task that is well worth whatever time is needed. Start by explaining briefly how peer conferences work. Emphasize that a peer conference empowers each attendee to participate in creating the conference they want. Then ask steering committee members how they feel about the approach, especially how they feel about providing significant time for peer sessions whose topics will be unknown until the conference is underway.

Ask any committee members who are still not convinced what they would like to get out of the conference. Remind them that at a peer conference they can ask for whatever they want. Then ask them whether they'd get that chance at a traditional conference. I find that when people realize that a peer conference gives them the opportunity to ask for what is meaningful to them and to shape what happens with other participants, they become enthusiastic about the possibilities for them personally and, by extension, for everyone at the conference.

Despite making your best effort, you should anticipate some lingering skepticism, even if your cohorts are willing to trust that things will work the "peer conference" way. Don't worry about this—time and again I've seen skeptics become believers as they experience their first peer conference!

3. Determine conference theme, target audience, and possible traditional program elements
If you've had preliminary discussions with individual steering committee members before the meeting, you probably won't find it too hard to agree on your theme. Deciding on the target audience may require more discussion; this is the time to introduce preliminary marketing and budget considerations. Don't worry too much about precise theme definition or audience targeting. The beauty of a peer conference is that your attendees will "fine-tune" your ideas on the conference theme, with the end result being an improvement over what the steering committee came up with. Just be sure that there is general agreement on what your conference is about and who may be interested in attending, so your marketing can accurately reflect these ideas.

Also discuss incorporating traditional pre-planned sessions into longer (two or more days) conferences. You don't need to decide on topics and presenters; it's enough at this point to rough out a range of possibilities for subsequent exploration.

4. Discuss conference length, dates, and site possibilities

At this stage, don't expect to settle on a cast-iron date, conference length, and site. Your goal should be to sketch out feasible calendar periods, get some bounds on the conference duration, and brainstorm a list of potential host locations. Narrowing down the resulting possibilities is the job of future committee meetings.

5. Brainstorm marketing strategies

Marketing your conference requires some serious planning. You'll need to turn fuzzy ideas about your target audience into promotional materials that entice prospective attendees to register. You'll need to create lists of prospective attendees who will receive your promotional pieces. That's why you should brainstorm marketing ideas at the first steering committee meeting; your marketing committee will need all the help it can get.

I've found the following approach useful for clarifying your marketing. Have each member answer these two questions:

- What would make this conference meaningful and useful for you?
- What do you think would make this conference a success?

Comparing members' answers provides information on how well their own conference goals align with their vision for the conference. If your steering committee reflects the target audience for the conference, the answers to the first question should expose plenty of useful marketing ideas.

Your discussion should clarify what the conference is about, and produce talking points about why your target audience should attend. Then brainstorm promotional ideas: sources for mailing and email lists, organizations that might be receptive to marketing to their members, other conferences or meetings where a conference announcement could be made, magazines and journals that would add your conference to their calendar, and any other marketing possibilities. Finally, realistically assess what your committee is capable of doing to create and carry out marketing, and what outside resources are needed to successfully promote your conference.

6. Present conference tasks and roles

Successful conferences don't just happen; there's plenty of work that goes into them. First there's the planning stage. Then before everyone arrives you'll need to prepare your site, and finally there's the work of actually running the conference.

At a minimum you'll need to plan and organize:

- Finding a site
- Marketing
- Finance
- Feeding attendees
- Session locations and timetable
- Registration
- Site preparation
- Running the conference

Depending on your conference plans, you may also have to provide:

- Accommodations
- Wiki and/or website management
- Vendor coordination
- Promotional items
- Coordination of traditional conference sessions

How do you get all this done? Working as a team, steering committee members have to first understand the tasks and then cooperatively distribute them, matching needs to talents, inclinations, and acceptable commitments. Loading jobs on reluctant volunteers (especially if they're not at the meeting where they're handed out) does not work; it leads to poor or incomplete performance, assuming that anything happens at all.

Before you ask for volunteers for any conference task, I suggest you present and describe all the jobs that will need to be done. Although this can take some time, it enables committee members to see the scope of the entire project and figure out what fits for them.

The conference tasks listed in Table 12.1 will be handled either by individuals or small committees. Steering committee members often will take on several roles and committees. An outline of the work is given later in this chapter, and in more detail in Chapters 13–24.

7. Agreements on conference tasks and roles

Once all the conference tasks have been described and you have clarified the scope of the related work, it's time to agree on who is going to do what. Flexibility is key here; people may be unwilling to take sole responsibility for a particular task and others may need to offer assistance. If you sense reluctance to take on a particular job, ask if someone else can help out.

TABLE 12.1 • Conference Tasks and Roles

TASKS	DESCRIPTION
Conference coordination	One person, the *conference coordinator,* who is responsible for keeping conference planning on track, and avoiding planning and execution snafus.
Pre-conference registration	Easily handled by a single committee member, the *pre-conference registrar,* who will liaise with the *treasurer* and *site coordinator* as registrations come in.
Site selection	Usually one to three people who research potential sites and report back to the steering committee.
Site visit	As many members of the steering committee as possible should visit the selected site.
Site coordination	You'll need a *site coordinator* to manage arrangements with the conference host you choose.
Conference hosting (when appropriate)	If someone interested in attending the conference works at your chosen nontraditional conference venue, ask him to join your steering committee as the *conference host.* The conference host liaises with host site personnel to negotiate site issues and is often deeply involved in site-specific administrative activities before and during the conference.
Program development	All steering committee members with relevant content experience should help develop the conference program. If traditional conference content is desired, the program committee needs to firm up this portion of the program early enough to enable inclusion of the details in conference promotional materials.
Meal and break planning	If the conference site is going to be responsible for providing conference meals and snacks for breaks, options should be discussed with the *site coordinator* and a representative of the food service during the site visit. Otherwise the *meals committee* will need to contact potential catering services and negotiate appropriate sustenance.
Marketing— promotional materials and publicity	During your initial steering committee meeting, discuss how much professional help you will need to promote your conference. Unless your steering committee includes members with professional marketing expertise, expect to use some outside help.
Website and/or wiki management	If you are going to use a website and/or wiki to market your conference and provide a platform for pre-conference communication, this will need to be set up by one or more of your steering committee members serving as *website or wiki managers.*
Finance	You'll need one or more *finance committee* members to develop a conference budget, which should then be approved by the steering committee. Have two committee members handle conference accounting, one who deposits incoming checks, and one who does the bookkeeping.

(continued on following page)

TASKS	DESCRIPTION
Accommodations	At a minimum, a committee member should create a list of accommodation options for registrants in the event they are unable or unwilling to stay at any accommodations available at the conference site.
Exhibit	Vendor solicitation (before conference) and coordination (at conference) can be significant work, requiring at least one *vendor coordinator*. A single person can usually handle vendor solicitation for a conference with fewer than 20 vendors, but sharing this job is not unusual. Vendor coordination during conferences can be a significant time commitment on Exhibit Day.
Site preparation	As many steering committee members as possible should arrive at the conference site in advance to help set up. Site preparation may include any or all of the following: arrangement of rooms, installing signs to help direct participants, providing and installing needed equipment such as flip charts, projectors, wireless microphones, and so on, and setting up the registration area.
On-site conference registration	The *pre-conference registrar* can also be responsible for registration at the conference, though this isn't always the case. Conference registration usually requires more than one person to welcome newcomers, sign them in, and hand out conference packets.
Entertainment	Optional. If included, have one or more members book appropriate entertainment that is within your budget.
Promotional items	If you plan to hand out promotional items (tee-shirts, mugs, etc.) to attendees or as thank-you gifts to steering committee members and others, you'll need to choose what you want, subject to budget, and get them personalized in good time for your conference. One person can do this; committees sometimes have a hard time agreeing on what to order.
Conference facilitation	You will need a facilitator and a couple of scribes for the roundtable, and a facilitator for spectives. You'll also need to choose the *conference announcer and timekeeper* (usually the conference coordinator) who will make announcements and take responsibility for keeping the conference running on time.
Evaluations	One steering committee member who is so inclined should be able to develop, distribute, and analyze conference evaluations, either paper-based or online.

Sometimes, no one at the meeting wants to volunteer for a specific conference task. If this happens to me, I ask for suggestions for people who might be interested in the job. So far I haven't had a problem finding the right person to cover the work that we need to get done. But don't let such gaps remain unfilled for long; your steering committee members need to know that all the conference organization work will be covered before they commit significant time and energy to making the conference happen.

Reaching agreement using Roman voting

How should a group make decisions? Common answers to this question include "by voting" or "by discussion and then the boss gets to decide." But what if we want a decision method that provides consensus, or as near consensus as we can get?

My favorite approach is a modified form of voting, called Roman voting, as described by Esther Derby in *Self-facilitation Skills for Teams* © 2004–2005, *Esther Derby*.

The following is excerpted with permission from Derby's article:

Agreeing On an Option

An individual making a decision may agonize over it, but when more than one person is involved, it can turn into an argument. Teams need a way to test their agreement, discuss concerns, and arrive at a decision that all can support.

The Romans indicated their will in the gladiator's arena with a thumbs-up or a thumbs-down. A modern modification of Roman voting helps teams arrive at a decision.

Thumbs-up = "I support this proposal."

Thumbs-sideways = "I'll go along with the will of the group."

Thumbs-down = "I do not support this proposal and wish to speak."

If all thumbs are down, eliminate the option. On a mixed vote, listen to what the thumbs-down people have to say, and recheck agreement. Be cautious about choosing an option if the majority are thumbs-sideways: This option has only lukewarm support.

This technique generates consensus. Consensus doesn't necessarily mean complete unanimity. Consensus means that everyone must be willing to support the idea, even if it's not his personal first choice.

Sooner or later, you'll have a situation where one person withholds support for any option. Manage this situation before it happens. At the start of the consensus process, set a time limit:

"We'll work really hard to reach consensus until the end of this meeting. If we don't have agreement by that time, we will turn the decision over to _____, or take a vote, or _____ (a technical expert, coach, manager) will decide."

Most people don't hold out to be obstinate; they are responding to a deeply held value or belief. Often the lone holdout will move on, but not at the cost of relinquishing an important belief. Respect the belief, use your fallback decision-making method, and move forward. However, when a group seldom reaches consensus, but instead relies on voting or deferring to authority, it's a sign there are deeper issues at play.

The keynote trap

The traditional conference model has molded most people's experiences and expectations so strongly that committee members will often push to have a keynote speaker at the conference, even when they have no idea of who the speaker might be. This is putting the cart before the horse. I have no problem with including a keynote speaker or predetermined presentation at a peer conference, provided the speaker is chosen due to her unique expertise, or the steering committee identifies a topic of great interest on which attendees have little knowledge and experts are available to present on it.

If committee members feel compelled to have a keynote speaker, have them discuss what they believe attendees want to hear about that they cannot obtain from their peers. You may discover that no particular topic comes to mind. Deciding that you must have a keynote first and then casting round for a subject is a clear sign that you're trapped in a traditional conference model. In my experience, keynote speakers chosen under such circumstances are generally a disappointing addition to a conference.

8. Scheduling future meetings

Before ending your first steering committee meeting, agree on any additional meetings and schedule them. Perhaps your marketing committee feels the need to brainstorm marketing materials and potential prospects, or the finance committee needs to hammer out a preliminary budget. You may well be able to conduct these meetings by telephone or online if the members are comfortable working together that way; if they live far apart, this may be the only reasonable option. While everyone's together, get out your calendars and decide on some possible site visit dates that allow as many steering committee members as possible to attend.

Steering committee tasks

This section describes in detail the scope of the work required to organize and run a peer conference. To provide some coherence, I've divided the tasks into the 19 discrete responsibilities or tasks summarized previously in Table 12.1, some of which may require more than one person. Since you'll have a dozen or fewer people on your steering committee, some members will have responsibilities in more than one area.

It's important that one person take the lead for each area. As David Allen points out in *Ready For Anything*, "When two or more are responsible for something, usually nobody is. . . . Shared responsibility works only when at least one person assumes that he or she will be totally responsible." As volunteers sign up for work, ask them whether they are willing to be the person with overall responsibility for the areas they choose.

Conference coordinator

Every peer conference requires a *conference coordinator*, one person who is responsible for keeping the conference planning on track; this is key to avoiding planning and execution snafus. If you have a business background, think of the conference coordinator as a *project manager*, with the project being your peer conference. The conference coordinator maintains a big-picture view of the conference creation process and is responsible for facilitating the work necessary to make the conference happen.

If you are a conference coordinator, familiarize yourself with the complete contents of this book. Other steering committee members can function well just knowing their specific responsibilities, but it is vital that *you* understand the details of how a peer conference is put together, the different tasks involved, and how they can be scheduled. This does *not* mean that you do the work. Your job is to create a good environment for the work to get done.

To minimize problems, monitor everything that's going on, track the progress of tasks that committee members have agreed to, and provide timely reminders of task timeframes and deadlines. When, despite your best efforts, your committee faces a challenge, it's up to you to facilitate a resolution.

The role of conference organizer, when it's going well, feels as though you are choreographing a dance, a dance in which each participant has abilities and limitations that you must learn, turn to good use, and respect in order to create a flowing performance. Be mindful of the delicacy and importance of your role, so that the resulting dance experience is enjoyable for the dancers, your committee, and your audience, the conference attendees.

Pre-conference registration

Pre-conference registration involves building and maintaining a database of conference registrations as they are received. One committee member can easily handle this work. The *pre-conference registrar* records participant registrations and forwards payments to the conference treasurer, liaises with the site coordinator to resolve any site or conference questions that come in with the registrations, and keeps the conference coordinator up-to-date on the number of people who have registered. Sometimes the same person processes conference check-in and last-minute registrations at the site.

A well-designed attendee database can manage and create most of the information and reports needed before and during the conference, including badges, the conference face book, attendee reports, mailing labels, conference packet labels, room occupant labels, room reports, attendee vendor reports, and more. On www.conferencesthatwork.com you'll find a user-modifiable FileMaker Pro conference database (compatible with both Macintosh and Windows operating systems) that will handle these conference tasks.

Site selection

The job of the *site selection committee* is to research potential conference sites, find viable candidates, and provide a site recommendation to the steering committee. Because follow-up site visits usually require significant time commitments, the site selection committee must carefully evaluate potential locations, to ensure time isn't wasted visiting a nonviable site.

Typically the site selection committee will have one to three members, who should be familiar with the criteria for a workable conference site described in Chapter 13.

If a potential site is local, site selection committee members should make a preliminary visit to confirm that this is a workable choice for the conference. For locations where a visit isn't practical, the committee needs to get in touch with the appropriate site contacts and determine the general feasibility of the site from afar before planning a site visit to nail down particulars.

Site visit

Chapter 14 describes in detail how to carry out a conference site visit. As many steering committee members as possible should visit the selected site; four people is a recommended minimum. The conference coordinator, site coordinator, conference host (if there is one), facilitator(s), and the vendor coordinator (if you're planning a vendor exhibit) should attend the site visit if at all feasible.

Site coordination

The *site coordinator* is responsible for communicating and making preparations with the appropriate contacts at the conference site. Often the conference coordinator will do double duty and take on this task, but if she's too busy, another committee member should handle the work.

Most of the site coordinator's questions should be answered at the site visit, but there are usually unresolved issues, such as details of meals and pricing, that require prompt follow-up after the visit so that conference publicity materials can be produced in a timely fashion.

Conference host (at nontraditional conference sites)

Sometimes, someone who works at your conference venue is involved with or interested in your conference theme. (Perhaps that's how you found your conference site in the first place.) If so, ask him to join your steering committee as the *conference host*. He'll work with your site coordinator, as the liaison between the committee and the host site. A conference host with an interest in your conference topic is a big plus for your conference; his personal motivation for the conference to succeed helps with overcoming any site-related problems that may arise, and he gets the personal satisfaction (and a reduced conference rate) from helping to create the conference.

Program development

At a minimum the *program development committee* must determine a workable schedule for your conference. If you're holding a pure peer conference, developing the program schedule is the *only* task of this committee. It can usually be done by one person and circulated to the steering committee for approval.

If traditional conference content (a keynote, presentations, panels) is desired, include everyone with relevant content experience on the program development committee. You want traditional session content to be chosen by as wide a representation of your target audience as possible.

Besides creating the program schedule, a program development committee for a peer conference that incorporates traditional content has two tasks: (1) to decide on the number, format, and content of traditional sessions, and (2) to agree on which committee members will organize each session.

Use a face-to-face meeting, phone conference, or wiki discussion page to work on these two tasks. Make sure that any financial, time, or space constraints are clear so that committee members don't waste time organizing a session that won't work.

Once the people responsible for each traditional session are determined, the conference coordinator monitors their progress and keeps them on track. Session moderators may not understand that their sessions must be firmed up in time for the marketing committee to include details in promotional materials; it's the coordinator's job to remind them.

Try to provide as accurate a conference program to attendees as far in advance as possible, but don't delay release of the schedule if some small details are still to be decided. Precise session start and end times are helpful, but not essential. If necessary, release the schedule with a brief explanation of any sessions that are still under development. Panel members can be listed as To Be Announced (TBA) if needed.

The early childhood education steering committee

Elissa jumped up to meet me as I entered her office. As the director of an agency special-izing in early childhood education, she had arranged for several colleagues to join us to organize a one-day conference for local early childhood educators.

"I'm really excited about the conference," she said, "though I have some questions." We were interrupted by the arrival of the other committee members, Muriel, Greta, and Shani. After introductions we sat down around a small table.

"I know that Elissa has talked to each of you about your ideas for this conference," I began. "Let's share them here. And this would be a good time for questions too!"

Muriel, director of a state-funded local agency, was the first to speak. "I see the conference as an excellent opportunity to reach out to day care directors. Many of them don't know what we do, or the ways we can help them. I'd like to have a place on the agenda for us to talk to childcare providers."

"Well, I meet regularly with many of them," Greta broke in. "I would like to go into depth on some of the issues that we don't have time to explore in our monthly lunchtime meetings."

"You know, there's a lot going on at the state level," added Shani, who had driven down from the capital. "I think it would be really helpful to hear about several early childhood intervention strategies that two neighboring states have introduced. We have only one day, and I think we should concentrate on big-picture ideas that can give participants some new ways to approach their work."

Elissa looked at me. "This is what I wanted to ask you about. I'm interested in hearing about everything that Muriel, Greta, and Shani have mentioned. Rose-Marie Chang, a well-known expert on early childhood education, has agreed to join us to give us a national perspective. How will she fit in?"

"I'm worried. We all have different ideas about what the conference can accomplish. Shouldn't we be setting up an agenda so that everyone has a chance to be heard? And how can we balance or prioritize all these difference viewpoints?"

Everyone looked at me. I drew a deep breath. Then I smiled.

"This always happens. I don't think I've ever worked with a steering committee whose members weren't worried that everything important to them would get covered. But you know what? It always works out. With the peer conference processes we'll use, the conference will automatically adjust to the needs of its participants. The people who want the big picture from Rose-Marie will have time and space to be with her, Elissa. The

regional issues, Shani, will be exposed too. Muriel, you'll get your chance to talk with day care directors. And your local network's needs, Greta, will also be addressed."

People looked skeptical. I tried again.

"OK," I said. "I can't guarantee that your ideas and viewpoints will be expressed in the form you have in mind right now. In fact, I'm sure that things will happen that you don't expect. There may be a different emphasis on your area; there may be more or less interest. But, and this is the crucial point, what happens will genuinely reflect attendees' needs, rather than being predetermined by us."

"That's why this process works, and why people enjoy it so much. Every participant will affect this conference in a way that's personally meaningful. Ultimately you have to trust the process. Every time I've done this, it's worked as well as it possibly could. In fact, in my experience it's the parts of the conference that are fixed and predetermined that people tend to enjoy and appreciate the least."

There was a short silence. "So when doesn't a peer conference approach work?" asked Elissa.

"Well, sometimes people are looking for answers and nobody's got any. I've seen peer sessions where that happens, and, when it does it's frustrating. But over the years I've developed a way to avoid scheduling topics where this seems likely to occur. We can usually seed the group with one or two people who have the experience the others need, or, at the worst, regretfully inform people that the group shouldn't be held because relevant experience is lacking among our attendees. So, no guarantees, but the odds of a useful group are very good. And for our conference, we've got experience and expertise at every level—the local level, Greta; the regional level, Muriel; the state level, Shani; and the national level via Rose-Marie! How can we lose?"

They weren't completely convinced. And why should they be? I was suggesting a new way of organizing a conference, a way they had not experienced before. But they trusted me enough to go ahead. And the conference went as well as I'd predicted. Though it was a small group of 30 participants, ranging from nationally known Rose-Marie to attendees running home-based day care, the peer sessions were well balanced and reflected the different participants' perspectives and experience.

Ultimately I don't know how to convince anyone that an agenda-less conference can work better than a conventional conference. The proof of the pudding is in the eating. It helps tremendously if someone on the steering committee has attended a peer conference, so the committee doesn't have to rely on trusting my zealous convictions. However, there's no

(continued on following page)

substitute for attending a peer conference and deciding for yourself. So if you have the opportunity to participate in one, seize it! And if you're organizing a peer conference, don't be surprised or disheartened when you hear reactions like those of Elissa, Muriel, Greta, or Shani. Consider the work you'll still need to do as—Early Conference Education.

HELP, HELP, HELP!

October 1996 found me with another annual conference to coordinate, and I was feeling depressed. The euphoria of the June conference had dissipated and the 1997 conference was only nine months away. We had chosen a location and dates, but had done nothing else. And, unlike other years, the volunteers who previously had taken on the various ongoing conference tasks seemed to have vanished. Up until now, a spontaneous energy had easily carried our group through the work required to make a conference happen. Now that energy was gone. The bloom was off the rose, and I was starting to wonder if our group was going to survive.

The more I thought about it, the more miserable I got. Sure, I could shoulder the jobs that needed to be done. But the thought of doing this was deeply unsettling to me. I had a busy professional life, and I was due for a sabbatical, which I planned to use touring around the Southwest in a camper with my wife and 11-year-old twins.

On Tuesday, October 29, I snapped, and sent out the following message to the group listserv:

Subject: HELP! HELP! HELP!

OK folks, I admit it. I NEED SOME HELP. After talking to Mary, who graciously agreed to help me solicit vendors and to lead us in our '97 Pictionary™ extravaganza, I have just realized I have the following tasks to get done, "real soon now":

  a. Get out the next newsletter
  b. Create a conference brochure
  c. Create a conference vendor mailing

I CAN'T DO IT ALL BY MYSELF! (Insert broken sobs here.)

  a. I have only two articles for the newsletter. I don't have an account of the '96 conference. Please, someone, offer to write one. Another article is needed. Come on guys, VOLUNTEER.

> b. Would someone with desktop publishing expertise please offer to design a '97 conference brochure? I can supply all needed copy, plus my amateur PageMaker attempt that was used for this year's conference.
>
> c. If the above is done by angelic folks, I will create the vendor mailing myself.
>
> My telephone and email await your soothing words.
>
> Is anybody there?

Yes, I asked for help.

Turning on my computer the next morning, I found the following message from Gayle:

> Subject: Re: HELP! HELP! HELP!
>
> Adrian,
>
> I'll do the '97 brochure. I'm not a desktop publishing expert, but I know my way around PageMaker pretty well.

My spirits soared. Help was out there! Someone cared!

But Gayle's message was only the first of many. By Sunday I had received multiple replies . . .

> Subject: THANKS! THANKS! THANKS!
>
> My pleas for help have been answered!
>
> I received six offers to produce the conference brochure—a big thank you to Gayle, Barbara, Jim, Jason, John, and Pathan. Gayle's doing it—an even bigger thank you to her.
>
> Another big thank you to Rob, who offered to write an account of the '96 conference for the newsletter.
>
> And Fred wrote an article for the newsletter. Whoopee! Fred, you rock!
>
> As you may have noticed, I was feeling somewhat overwhelmed when I asked you for help. I feel so much better now. Thank you everyone! Next time I'll remember to ask for help sooner, before I get so bent out of shape.

Coordinating a conference, no matter what size, can be a difficult and taxing experience. But it doesn't have to be that way. If you start to feel put upon and stressed, first recognize how you're feeling. And then ask for help. You'll be surprised what happens.

Meals and refreshments

I'm a big believer in having the best possible food and refreshments at conferences. Mealtimes and refreshment breaks offer natural opportunities for socializing, and providing great food and drink will significantly enhance everyone's conference experience. Organizing excellent conference nourishment is the job of the *meals and refreshments committee.*

When a site will be responsible for providing conference meals and refreshments, options should be discussed with the site coordinator and a representative of the food service during the site visit.

If you're using a nontraditional conference site, the meals and refreshments committee will need to contact potential catering services and negotiate appropriate sustenance.

Arranging food service for a conference at a nontraditional site can be challenging, and generally requires more work than contracting with an embedded provider at a traditional conference location. On the other hand, external food services often can provide a better fit to your exact meal requirements, as well as offering some novel options that a hotel or conference center food service may be unable or unwilling to supply. I've enjoyed conference meals catered by trainees from the Culinary Institute of America, tiny mom-and-pop catering services, and professional chefs at private schools. If you're going this route, here are a few suggestions that can make your job easier.

Start by asking your contact at the conference site about any restrictions or concerns about using an external food service vendor. (If you're planning to serve alcohol during the conference, check site and local restrictions.) Ask for suggestions and recommendations of potential providers, especially vendors who have provided meals at the site before. You may now have plenty of avenues to explore. If not, research local food service providers. Check local restaurants; many are accustomed to catering off-site meals or can suggest businesses that will.

There may be gaps in the service an outside food service supplier can offer. You'll need to be clear on what isn't provided and figure out how you can supply the missing pieces. If, for example, the supplier can deliver all needed food and serving supplies, but can't set up and serve meals, you could use volunteers to set out a delivered buffet-style lunch, or hire some local teenage help if several meals are involved. Simple creative solutions like these can make your conference meals and refreshment breaks an agreeable time for attendees to deepen their connections, and enjoy themselves in the process.

Marketing

Although input on conference marketing can be solicited from everyone on the steering committee, one to three members should form a *marketing committee*. Chapter 17, on conference marketing, will help you understand the scope of this committee's work. If you're lucky enough to have people with marketing or graphic design experience, ask them to join the committee.

During your initial steering committee meeting, determine how much additional outside help you'll need to market your conference. Although it's possible for amateurs to do a good job reaching potential attendees, I recommend using a professional designer to create attractive marketing materials.

Determining and pricing your conference marketing strategy are key responsibilities of the marketing committee. A long conference, marketed to thousands of potential attendees via a mailed, professionally produced, color brochure, can cost thousands of dollars to promote, while a one-day conference promoted via email to a small existing group of potential attendees can cost very little. It's important for the marketing and finance committees to agree on a realistic marketing budget for the conference at an early stage.

The marketing committee needs timely information from the site visit, program development, and finance committees so it can provide accurate and informative promotional conference materials and distribute them well in advance of the conference. The conference coordinator is responsible for overseeing communications between these committees.

Website and/or wiki management

Although it's certainly not essential, there's a lot to be said for using a website and/or wiki to market your conference and readily enable pre-conference communication, especially if your conference is long and contains significant traditional content. A conference website provides an attractive platform for your marketing materials, and can be used to register conference attendees. Sometimes you may be able to add web pages for your conference to a preexisting website belonging to an allied or sponsoring organization. Wikis are websites that allow visitors to easily add and edit content; they are ideal for hosting pre-conference discussions, attendee bios, and ideas for peer sessions, as well as providing a convenient place to post conference session transcripts, resources, and notes. Chapter 21 contains more information on using wikis before and during your conference.

If you decide to use a website and/or wiki, it will need to be set up and managed by one or more of your steering committee members: the *website committee*. This committee works closely with the marketing committee so that their combined efforts provide a coherent and complete view of the conference.

Finance

The *finance committee* develops a conference budget (which is then reviewed and approved by the steering committee), finds seed money to cover initial expenses until registration fees arrive, tracks and disburses funds, and provides a final conference accounting to the steering committee. Typically, one person (the treasurer) does most of the work, described in detail in Chapter 18. However, to reduce the potential for theft, I recommend that two committee members handle conference receivables, one to process and deposit incoming payments, and one (the treasurer) to record receipts in the conference accounts.

Accommodations

If you've arranged for attendees to stay in school dormitories, some people may desire more luxurious lodgings. At a minimum, the *accommodations committee*, usually one person, creates a list of alternative places to stay for registrants who are unable or unwilling to stay at on-site accommodations. If there are reasons to expect a significant number of attendees will stay off-site, the committee also researches and negotiates available group rates and discounts. When conference speakers need a place to stay, the accommodations committee makes the necessary arrangements.

Vendor exhibit

If you know of vendors who would be interested in marketing to your conference attendees, and your attendees would like the opportunity of meeting these vendors in a low-key, low-pressure environment, you may decide to hold a vendor exhibit during a multiday conference. It's hard to predict the number of vendors who will attend a specific conference, but the typical number is around a dozen. Sometimes just one or two vendors are appropriate, and they can be treated more as conference sponsors.

Organizing a vendor exhibit entails significant work. The *vendor exhibit committee* must identify potential vendors, contact them to arrange their presence at the conference (often multiple times), and coordinate the vendor exhibit during the conference. One person can handle vendor solicitation for a peer conference, but the job is sometimes shared, especially when there are many vendors. Vendor coordination at the conference can be a significant time commitment on Exhibit Day, and usually involves the coordinator missing one or two conference sessions. Chapter 19 describes in detail the work involved in putting together a vendor exhibit.

Site preparation

The *site preparation committee* is responsible for obtaining any additional equipment needed for the conference, such as flip charts, projectors, wireless microphones, and so on and setting up the site before attendees arrive. To the extent possible, steering committee members should plan to arrive early to help with site setup. At a short conference this can often be done the same day; for longer conferences it's best for at least some of the committee members to arrive the day before the conference starts.

Site preparation includes room setup, installing signs to help direct participants, setup of a registration area, and installing all necessary equipment.

On-site conference registration

The pre-conference registrar can also be responsible for *on-site conference registration*, though this isn't always the case. Conference registration requires a crew of two to four people (depending on the conference size) who welcome newcomers, collect unpaid registration fees, take photographs for the face book, hand out conference packets and promotional items, and help attendees find their rooms if they're staying on-site.

Entertainment

Conference entertainment is optional. If you decide to include some, create an entertainment committee with one or two members who have responsibility for booking appropriate entertainment that's within your budget. Some examples of entertainment options are given in Chapter 13.

Promotional items

Some people think of promotional items as marketing. However, in my experience, people don't attend a peer conference because they've been told they'll receive a free mug; I like to think of "promotional" items as extra fun freebees that attendees appreciate, rather than a cornerstone of conference marketing. If you plan to hand out promotional items (tee-shirts, mugs, etc.) to attendees or as thank-you gifts to steering committee members and others, you'll need to research and choose what to give, subject to budget, and get the items personalized in good time for your conference. I suggest you have a short steering committee discussion of possible promotion items and budget, but leave the final choice to one person; committees often spend an inordinate amount of time coming to agreement on exactly what to order, and this should be a minor concern compared to the rest of the conference planning.

Conference facilitation

You will need a facilitator and a couple of scribes for each conference roundtable, and a facilitator for each personal introspective and group spective. Of course, you don't have to use the same facilitator for these peer conference sessions. In addition, you'll need someone to collect and post the notes of peer session scribes, as well as an appropriate number of people to welcome attendees at the start of the conference, make announcements, and keep the conference program on schedule. The conference coordinator is responsible for ensuring that these activities run smoothly.

Determining your audience

You probably already know the target audience for your conference. People like you. People who have the same interests, people who have some of the same questions you do, and who may have some of the answers.

Try this with your steering committee members. Give yourselves a few quiet minutes to think about this question:

> Who would *you* want to come to your conference?

Then discuss.

You certainly want to have people who can help you learn more about your interests, who share and understand the passion you have and the difficulties you face—people who know something of what it's like to be in your shoes. In some ways this is the model of an ideal traditional conference, where you learn, one-way, from others who answer your questions and teach you what you want to know—where you sit back and receive knowledge.

What may be less obvious is that you might well find it equally rewarding to spend time with people who can learn from you, with whom you can share your own expertise, your triumphs over difficulties, and your insights. This is what happens naturally in a peer conference—an example of "from each according to his abilities, to each according to his needs" in action.

Think about when you work and learn most effectively. I'll bet your experience is like mine—the best learning and productive work happens when you're with a small group of people, and the best experience is when everyone contributes.

The trick is to create a conference with the right people, people who will mutually learn from each other, people who will enjoy the process. You don't want too many people, because you can't learn effectively from a large group. A peer conference is an environment designed to maximize the opportunities for each attendee to learn and share.

How do we create a conference where we can get a small number of the right people to attend? One way, of course, is to put an upper limit on the number of attendees. Make registration on a first-come first-served basis. Because you never know for certain how many will be attracted to your conference, it's a good idea to decide on and publicize an upper limit to any peer conference registrations. I limit attendance at any peer conference to a hundred people, though your location or other considerations may lead you to choose a lower number than this.

Although receiving a glut of registration requests for a conference may seem like a good thing, there is a downside. Too many people interested can mean that your conference theme is too general, which implies that the people who come will have a broader range of interests than if the conference was more narrowly targeted. There may be times when this is what you want, but you may end up with a group of attendees who have less in common with each other than works well for this format. Consider this as you decide the scope of your conference theme; I suggest you recall my initial question—who do you want to come to your conference?

In some ways, a conference where attendance is below the number of people that could be handled may be better than an oversubscribed event. I have run excellent conferences with 30 attendees who greatly appreciated the intimacy and sharing possible in a small group of their peers. As numbers increase there is often a trade-off. There may be more expertise available in the group as a whole, but it's more likely that important personal connections may be missed. I have attended multiday traditional conferences with 80 people where I made an important connection with someone on the last day. I sometimes wonder whom I never got to meet.

Controlling the appeal of your conference

You can control appeal by defining your conference:

- Theme
- Geographic reach
- Duration

Suppose your group wants to hold a genealogical peer conference in the United States. You know that traditional national genealogy conferences attract thousands of attendees, far too many for a peer conference. Your interests are more focused. Are you amateur or professional genealogists? Perhaps you're interested in the genealogy of an ethnic group, like Hispanics, or a religious group like the Quakers. You may have a specific geographic or historic focus. Perhaps you are interested in using computers to manage genealogical information. By narrowing your theme and geographical reach, you can create the kind of focused conference you want.

Your choice of target audience can further fine-tune who comes. All other things being equal, a conference pitched to a larger constituency will attract more people than one that is narrowly focused. A conference for people who work with seniors will attract more interest than a conference for home health aides; a conference for nonprofit agencies will have a broader appeal than one for arts agencies. By carefully defining your desired peer group, you shape your conference's appeal.

When you've successfully zeroed in on your target audience, you should be able to define them in a single phrase. Make sure that your target audience is consistent with the kinds of conference topics you have in mind. For example "medical interns at large hospital X" may be working in many different specialties, so a peer conference for them might revolve around common issues such as working conditions rather than the practice of medicine itself. On the other hand, a peer conference for "geriatric consultants in city *Y*" would be more likely to deal with medical issues, since attendees would all be practicing in the same area of medicine.

The number of days you choose for your conference will also affect who comes. One-day peer conferences are typically local in scope, whereas a three- or four-day conference can attract national attendance.

It may seem that your choices are overwhelming. Don't get blocked from acting for fear of making a mistake. My experience is that people who have a feel for their conference subject and target audience are surprisingly good at determining the appropriate combination of theme, geographic reach, and duration that will attract the right number of people. In general, I've found it possible to predict attendance within a factor of two. And, as described in the budget section later in this chapter, it's possible to design a conference financial structure that can handle this range of uncertainty. Trust the intuition of your group and come up with an audience definition you feel good about.

Once you've narrowed in on your target audience, research traditional conferences that could compete with what you're planning to offer. Although the peer conference approach is novel in itself, avoid scheduling your conference at the same time as an established event that ostensibly covers similar ground. Make sure that there's something unique about your conference—the target audience, the theme, or the geographic focus—and you should be fine.

Conference timing: start, end, and duration

Peer conferences generally run for between one and four days. The duration of your conference affects its character in several key ways, which I cover below. But first, let's examine when you should start and end your conference.

When to start a peer conference

In the last few years I've become a big fan of starting all but one-day peer conferences in the early afternoon. Not only does this allow attendees who live nearby to arrive on the first day of the conference, but, more important, an afternoon start provides the right amount of time on the first day to hold the conference roundtable, peer session sign-up, and an informal dinner where people can get to know each other. By the end of the day, conference connections and themes have been established. At the start of the second day, attendees are fresh and ready to dive into the peer session topics they have chosen through their work the previous day.

If you can't start your conference after lunch, a morning start is perfectly feasible. For conferences longer than a day, you can still have peer sessions start on the second day if you schedule

When to hold your conference

Deciding *when* to hold your conference is a critical choice that can, if poorly made, wreak havoc on the level of attendance. Most education conferences, for example, are held during school vacations, not while school is in session. Check with a significant sample of likely attendees to see whether the proposed dates work for them, and research conflicting or closely scheduled events that may draw off attendance. Finally, consider seasonal factors—high-season prices can stretch attendees' budgets, and three days in North Dakota in January may not appeal to everyone!

a keynote or other traditional sessions on the first day, along with the introductory peer conference sessions.

When to end a peer conference

When should a peer conference end? Unless your conference is held on a remote island with one ferry going to the mainland once a day at 3 p.m., or you have some equivalent logistical constraint, I recommend that you end your conference at the end of the workday. To understand why, I first need to bring up an unpleasant truth.

At every conference, people leave early. Perhaps there's a plane they need to catch, perhaps they want to miss the five o'clock rush hour traffic, perhaps they need to get home and make dinner for the rest of the family, perhaps they don't think that a personal introspective or group spective is worth their time. Whatever the reason, it's a good reason as far as they're concerned, and they *will* leave early. Don't take it personally! I can't tell you how many people have come up to me on the last day of a conference, told me how great it was and then started to apologize for having to leave early. When this occurs, I thank them for coming and commiserate with them that they can't stay until the end.

How does this affect deciding when a conference should end? I've found that if your last conference day is not a full day, some people will seriously consider skipping the final partial day completely. If they haven't attended a peer conference before, they may view personal introspectives and group spectives as unimportant. Seeing only one or two remaining sessions on the last day's schedule, they wonder if it's worth their while to come for the final day.

You can't prevent people from leaving early. But making the last day of your conference a full day will, in my experience, maximize the number who stay to the end.

If you want to provide an incentive for attendees to stay to the end of the conference, consider adding a few minutes before everyone leaves to hold a conference raffle. If you're holding a vendor exhibit, your vendors may be willing to donate some prizes. Otherwise, prizes as modest as a few hanging baskets of flowers, gift certificates to local or online stores, or other appropriate gifts can be surprisingly effective at enticing attendees to stay to the end.

Conference duration

I divide conferences into *short* (1–1.5 days), and *long* (2+ days). In this section I'll outline the essential characteristics of conferences of various lengths. In Chapter 16 you'll find detailed model schedules for each variation, which will help you zero in on the conference length that's right for you.

Short conferences

Short conferences are usually local or regional. When your attendees can't or won't travel long distances or stay overnight, you need to provide a short conference. Such conferences can be completely agenda-less—no pre-planned keynotes, presentations, or panels. Besides providing a heady dose of connection for attendees, these conferences are great for discovering regional issues and acting as a springboard for future group initiatives.

One-day conference

I have held a number of one-day peer conferences. One (very full!) day is the minimum time needed to process the essential components of a peer conference: the roundtable, some peer sessions, and a minimal spective. Frankly it's a rush to complete even these basics in a day.

But although a single day is a little brief for an optimum peer conference, it's sometimes necessary. I once organized a peer conference for childcare providers. It was a struggle for them to schedule a day away from their demanding, understaffed agencies, and I remember that many of them had to leave early to pick up their kids from school. A longer conference simply wouldn't have been feasible for this group.

I'd advise limiting registration for a one-day conference to 50 or fewer. It's hard for members of a bigger group to discover meaningful connections in a single day.

One-and-a-half-day conference

This is my favorite format for a short conference. On the first day, you start in the afternoon and run the roundtable and peer session sign-up before an evening meal. The next day you're ready for a full day of peer sessions plus a personal introspective and a group spective. This is an ideal timeframe for a short local conference. The initial half-day teases out the conference themes, and the overnight pause allows people to be fresh for their peer session work on the second day.

Because the conference includes an overnight, attendees will need somewhere to stay, and this means that a one-and-a-half-day conference should be designed for mostly local attendees who live close enough to drive home for the night. If you have pre-planned program sessions, any outside presenters may come from further afield.

Long conferences

Peer conferences that span two or more days have a more relaxed atmosphere and can attract a national audience. Such conferences require you to offer accommodation options (even if you just provide a list of nearby hotels), because nonlocal attendees will need to stay somewhere for at least a couple of nights.

Longer peer conferences usually include traditional conference elements, such as pre-planned speakers and panels, vendor exhibits, organizational business meetings, outings, and so on. Because most people have never attended a peer conference and may be cautious signing up for something out of the ordinary, including traditional content can help attract people to your event. I'll have more to say about this in Chapter 16. A two-day conference can have 0–40 percent traditional content, while three- to four-day conferences typically contain 30–60 percent.

My preferred duration is two and a half or three and a half days. I haven't run any longer conferences. Three and a half days seems to be enough time for most significant connections to be made, and for most of the useful interactions to occur. Because peer conferences can be intense, I suspect that attendees' energy levels would flag toward the end of a longer conference, in addition to the practical issues of cost and time away from work and home.

Choosing a Conference Site

Before you seek a peer conference venue you'll need to decide what kind of conference facility you're interested in using: *professional* or *nontraditional*. Professional conference facilities are stand-alone conference centers or hotels with attached conference spaces. In contrast, nontraditional conference spaces can be anywhere that people can meet that will work for a peer conference.

Which you choose will depend on a number of factors, summarized in Table 13.1.

Before you decide to check out a potential conference site, be sure to read the following section, which describes minimum and desired site requirements for a peer conference.

Using a professional conference venue

There's a lot to be said for using a professional conference venue. If you've never handled conference logistics before, a professional conference facility can relieve you of much of the work needed to host a successful conference. Conference centers are set up specifically to supply the range of services that your conference needs—space to meet, meals, accommodations, equipment, and administrative support. Hotel conference facilities can do a decent job of providing many if not all of these requirements, potentially saving you much work and many headaches.

In general, you don't have to worry too much about the location of a professional conference site. Most commercial facilities are located in areas with good travel connections.

TABLE 13.1 • Professional versus Nontraditional Conference Venues

CONSIDERATIONS FOR:	PROFESSIONAL	NONTRADITIONAL
Cost	Expect to pay for meeting space; sometimes free if enough attendees book accommodations. Non-local attendees must pay hotel rates, which may be reduced if you can book a block of rooms in advance.	Accommodations and/or meeting space may be available at nominal cost. Rural locations can cost less than urban facilities.
Attractiveness	Stand-alone conference facilities can be attractive; hotel conference facilities are often generic window-less rooms.	Nontraditional conference venues can be very appealing, a welcome change from standard conference facilities. Rural sites can be in unique, welcoming settings.
Site convenience	Usually compact design with rooms close to meeting space. This can provide an intimate social environment for the conference.	Meeting spaces may be scattered, and not close to available accommodations. This can lead to logistical problems that must be carefully considered.
Workload	Some conference pre-planning and conference operations can be delegated to the professional conference staff. However, careful supervision is still needed.	You must plan and perform conference functions not delegated to others (e.g., catering services, room check-in). A plus: You can do these things the way *you* want to, rather than be limited by professional conference venue procedures/requirements.
Location	Often, but not always, in a convenient place for attendees to travel to, usually urban. Can be in an area where desirable conference services or attractions are expensive.	May be rural, novel, and spacious, which can appeal to attendees. Check that travel options will be acceptable to the target attendee, and avoid locations that are hard to reach in bad weather.

In addition, you'll get an often-overlooked benefit from holding your conference in a well-designed facility or a hotel, where your meeting space is close to attendees' rooms. When attendees don't have a 15-minute trip from the meeting location to their rooms, it facilitates an intimate conference where people stay around talking informally during conference breaks. If someone needs something from their room, they can get it and be back in five minutes. Conversely I've noticed that attendees with off-site hotel rooms often disappear in the evening, not to be seen until the next morning, while the folks who are staying on-site hang out together until late into the night.

If you're holding your conference at a professional conference facility, you'll still need to closely supervise the work that you've effectively delegated to the facility and its staff. Even the best professional conference staff can't read your mind about when food should be available, how to arrange chairs and tables, your projection and Internet needs; in short, all those things that make an event go smoothly and according to plan. And even if you've meticulously planned every last detail and communicated your plans flawlessly, there's no guarantee that the facility staff will carry out your desires as you expect. Making "trust but verify" your motto, doing some contingency planning, and staying flexible are all good strategies for minimizing the chances that something will go wrong and significantly disrupt your conference.

Using a nontraditional conference venue

Although it can be more work, I encourage you to explore the possibility of holding your conference at a nontraditional venue. Some of the best conferences I've organized have been held in settings that are rarely used for such events. I've organized them in huge barns, at private schools, and in donated corporate retreat centers. There is something very liberating in holding a conference in such idiosyncratic spaces. I have seen enough conference evaluations to convince me that, provided there are no major drawbacks, attendees love being in these unusual venues.

Any facility that people use to meet can be a potential site for a peer conference, so don't limit yourself to traditional venues. To get you started, here's a list of nontraditional sites to consider:

- Schools
- Places of worship
- Company offices
- Hospitals
- Human service agencies
- Town offices
- Senior centers
- Libraries
- Community centers
- Social clubs
- Art centers
- Museums
- Summer camps

Not only do you have the novelty of an unconventional meeting place, you also have the freedom to do things at the conference *your* way. Food is one example. A professional conference facility or hotel will usually expect you to use their food service (though some venues can be more flexible). At a nontraditional site, when you find out that over half your attendees have requested vegetarian meals, you can decide to contract your food service with the chef at that great nearby natural foods restaurant. Or, perhaps you will arrange for dinner on a boat cruising slowly down a nearby river, lake, or ocean. The possibilities are only limited by your imagination, your energy, and, sadly sometimes, your budget.

Some nontraditional sites offer facilities that simply aren't available at most conventional conference venues. For example, I've held many conferences at private schools, which often have luxurious sports facilities. It's often possible, with a little ingenuity, and sometimes a small fee, to arrange for partial access for conference attendees. An evening discussion over a game of pool? Blow off steam with a quick game of squash? A midnight swim in the Olympic-size pool? All possible! Look for opportunities like these at any site you're considering.

Some nonprofits respond very positively to the idea of a conference being held at their site, especially if you are the first group to approach them. They can see hosting a conference as part of their mission, feel flattered, and bend over backwards to make things work for your group. Other "hooks" for their involvement may be increased exposure for their institution, the potential for their staff to attend for free or greatly reduced admission, positive public relations, and direct exposure of your attendees to their activities.

So, why would anyone *not* want to hold a conference at a nontraditional venue? As usual, with freedom comes responsibility. Sure, there may be great potential to do cool things at a nontraditional conference site, but it's up to you to make it all happen. Professional conference venues often have event planning staff with intimate knowledge of possible local activities and options for their facility. Finding interesting conference activities and implementing them can be as simple as asking these people what's available and signing a contract for whatever you choose. In a nontraditional facility you'll need to do this work yourself. But often you can get a good head start by brainstorming possibilities with your conference site contact, who may have some great ideas that can be investigated further.

Let's be clear; there *can* be significant drawbacks to a nontraditional conference site. Scattered meeting rooms, uncomfortable chairs, food service limitations, far-off accommodations, and time restrictions on facilities use are all real possibilities. You'll need to maintain a creative, open approach for resolving potential problems. The good news is that such issues can often be circumvented, or may turn out to be minor inconveniences that are outweighed by the additional charm and possibilities your site brings.

Finding a nontraditional conference venue

The process of securing the right nontraditional venue for your conference can be frustrating. Perhaps your first choice is not available when you need it; at the next potential site, there's no place large enough for everyone to meet comfortably, or there is but the seating is fixed and doesn't work for the roundtable; at another location, meals can't be provided at the right times or they can, but they cost too much, or peer session rooms are scattered around a meandering site, and no one's going to get there anyway if the heavens provide a snowstorm (I am speaking as a Vermonter here).

Negotiating for a nontraditional conference site can be exasperating. This is particularly true if the potential host is not accustomed to hosting conferences. If you're hoping to hold your conference at a friendly organization's building or campus, your site contact often doesn't have the authority to approve your request. Negotiation may have to be done with others in the organization prior to final approval, adding delays and frustration to what is already a complicated process. So allow ample time, and be patient and persistent.

I've experienced false starts, clashing schedules, and incompatibilities galore in searching out peer conference venues. It is rare to come across a nontraditional site where the availability, location, meeting space, meals, and accommodations all dovetail perfectly with your conference ideals. But the possibility of creating a conference environment that is especially appealing to attendees inspires me to look for that unusual site and creatively solve the unique problems it poses. In my experience, the end result is worth the extra work. But that's me. If this is the first conference you've organized, you may want to minimize your work and pay for the assistance and support that a professional facility can provide. It's your call.

Timing

Before you call your site contact, be clear on the conference length, desired starting and ending times, dates that would work, and any you need to avoid (perhaps because they conflict with another conference that your potential conferees may want to attend).

Minimum and desired site requirements

Table 13.2 lists the issues you will want to inquire about in order to determine the acceptability of a conference venue. Before you fly or drive to check out a potential site, give the site representative a call and go through these requirements with them. If you've gone through the list of topics and the site sounds promising, ask the site contact what else you should know about

TABLE 13.2 • Site Screening Issues

SITE SCREENING ISSUES	NOTES
Other groups meeting at the site, and any simultaneous construction or renovation projects	
Space suitable for:	
roundtable and spective(s)	Large enough to seat all attendees in a circle
peer sessions	
refreshment breaks	Close to where sessions are held
on-site registration	Near entrance to facility, easy to signpost and find
evening socializing	Provide a mixture of social areas, including quiet spaces
vendor exhibit & presentations, if any	Check on power, Internet connectivity, access for vendor vehicles
traditional conference sessions	
conference meals	Meals should be available on-site
peer session sign-up	Use notice boards or walls with tape or tables without chairs
other conference functions	Business meeting, softball game, etc.
Conference site facilities that may be of interest and available to attendees	Sports and exercise facilities, libraries, stores, etc.
Accommodation options, on- and off-site	Even if on-site accommodations are available, inventory alternatives in case some attendees prefer to be off-site
Food service: menu and refreshment options	
Parking space	
Cell phone coverage and Internet availability	
Availability of local computer network storage space for conference documents	
Availability of conference support items	Seating and tables, wireless microphones, A/V equipment, flip charts & markers, notice boards, computers, electrical power
Brochures/photos/images of conference site	
Local leisure, entertainment, and outing options	
Conference site staffing options	
Travel to site	Site map, directions, shuttles & taxis, nearby airports and train stations
Insurance issues	

the site that you haven't already asked about. Often your contact will volunteer one or more tidbits that are important for you to know.

Sometimes you may already be quite familiar with a local site. If after reviewing the requirements given in this section, you're pretty sure it's suitable for a peer conference, schedule a site visit and check out the details.

Note that a telephone call cannot take the place of a site visit. In my experience, there is no substitute for visiting a potential site.

While a good deal of the site screening can be done through telephone contact, there are other aspects that will have to await your site visit. Even if a site seems like it will work very well after you've been through your "laundry list" on the phone, only in person can you evaluate certain aspects to truly rule a site in or out as a viable location for your conference. Let's look at these issues one at a time.

Checking on-site use and availability during the conference

Ask whether other groups are scheduled to be on-site during your conference. If so, find out how this might affect your plans. Discovering that your venue is packed to the gills with other events is not necessarily a deal breaker, but it's one more factor to consider when deciding on a site. Can you do conference setup the day before, or will you have to rise early on the morning that the conference starts in order to get everything ready in time?

Also ask about any construction or renovation projects in process, and take into consideration any resulting noise or circulation issues. If you're planning to use a school during a school vacation, this is often when construction or maintenance is scheduled. I've had sessions disrupted by nearby noisy power tools, and attendees forced to take circuitous routes around construction areas that didn't exist when we did the site visit six months earlier.

Keep this information in mind during your visit, especially when choosing locations for conference activities. Finally, as you tour the conference site, look for handicapped access to the conference locations you choose.

Determining suitable space for meeting and other conference activities

At a traditional conference center, determining suitable locations usually involves choosing from a few predetermined possibilities. Spaces for sessions are generally designed to be close to each other, with accommodations and places for refreshments and socialization nearby.

At a nontraditional conference site you'll often have a number of rooms to choose from for your conference sessions, so be prepared to spend some time examining your options. While you can get a description of options on the phone, that's not sufficient. You'll need to tour the site in order to consider the room's size, layout, seating options, lighting, acoustics, comfort, attractiveness, access, ambient noise, and its proximity to other conference locations. Be sure to check that the chairs you will use are comfortable, particularly those used for the round-table and spective sessions, when attendees may be sitting in one place for long periods.

Keeping the locations for different conference sessions near to each other is important. A lot of time and energy can be wasted if attendees have to walk long distances between sessions.

The Main Room: roundtable and spectives

I've been using roundtables to start conferences since 1992. When I began organizing confer-ences, I didn't think much about the space I used for the roundtable and spectives: the "Main Room." As long as the room held everyone, even if we were somewhat cramped, and we were nominally facing each other, I was happy.

Over the years I've become much more particular about requirements for the Main Room, its size and how it's set up. I've discovered that the setting where everyone meets together signifi-cantly affects how well the resulting group sessions work. Chapter 23 describes the ideal Main Room in more detail. Ultimately, however, the only essential requirements are that the room is large enough to comfortably seat everyone in a circle and that it has movable seating. In Appendix 10 I have included a table from which you can look up the minimum dimensions of the space you need, given the number of attendees and the width of the chairs used.

With *60 or fewer attendees*, you can hold the conference roundtable and spectives in the same room, which I'll call the Main Room. This room must be large enough to comfortably hold a perfect circle of chairs, one for each attendee.

If you are expecting *more than 60 attendees*, aim for three separate locations, one which can accommodate everyone in classroom or circle seating (Main Room) and two others large enough to hold simultaneous roundtables (Rooms B & C), each comfortably accommodating a seated circle of half the attendees. Check that you'll have enough chairs (two for each attendee). The Main Room must have movable seating to accommodate spective sessions. If three appropriate rooms aren't available, you can get away with using the Main Room and Room B, though you'll need to rearrange half the Main Room chairs into a circle when the roundtables start.

The ideal Main Room space is beautiful, well lit, has good acoustics, and has plenty of room for a perfect circle of chairs. Nontraditional conference sites have often been able to provide me with this environment. I have held roundtables and spectives in open theater space inside a huge barn, in ancient school assembly rooms with portraits of the founder beaming down on everyone, and in beautiful church chapels with light streaming through stained glass. In my opinion, this definitely beats sitting in windowless air-conditioned conference rooms, no matter how nice the carpet.

Although an attractive Main Room space is desirable, in the end all that really matters is that the space is large enough. It should be open, with no pillars or objects that could block attendees' views of each other, and large enough to easily hold all the conference attendees when seated in a circle of chairs that has several gaps to allow attendees to arrive and leave.

It's fine if the room is much larger than necessary. In fact, I prefer to hold sessions for the entire group in a large open room. The open space inside and outside the circle creates an intimate yet intense group environment that maintains attendees' attention. Make sure that the room lighting is good so attendees can see each other clearly.

Other peer sessions

Besides rooms for the roundtable and spectives, you'll need space for peer session sign-up and the peer sessions themselves.

Describing over the phone what constitutes a suitable space for peer session sign-up is difficult. You're looking for blank, unobstructed walls, notice boards, or tables. Ask whether you can tape sign-up sheets to walls. Sign-up surfaces should have at least ten feet of open space in front of them to allow attendees to mingle and see topics easily. When tables are used for sign-up, they must be free from chairs or benches. You'll need *a minimum* of five horizontal inches of notice board or ten inches of tabletop width for each attendee. If the sign-up is scheduled during meals or social events, choose a location close to where the food is served or people will congregate.

Peer sessions require enough rooms to handle the maximum number of simultaneously scheduled sessions. I like to have four additional rooms available. This should be sufficient for any peer conference, though with less than thirty attendees two or three extra meeting places may suffice. Peer session rooms should have movable seating. Pick spaces with whiteboards or blackboards and computer projection, if possible.

Refreshment breaks

As you pick conference session locations, look for spaces where *refreshment breaks* can be set up. Central areas close to where the sessions will be held are best. Avoid cramped spaces where it would be awkward for attendees to pick up snacks and drinks.

On-site registration

You'll need a place to hold *on-site registration*. Pick an area close to the entrance of the conference facility. It should be as close as possible to where attendees arrive, and must be clearly sign-posted and easy to find. Make sure it's large enough. You'll need space for welcoming attendees and to hold the peak inrush of arrivals, space for any conference swag (attendee gifts) you're giving attendees plus a refreshment table. You may want to choose a registration area that can be locked to protect registration equipment and conference swag when staff isn't around. If you're holding your conference at a school, the staff lounge can usually be secured and often contains comfortable sofas in which people can relax while waiting to register.

Evening socializing

Most conference sites will have several options for *places to socialize* at breaks or in the evenings. Choose one or more locations that include some calm spots, so that people who want to hold quiet conversations don't have to leave the conference site. Make sure that refreshments will be available wherever people are socializing.

Vendor exhibit

If you're planning a *vendor exhibit* at your conference, you'll need to pick a suitable space. If at all possible, choose a space that is not needed for any other conference sessions. This allows the vendor coordinator and crew to set up vendor tables, power, signage, and so on without having to worry about coexisting with other conference activity. I like to schedule vendor exhibits over lunch and include a buffet lunch with tables and chairs in the exhibit area. Some vendors may bring booths; some may be satisfied with a linen-draped table. Your vendor coordinator will need to organize this. Other considerations for the vendor exhibit include the availability of power and Internet connectivity, and appropriate access to the exhibit space for vendors to set up displays.

During the site visit, once you've chosen the space for your vendor exhibit, sketch the room. Include in your sketch entrance and exit locations, any obstructions or barriers, and the locations and capacities of power outlets and Internet access points, if needed. Your sketch will prove invaluable for designing a vendor booth layout as vendor registrations arrive.

You may decide to let your vendors give short presentations on vendor exhibit day. If so, choose an appropriate number of rooms near the vendor space and note any presentation facilities that vendors may find useful.

Traditional conference sessions

Your conference site contact will probably have suggestions for where traditional conference sessions can be held. Avoid spaces that are designed for much bigger groups; they will feel cavernous and awkward.

Conference meals

Meals should be served on-site if at all possible. If there are several locations where meals can be served, try to take advantage of them during the conference. Have a cookout on the lawn one night, a formal sit-down dinner the next. If your conference site is close to a picturesque town with a variety of dining choices, consider providing transport there one evening and letting attendees make their own dinner choices.

Peer Sessions

For peer sessions choose four smaller spaces, one for each simultaneous session. These rooms should be near each other and a mixture of sizes, with the smallest able to comfortably hold 10 to 20 people. It's possible to hold peer sessions in different parts of a large room, but people get distracted and I don't recommend it. You'll also want to have a couple of large rooms available, in case one or two popular peer sessions monopolize a time slot.

During the site visit, check that chairs will be available, and look for rooms with flexible seating that can handle a discussion, panel, or presentation format. Built-in whiteboards are a plus; if a room doesn't have one, make a note to have a flip chart available. Also note whether the room has projection equipment.

Other conference functions

Perhaps your conference provides an opportunity for an associated nonprofit's business meeting. Or you think an informal softball game might provide an enjoyable conference break. If you're planning additional functions like these, choose good locations during the site visit. I like to hold an annual business meeting after dinner in one of the socialization areas.

Conference site facilities

Inquire about facilities that may be of interest to attendees, and take note of these when you tour the site. Many schools, for example, have sports and exercise facilities that could be made available to you. I have organized conferences where squash courts, swimming pools, lake canoes, and extensive exercise rooms were open for attendees to use. Amenities like these are attractive to potential conference-goers; be sure to describe them in marketing materials.

Meals and refreshment breaks

Even at a one-day conference people need to eat, and at a nontraditional site you'll need to determine how to provide meals and refreshments. Can meals be cooked and served on-site, or will you need to hire an outside catering service, or perhaps even bring in morning coffee and a buffet lunch yourselves? Your site contact should be able to give you some preliminary answers.

If your conference meals and refreshments will be provided by or contracted with the conference site, you should schedule a meeting with the catering manager (CM) during the site visit to outline your needs and discuss your options. Ask whether you can also meet with the head chef. During the meeting, describe what meals and refreshments are needed on what days, and listen to the CM's and chef's meal ideas. Make sure that vegetarian options are available, and ask about accommodating special dietary needs. If you're planning to have alcohol available you'll need to discuss serving options, and cost and liability issues with the CM.

Give the CM an estimate of how many attendees you expect, and ask when she needs an accurate count. This will usually be several days before the conference begins. Don't expect to receive detailed proposals and costs on the spot; ask when the CM will have them available.

Accommodations

A one-day local conference doesn't require overnight accommodations, but longer or regional conferences will. Using a professional conference site or hotel ensures that attendees will have rooms located nearby; in your initial call, confirm that they're appropriate, available, and affordable. Also ask about minimum reservation requirements and associated nonrefundable obligations.

On the other hand, a nontraditional site may have nowhere for attendees to stay, or perhaps offer minimal facilities, such as college dormitories, which may or may not be adequate. Even if a nontraditional site offers some form of accommodations, you should ask about the availability of nearby hotel rooms or bed and breakfasts for those attendees who would prefer a conventional place to stay. During your initial call to a nontraditional site, ask about:

- Air conditioning if the conference is being held during the summer;
- Bathroom access, private or shared;
- Room security;
- Number of available rooms and whether people will need to share;
- Room availability, including if attendees can arrive the day before, or stay the night the conference ends;
- Room costs; and
- Other amenities that may be missing from rooms, such as curtains and task lighting.

For both traditional and nontraditional sites, seeing the rooms where attendees will stay is an essential part of your site visit. Traditional conference facilities offer hotel rooms with standard amenities. Check to see whether you can negotiate a conference rate for a block of rooms, and determine the conditions for receiving the rate. Also discuss rates and conditions for attendees who wish to arrive early or stay after the conference is over.

On-site accommodations at nontraditional conference locations are usually rudimentary and inexpensive. Student dormitory rooms, for example, are vacant during school holidays and can provide a cheap, if basic, place to stay. Often such rooms can be used for little more than the cost of linens and cleaning services. This keeps the cost of the conference down for attendees who are prepared to stay in basic rooms with few amenities. In my experience, most attendees find inexpensive simple accommodations acceptable. Some will not, and they are free to choose off-site alternatives from the list you provide.

If you are considering nontraditional accommodations, confirm whether they have air conditioning and/or heating, if relevant. Overhead room lighting may be minimal or nonexistent, and bedrooms may not have curtains. Bathrooms are often shared; consider whether this is acceptable. Also check on room security. Once you've established what's available, be sure to accurately describe any limitations of the accommodations in the conference marketing materials, and provide a list of any useful things to bring (a small desk lamp, a fan, etc.) in your registration confirmation letter.

During the site visit, discuss options for attendees who want to arrive early and/or leave late. You may decide not to provide early and late arrival options if nontraditional accommodations are going to be used. For larger non-local conferences I recommend having at least some of the steering committee stay the night before the conference starts, so they can check on and assist with pre-conference preparations.

Determining your cost for nontraditional conference accommodations depends on the site. Some places will estimate their incremental cost for attendees staying on-site and charge you accordingly, some will hire external service providers and charge you their actual costs, and some will come up with a cost per room that bears little resemblance to their actual costs. If the conference site is also providing food service, the host site has many ways to calculate your final cost per head. When discussing accommodation costs, stay flexible, ask for what you want, and look for solutions that work for both you and the conference site.

Parking

Check to make sure that adequate parking will be available for attendees. If there are parking fees, see whether the conference site will waive or discount them.

Phone and Internet availability

As you tour the site, check the signal strength on your cell phone, and ask your tour guide about the quality of local cell phone reception. Note whether wired phones are available in the rooms where attendees will be staying, and ask for a list of public phones if telephone availability is poor. Check both session rooms and accommodations for wired and wireless (Wi-Fi) and Internet availability. Sometimes the conference site will be amenable to installing temporary Wi-Fi access during your conference.

Computer network support

Many attendees nowadays bring personal computers along to the conference. If you don't have a conference wiki, ask whether your site can supply local network storage space for conference schedules, handouts, session notes, and other useful conference documents. This can be helpful in providing a single repository for the materials needed for and generated by the conference. If your site can provide this, make sure that a handout that describes how to access the shared storage is written and available at conference registration. Tested directions for both PC and Apple computers should be included. Printed copies of the conference documents will also be needed for all attendees; check to see what printing facilities will be available during conference setup and the conference itself.

Conference support items

Determine the conference support items that will be available to you. You will need to rent missing items from an outside supplier or arrange for steering committee members with access to these items to bring them to the conference. Make sure to cover the following list during your site visit:

Seating and tables. For each meeting room, determine whether existing seating and tables are adequate, or are available elsewhere on-site. Note any needed room setup. If you are supplying tables for a vendor exhibit you may want to rent tablecloths and table skirts.

Audiovisual (A/V) equipment. You'll need a couple of wireless microphones feeding an effective sound system at each roundtable and the spectives, unless their rooms' acoustics are superb or the conference group is small. Have available a lavaliere microphone for the session facilitator, and a handheld microphone for attendees. Peer sessions are usually small enough not to need audio equipment, but try to arrange for computer projectors and screens to be available for peer sessions, in case they are needed. Traditional sessions may need A/V equipment too.

Flip charts and markers. Plan on two flip charts (on easels) and broad markers for each roundtable. All peer session rooms should have a flip chart available too, unless there's a whiteboard in the room. Count up the number of flip charts you'll need and check on availability at the site.

Notice boards. Arrange for a notice board at registration for posting general conference information. If the site has additional notice boards, consider using them for peer session sign-up. You'll need at least 20 horizontal feet of notice boards for enough sign-up sheets for 50 people.

Computers. If you're holding the conference at a school, nonprofit, or business, there may be public computers that attendees can use. Check whether this is possible at your site, and come to an agreement as to what equipment will be available, where, and when. Mention these facilities in your conference marketing.

Face book production equipment. During the conference you'll need to be able to print multiple copies of the attendee face book with photographs (see Chapter 23). Many copying machines are not capable of the quality needed; you may need to use a fast laser printer. Investigate the printing options available on-site and plan accordingly.

Materials for conference marketing

While on-site, ask for materials that can be used to support marketing the conference, and make sure you have permission to use them. This includes attractive images of the location or surrounding area. Be on the lookout for interesting information that can be included in marketing materials. For example, while touring a private school, my guide mentioned that a well-known, upbeat movie had been filmed there. That information went into the conference marketing materials, providing registrants with an appealing pre-conference picture of where they'd be meeting.

Local leisure, entertainment, and outing options

Although you can certainly hold a peer conference where attendees are happy never leaving the site, interesting local leisure, entertainment, and outing options may influence your choice of one site over another for multiday conferences. Ask your site conference contact for ideas of local trips and entertainment. I like to weave unique local opportunities, if practical and affordable, into conference evenings. Over the years I've organized numerous dinner cruises, a trip to a nearby casino, hilarious dinner theater, hula demonstrations, and many other enjoyable conference diversions. Don't feel you must provide comparable, or indeed any, entertainment. Rather, look for opportunities that are locally available and, perhaps, unique to the region—that can be easily be added to your conference program.

Conference staff

It can be helpful to have the conference site supply staff to assist with site-related issues like accommodations, room setup, and access to facilities. Traditional conference sites usually have these arrangements in place; you'll need to clarify the functions that are being covered, who is covering them, and any associated costs. At nontraditional venues, discuss staffing needs and options with your site contact during your visit. Be prepared to decide what your committee can do, and what you need help with. At schools, students can often be hired inexpensively to help with registration, showing attendees to their rooms, and running errands.

Travel arrangements

Your visit is the best time to pull together information on travel to and from the site. If your conference is local, driving directions may be all you need. Otherwise, get the locations of nearby airports and train stations, and ask about car rental, taxi, public and hired bus, and shuttle options. Make sure to obtain travel times for ground transportation to the site from nearby metropolitan areas, local airports, and stations. Ask whether the conference facility has its own shuttles to transport attendees. Confirm the accuracy of this information and incorporate it into the conference marketing and registration materials.

Insurance

Ask your site conference contact whether they have any insurance and liability concerns. A few nontraditional conference facilities may want attendees to sign individual liability waivers when they register.

CHAPTER 14

The Conference Site Visit

A conference site visit is essential, unless you've used the conference facility before. During the visit, steering committee members view the proposed conference facilities, plan where the different parts of the conference will be held, discuss food and accommodation issues, and get information on costs and travel.

The site visit should be scheduled well before promotional materials are needed, so that costs, accommodation, and travel information are available in good time.

Try to have as many of the steering committee members as possible attend the site visit. If the potential site is far away, financial considerations may make it impossible for everyone to go, but aim to have at least four people at the site visit, and check that other steering committee members feel comfortable relying on the recommendations of the visiting group. The conference site host, the conference facilitator, the conference coordinator, and the vendor coordinator (if you're planning a vendor exhibit) should attend the site visit if at all possible.

At a traditional conference venue, the site visit may consist of a quick tour of the available conference facilities plus a meeting with the professional conference staff to discuss food and accommodation options and associated costs. Nontraditional sites usually require a more extensive tour to select appropriate spaces for the various parts of the peer conference. Schools, for example, usually have a variety of assembly rooms and classrooms that can be used for group and peer sessions, and it can take some time to determine the combination of spaces that will work best.

What to bring on a site visit

You'll need *a way to take notes* while you're walking around the conference site. I like to use 3 × 5 cards and assorted color pens, but you may prefer a yellow pad, a laptop, or a tablet PC.

Bring a *tape measure*, 25 feet or more, to check room dimensions. Although your conference site contact may know a room's capacity when using conventional seating, she probably won't be able to tell you how many people will fit in the space when they're seated in a circle. Use your room measurements and the table in Appendix 10 to calculate whether the space is large enough.

You may also want to bring a *camera*, perhaps even a video camera, especially if not all your steering committee can attend the site visit. Bring a wide-angle lens, if you have one, to take pictures of rooms; regular lenses are rarely able to capture an entire room in a single shot. Photographs provide a useful record of site features for reference before the conference, and a short video can give other committee members a useful sense of the location.

Some sites will have a *map* of the conference buildings and/or rooms. Bring this with you as you tour the site. If there's no official map, sketch your own and annotate it as you make decisions—it can prove invaluable six months later when you're trying to remember exactly where you decided to hold registration.

It's unlikely that by the end of your site visit you'll have answers to all the questions and concerns I've listed. But before you leave, you should have developed a clear plan and timetable for obtaining any missing information and deciding any remaining issues.

Write up your notes on the site visit as soon as possible after your return. I try to type them up on the airplane when I fly home. Promptly circulate the write-up to the committee, solicit needed discussion, and tie up any loose ends.

Oh for a golf cart!

I was late for my pre-conference meeting. The school campus held a bewildering number of classroom buildings, lecture halls, and housing, and, despite the map Joel had sent me I took several wrong turns before I found the faculty housing. The next moment I saw Joel's familiar figure ambling toward me.

"There's been a slight change of plan," he told me a few minutes later. "The contractors are still working on the classroom building we were going to use for the peer sessions. But don't worry; I arranged for us to get the brand-new one over there." He pointed to a

(continued on following page)

gleaming edifice a few hundred yards away. "I'm glad you could make the switch," I said. "Let's take a look."

We strolled over, and everything looked great. There were plenty of classrooms available, with comfortable chairs, whiteboards with fresh markers, and brand new digital projectors and screens. "Even better than the place we were going to use" was Joel's comment, and I agreed. I thanked him for saving the day and we walked over to check out the registration setup.

As it turned out, we had overlooked something. Our peer session building was now nearly 10 minutes' walk from the lecture theater where we were holding our traditional conference sessions. And the registration area, where the conference face book and administrative services were located, was in a third building hundreds of yards from the others. Significant distances now separated the three main centers of conference activity.

It was very hot that week. I spent the next three days sweating across innumerable playing fields, carrying my heavy laptop, backpack, sheaves of handouts, and other assorted items. I was miserable. Attendees didn't have enough time to get to their next destination. Sessions started late, and, though the conference overall was deemed successful, the excessive distances we had to walk sapped everyone's energy and led to a number of complaints.

Frequently, as I trudged to and fro, I wished desperately for an air-conditioned golf cart. I fantasized about providing a cart for everyone, visualizing a swarm of gaily-painted vehicles crisscrossing the campus, converging on the next session location followed by the screams of angry maintenance staff as they discovered the ruined football fields. They were pleasant fantasies that distracted me momentarily from unpleasant reality, but fantasies they remained.

Unless you can afford a fleet of golf carts, or are confident that your attendees will enjoy frequent strenuous exertion throughout your conference, make sure to locate all significant conference activities close to one another. Your conference will have a more communal feeling, energy levels will be higher, trips for missing stuff will be less harrowing, and you'll have a much easier time keeping your conference on schedule. And you and your attendees will be spared an unexpected forced exercise program!

CHAPTER 15
Food and Refreshments

This is a short chapter, with one message.

Offer the best food and refreshments you can.

I've read hundreds of attendee conference evaluations, and am always struck by the sheer quantity of comments, both positive and negative, about meals. Often, these comments are the most detailed offered on an evaluation! As much as I would like to believe that attendees are enthralled and delighted by the peer conference approach, it's clear that the perceived quality of many, if not most, attendees' conferences is significantly affected by their dining experiences.

I'm not suggesting that you make every meal a peak experience. You don't need to regale your attendees with ambrosial dishes they've never seen before, served with rare and costly wines and nectars. Instead, I'm proposing a more modest goal: *fine food and refreshments, well cooked, and attractively served.*

I can't help you much in reaching this goal, only urge you to put energy and creativity into achieving it.

Bear in mind that the cost of conference food and refreshments is usually the largest conference budget expense. If you're spending so much money, spend it wisely.

If at all possible, meet with the people who will actually prepare your food. Unfortunately, the skills and motivations of food service folks are habitually taken for granted and not appreciated.

I've found that letting the food staff know directly that you appreciate good food and asking what they can do for you is often all it takes for the chef to get excited and start proposing all kinds of delicious-sounding menus. Of course, your budget isn't limitless, but the difference in cost between an adequate and a great meal is usually quite small. So start by asking for the quality you'd really like, and only scale back if the estimated cost is too high.

Finally, if the food provided during your conference is great, let the staff know it. At several conferences I've seen attendees spontaneously cajole the food staff out to the dining area, publicly thank them, and lead everyone in a round of applause. Giving out conference tee-shirts or tote bags to the staff is a nice little extra thank-you too. And, as I know from personal experience, if you ever hold a conference at the same location again, they'll really treat you right!

Determining the Conference Program

Y our conference program must be designed early in the planning process so you can create appropriate and timely marketing materials. This section describes the steps to organize a conference program, and provides model schedules you can use to get started.

Peer conference programs

If you are holding a pure peer conference, that is, one with no traditional sessions, determining the conference program involves little more than designing a schedule for the peer conference elements. The initial schedule needn't be highly detailed; it's enough at this stage to draft a realistic timeline that shows when the major peer conference sessions will take place. You can fine-tune your program closer to the conference, when practical considerations like meal, entertainment, and travel times are nailed down.

Here are the steps to use when drawing up a conference schedule:

- Estimate the time available for sessions by subtracting meal and break times from the total time available for the conference.
- Reserve time for the roundtable, peer session sign-up, and the spective(s).
- If you're holding traditional conference sessions, reserve time for them. (Should you include traditional conference sessions? See the discussion below.)

- Calculate how many peer session slots can be scheduled in the remaining time.
- Decide on the order for the resulting sessions.
- Build a draft schedule using the session times and order determined in the previous steps.

How long should sessions last?

To create a realistic conference schedule, it's important to allocate appropriate times for peer conference sessions. Table 16.1 summarizes my recommendations for session lengths. Reading this book's detailed session descriptions in Chapter 25 will help you choose the right duration for your conference.

Schedule as much time as practical for on-site registration, at least one minute per registrant, preferably two minutes. At a multiday conference that starts in the afternoon, offer a two- to three-hour period for attendees to register. Conferences that start in the morning usually have tighter scheduling constraints. Allow at least an hour—more if there are over 50 registrants. Include, but don't publicize, a 15-minute gap between the announced end of registration and the start of the conference. This will give you time to process the inevitable last-minute arrivals.

Use a conference *Welcome* of 15 to 30 minutes to thank attendees for coming, provide necessary introductions, cover site housekeeping issues, and answer any questions. A one-day conference calls for a short, efficient welcome; the welcome for a multiday conference can be more relaxed.

TABLE 16.1 • Recommended Session Lengths

SESSION	TIME ESTIMATE
On-site Registration	As long as possible; schedule at least one minute per attendee
Welcome	15–30 minutes
Roundtable	60–150 minutes, depending on conference size and duration (Use Table 16.2 to estimate roundtable length.)
Peer Session Sign-up	30–45 minutes (Can be held during meals or breaks.)
Peer Sessions	45–60 minutes
Personal Introspective	75–90 minutes
Conference Spective	90–120 minutes

TABLE 16.2 · Estimated Roundtable Length (minutes)

		NUMBER OF ATTENDEES							
		30	**40**	**50**	**60**	**70**	**80**	**90**	**100**
CONFERENCE DURATION	1 day	60	75	90					
	1½–2 days	75	95	115	135	115	125	135	145
	> 2 days	90	115	140	150	132.5	145	150	150

←———————1 roundtable———————→ ←———————2 roundtables———————→

The *Roundtable* session is held immediately after the welcome and lasts from one to two and a half hours, depending on the conference size and duration. Stay within this range; a roundtable shorter than an hour lacks cohesion, and anything over two and a half hours is grueling. If you have more than 60 attendees at a longer conference, you will need to run two simultaneous roundtables. Use Table 16.2 to determine how much time to allocate to your roundtable.

Allow 30–45 minutes for *Peer Session Sign-up*. If your conference starts in the afternoon, you can hold the sign-up during the evening meal. At a one-day conference, use a midmorning refreshment break or lunch. Make sure to schedule sufficient time for determining peer sessions between the end of the peer session sign-up and the start of the first peer session! You may want to have a second peer session sign-up "recap" at a long conference; if so, I suggest you hold it during breakfast at the mid-point of the conference.

Peer Sessions typically last between 45 and 60 minutes. Use the longer duration at longer conferences. Provide at least a five-minute break between consecutive peer sessions; provide appropriate longer breaks if any of the peer session locations are not near the others. Schedule no more than two consecutive peer sessions before a meal or refreshment break.

If you are holding a *Personal Introspective*, allow between 75 and 90 minutes. Schedule it just before the group spective at a two-day conference, and after breakfast on the last day of longer conferences.

A *Group Spective* lasts between one and a half and two hours. It is the last conference event.

If you want to provide an incentive for attendees to stay to the end of your conference, consider adding a few minutes before everyone leaves for a *conference raffle*.

Getting from one session to the next

Ideally, all conference session locations will be close to each other. Sometimes, particularly at nontraditional conference sites, this is not possible. When significant time is needed to get from one conference location to another, make sure this is reflected in a realistic schedule, so that attendees don't have to rush to get to their next session.

Traditional conference sessions

If your peer conference lasts less than two days, there's rarely time for more than a keynote. Longer conferences can include traditional conference sessions. So, should you include keynotes, presentations, and panels in your peer conference?

Steering committee members often feel compelled to incorporate traditional conference content in a peer conference program. They worry that no one will come to a conference without predefined sessions; they are puzzled about how to market a self-organizing conference. These concerns can translate into pressure to include "at least a keynote," offering a format that is more familiar and feels "safer."

Resist pressure to include traditional content in your peer conference for such reasons. If you have the opportunity to snag a great keynote speaker, whom you are confident your attendees will enjoy and value, by all means add her to your program. But don't decide you must have a keynote, and then look around for someone who can fill the time slot. Let the appropriateness and availability of excellent traditional content drive its inclusion in your conference, not the fact that there are time blocks that must be filled.

How much traditional content to have is your decision, but don't agonize about getting the balance exactly right. For a longer conference, I suggest you schedule between four to six slots for peer sessions, and then see how much time is left in your conference schedule. This gives you a starting place to think about the quantity of traditional content you might want to include. If you have time left, you can always add another peer session.

Brainstorming a set of topics among program committee members and then choosing a few to examine further can take a while. Sometimes prospective speakers don't return your calls, or won't commit right away. Discuss whether you want to include a keynote, and decide on the number and nature of session topics. You must confirm availability of the keynote speaker and any other presenters and panelists for time slots that fit with your conference schedule.

Some conferences benefit from a small vendor exhibition. If this is appropriate for your conference topic and audience, vendor exhibits can be an added draw for attendees. When scheduling an exhibition, balance the amount of time assigned against other conference needs. I often schedule exhibits around lunchtime, with buffet-style food and drinks available at tables in the exhibit area. This gives vendors time to set up their booths in the morning, and allows attendees to allocate their time between the exhibit, lunch, and socializing.

Vendors appreciate not having conference sessions scheduled during their exhibit time. They also appreciate a short time to introduce themselves to the entire body of attendees, which can often be scheduled at the end of a traditional session right before the exhibit opens. If you restrict vendors to a one-minute introduction each, the whole process will take less than 20 minutes. Vendors will occasionally ask whether they can give short talks on their products and services in a private space. If this fits for you, schedule the sessions during the exhibit time, assign rooms for the purpose near the exhibit location, and provide an exhibitor talk schedule.

Until the nature and schedule of traditional content has been decided, you won't be able to create detailed marketing materials for your conference. Programming such sessions often takes longer than you expect, so allow plenty of time to choose and confirm traditional conference sessions.

Some thoughts about entertainment

For many years I put a lot of effort into arranging entertainment at longer conferences. (There just isn't enough time for entertainment at a one-day conference.) My conferences have included: dinner cruises, a trip to a casino, a winery tour, dinner theater, a hula dancing demonstration, a magic show with audience participation, and a close-to-X-rated game of Pictionary™ between two teams of conferees. These events were a lot of fun, though not everyone participated. But nowadays I am much less invested in the need for entertainment at a conference.

Why? I've come to realize a successful conference doesn't need traditional entertainment events. In fact, such events can break the "conference trance." I've found that most people are happy to immerse themselves in a set of conference topics that are dear to their hearts. A prolonged break, when their attention is dragged elsewhere, can make it difficult for them to return to the intense experience they were having before the interruption.

That said, I'm not opposed to supplying conference entertainment, and if there is an obvious opportunity to relax (e.g., a nearby beautiful or unique locale or a well-known show) by all means explore the option of incorporating it into your conference. But don't feel that you need to provide entertainment for your attendees regardless of circumstances, and then hunt high and low for something that might fit the bill. Do a good job on the conference content and process, and your group will entertain itself!

Model conference schedules

This section includes a number of model conference schedules. Use them as a jumping-off point for your own schedule. Consult your map of the conference site to ensure that the schedule allows plenty of time for attendees to leave each session and arrive at the next one on time.

FIGURE 16.1 • One-day Conference Schedule with 45-minute Peer Sessions

TIME	ACTIVITY
08:00AM–08:30AM	Registration
08:30AM–08:50AM	Welcome & introduction
08:50AM–10:35AM	Roundtable
10:35AM–11:20AM	Refreshments and peer session sign-up
11:25AM–12:10PM	Peer session 1
12:15PM–01:15PM	Lunch
01:15PM–02:00PM	Peer session 2
02:05PM–02:50PM	Peer session 3
02:55PM–04:30PM	Group spective

FIGURE 16.2 • One-day Conference Schedule with Short Keynote

TIME	ACTIVITY
08:00AM–08:30AM	Registration
08:30AM–08:45AM	Welcome & introduction
08:45AM–10:15AM	Roundtable
10:15AM–10:30AM	Refreshments
10:30AM–11:30AM	Keynote
11:30AM–12:30PM	Lunch and peer session sign-up
12:30PM–01:15PM	Peer session 1
01:20PM–02:05PM	Peer session 2
02:10PM–02:55PM	Peer session 3
03:00PM–04:30PM	Group spective

FIGURE 16.3 • One-and-a-half-day Conference Schedule with 55-minute Peer Sessions

DAY 1

01:00PM–03:00PM	Registration
03:00PM–03:15PM	Welcome & introduction
03:15PM–05:30PM	Roundtable
06:30PM–08:00PM	Dinner and peer session sign-up
08:00PM–	Informal chat and recreation

DAY 2

07:30AM–08:30AM	Breakfast
08:30AM–09:25AM	Peer session 1
09:30AM–10:25AM	Peer session 2
10:30AM–11:25AM	Peer session 3
11:30AM–01:00PM	Lunch
01:00PM–01:55PM	Peer session 4 or personal introspective
02:00PM–04:00PM	Group spective

With two days for a conference you have more flexibility. If participants are traveling some distance, consider offering registration for a few hours the evening before the conference starts.

FIGURE 16.4 • Two-day Conference Schedule with One Traditional Session

DAY 1

08:00AM–09:30AM	Registration & breakfast
09:30AM–09:50AM	Welcome & introduction
09:50AM–12:00PM	Roundtable
12:00PM–01:30PM	Lunch and peer session sign-up
01:30PM–03:00PM	Presentation/panel session 1 or keynote
03:00PM–03:20PM	Refreshments break
03:20PM–04:15PM	Peer session 1
04:20PM–05:15PM	Peer session 2
06:00PM–08:00PM	Dinner
08:00PM–	Informal chat and recreation

DAY 2

07:30AM–08:30AM	Breakfast
08:30AM–10:00AM	Presentation/panel session 2
10:00AM–10:10AM	Refreshments break
10:10AM–11:05AM	Peer session 3
11:10AM–12:05PM	Peer session 4
12:05PM–01:20PM	Lunch
01:20PM–02:15PM	Peer session 5
02:20PM–03:15PM	Personal introspective
03:20PM–04:50PM	Group spective and evaluations

FIGURE 16.5 · Two-and-a-half-day Conference Schedule with Keynote Address

DAY 1

01:00PM–03:00PM	Registration
03:00PM–03:20PM	Welcome & introduction
03:20PM–05:40PM	Roundtable
06:30PM–08:00PM	Dinner and peer session sign-up
08:00PM–	Informal chat and recreation

DAY 2

07:30AM–08:30AM	Breakfast
08:45AM–10:30AM	Keynote
10:30AM–11:00AM	Refreshment break
11:00AM–12:00PM	Peer session 1
12:00PM–01:00PM	Lunch
01:05PM–02:05PM	Peer session 2
02:15PM–03:15PM	Peer session 3
03:15PM–03:35PM	Refreshment break
03:35PM–04:35PM	Peer session 4
05:30PM–08:00PM	Dinner
08:00PM–	Informal chat and recreation

DAY 3

07:30AM–08:30AM	Breakfast
08:40AM–10:00AM	Personal introspective
10:00AM–10:15AM	Refreshment break
10:15AM–11:15AM	Peer session 5
11:15AM–12:15PM	Peer session 6
12:15PM–01:15PM	Lunch
01:15PM–02:15PM	Peer session 7
02:20PM–04:00PM	Group spective
04:00PM	Boxed dinner to go

A two-and-three-quarter-day conference could be run as a Wednesday-to-Friday conference, with the last day ending with a late lunch, after which participants travel back home for the weekend.

FIGURE 16.6 · Two-and-three-quarter-day Conference Schedule with Three Traditional Sessions and Vendor Exhibit

DAY 1

08:00AM–09:30AM	Registration & breakfast
09:30AM–09:50AM	Welcome & introduction
09:50AM–12:10PM	Roundtable
12:10PM–01:40PM	Lunch and peer session sign-up
01:40PM–03:10PM	Presentation/panel session 1 or keynote
03:10PM–03:20PM	Refreshment break
03:20PM–04:15PM	Peer session 1
04:20PM–05:15PM	Peer session 2
06:00PM–08:00PM	Dinner
08:00PM–	Informal chat and recreation

DAY 2

07:30AM–08:30AM	Breakfast
08:30AM–10:00AM	Presentation/panel session 2

10:00AM–10:10AM	Refreshment break
10:10AM–10:30AM	Vendor introductions
10:30AM–01:00PM	Vendor exhibition
12:00PM–01:00PM	Lunch
01:30PM–02:25PM	Peer session 3
02:30PM–03:25PM	Peer session 4
03:25PM–03:45PM	Refreshment break
03:45PM–04:40PM	Peer session 5
04:45PM–05:40PM	Peer session 6
06:00PM–08:00PM	Dinner
08:00PM–	Informal chat and recreation

DAY 3

07:30AM–08:30AM	Breakfast
08:30AM–10:00AM	Presentation/panel session 3
10:00AM–10:20AM	Refreshment break
10:20AM–12:20PM	Group spective
12:30PM–02:00PM	Lunch

A three-day conference could be scheduled as a Monday-to-Wednesday conference, with accommodations available for long-distance attendees Sunday night.

FIGURE 16.7 • Three-day Conference Schedule with Three Traditional Sessions and Vendor Exhibit

DAY 1

08:00AM–09:20AM	Registration & breakfast
09:20AM–09:40AM	Welcome & introduction
09:40AM–12:00PM	Roundtable
12:00PM–01:30PM	Lunch and peer session sign-up
01:30PM–03:00PM	Traditional session 1 or keynote

03:00PM–03:20PM	Refreshment break
03:20PM–04:15PM	Peer session 1
04:20PM–05:15PM	Peer session 2
06:00PM–08:00PM	Dinner
08:00PM–	Informal chat and recreation

DAY 2

07:30AM–08:30AM	Breakfast
08:30AM–10:00AM	Traditional session 2
10:00AM–10:10AM	Refreshment break
10:10AM–10:30PM	Vendor introductions
10:30AM–01:00PM	Vendor exhibition
12:00PM–01:00PM	Lunch
01:10PM–02:05PM	Peer session 3
02:10PM–03:05PM	Peer session 4
03:05PM–03:30PM	Refreshment break
03:30PM–04:25PM	Peer session 5
04:30PM–05:25PM	Peer session 6
06:00PM–08:00PM	Dinner
08:00PM–	Informal chat and recreation

DAY 3

07:30AM–08:30AM	Breakfast
08:45AM–10:00AM	Personal introspective
10:00AM–10:15AM	Refreshment break
10:15AM–12:15PM	Traditional session 3
12:15PM–01:15PM	Lunch
01:15PM–02:15PM	Peer session 7
02:15PM–04:00PM	Group spective
04:00PM	Boxed dinner to go

FIGURE 16.8 • Three-and-a-half-day Conference Schedule with Three Traditional Sessions and Vendor Exhibit

DAY 1

01:00PM–03:00PM	Registration
03:00PM–03:25PM	Welcome & introduction
03:25PM–05:55PM	Roundtable
06:30PM–08:00PM	Dinner and peer session sign-up
08:00PM–	Informal chat and recreation

DAY 2

07:30AM–08:30AM	Breakfast
08:45AM–10:30AM	Keynote
10:30AM–11:00AM	Refreshment break
11:00AM–12:00PM	Peer session 1
12:00PM–01:00PM	Lunch
01:05PM–02:55PM	Traditional session 1
02:55PM–03:15PM	Refreshment break
03:15PM–04:15PM	Peer session 2
04:30PM–06:30PM	Social
05:30PM–09:00PM	Dinner & business meeting
09:00PM–	Informal chat and recreation

DAY 3

07:30AM–09:00AM	Breakfast & peer session recap
09:00AM–11:00AM	Traditional session 2
11:00AM–11:20AM	Refreshment break
11:30AM–12:00PM	Vendor introductions
12:00PM–03:00PM	Lunch & vendor exhibits
03:00PM–04:00PM	Peer session 3
04:00PM–04:15PM	Refreshment break
04:15PM–05:15PM	Peer session 4
06:00PM–10:00PM	Dinner out in town

DAY 4

07:30AM–08:30AM	Breakfast
08:45AM–10:00AM	Personal introspective
10:00AM–10:15AM	Refreshment break
10:15AM–12:15PM	Traditional session 3
12:15PM–01:15PM	Lunch
01:15PM–02:15PM	Peer session 5
02:15PM–04:15PM	Group spective
04:15PM	Boxed dinner to go

After creating your conference schedule, check it carefully. Have more than one person review it. Confirm that you have:

- Allocated reasonable time for each session;
- Allowed enough time for attendees to get from one session to the next; and
- Included appropriate meal and refreshment breaks between sessions.

Once your schedule is drafted, circulate it to your steering committee for comments and sign-off, and then pass the schedule to the marketing committee members, so they can begin their work.

Marketing Your Conference

Once you've determined your conference audience and a preliminary program, it's time to market your conference. Marketing gets the word out about your conference to the right people, gives them the information they need to determine whether your conference is right for them, and gets them sufficiently interested and excited to register and attend.

To market your peer conference, you need to decide *how* you will reach your target audience, and *what* you will tell them. In this chapter I'll explain the differences between peer and traditional conference marketing, describe ways to reach the right audience, and supply some marketing samples to help you get started.

Marketing a peer conference

Peer and traditional conference marketing employ the same methods for reaching potential attendees: advertisements, trade journal and magazine announcements, brochures, fliers, email, Web 2.0 social networking "buzz" tools like Twitter, and conference websites. The difference between the two is the *content* of the marketing materials.

Traditional conference materials provide considerable information about the conference content. Assuming that monetary and logistical factors are not a barrier to attendance, prospective conferees expect to receive a detailed program of speakers, topics, and events;

they make their decision to attend based largely on whether they find the overall content compelling.

A pure peer conference has no pre-planned schedule of speakers, panels, and sessions. It offers instead a dynamic, structured experience for conferees to learn and share about their common interest—something very different from traditional conference fare. Because a peer conference program is short on specifics, marketing can seem a daunting task.

To successfully market a peer conference, you must be up-front about the peer focus of the conference and sell it to prospective conferees. You needn't explain each component of the peer conference in detail. In fact, you don't need to mention the components at all, although I like to include brief descriptions of the roundtable and peer sessions in the publicity for longer conferences. What's important is that your marketing materials clearly convey the core aspects of a peer conference: an intimate and supportive learning environment, rapid learning about the other attendees and their interests and experience, and the discovery and subsequent discussion of relevant conference topics.

Be clear about the interactive focus of peer conferences in your marketing materials so you do not attract attendees looking for a passive conference experience. A conferee who is over-worked and looking chiefly for a rest, good food, attractive surroundings, and a few rounds of golf is unlikely to provide much of a contribution to your conference, and is more likely to get what he wants at a traditional conference. Emphasize the active and participatory nature of your conference, and you will attract people who are open to playing an active role, supplying an essential ingredient of the peer conference process. Aim your marketing materials at people who want to come because of their innate interest and passion for the conference topic, rather than those who are looking for Continuing Education Credits, or have been told by their boss that they should attend a conference this year.

Longer conference programs often incorporate traditional keynotes, presentations, or panels. Providing descriptions of these sessions in your marketing materials gives prospective conferees a comfortable and familiar introduction to your conference's theme. Those unfamiliar with the peer conference approach will see that the conference will provide pre-planned sessions they value. Over the years I have met innumerable attendees who came to a conference because they were attracted by the promise of traditional sessions but ended up enjoying and appreciating the peer sessions more.

If your conference is a repeat event, there's an easy way to help potential attendees see whether the conference fits for them. Simply include a list of peer session topics from earlier conferences in your marketing content, eliminating any that are out of date. This reassures prospective conferees that the peer conference process leads to topics relevant to their needs and interests.

If your conference includes a vendor exhibit, provide a description in your promotional materials. If you have the names of some of the vendors, include them, or include a list of vendors who exhibited at your prior conferences. This helps prospective attendees determine whether your conference has appeal for them.

Make a PDF file of any paper-based conference marketing materials. The PDF can be attached to emails, providing recipients with an attractive copy of your conference promotional content without the expense of printing or physical mailing.

What's in a name?

Decide on a short name that reflects your conference theme. Leave long-winded titles to big traditional conferences; even if you select one, people will shorten it or turn it into an acronym. If your conference is built around members of an existing group, you can use the group's name, for example, "edACCESS 2007" or "The NASMAN Conference." If the conference is popular and there's energy to repeat it, your conference name will become your brand for future events.

How to reach potential attendees

When deciding how to reach potential conference attendees, your steering committee is the first place to go for ideas about generating conference leads. Brainstorm promotional ideas; think about sources for mailing and email lists, organizations that might be receptive to marketing to their members, other conferences or meetings that might agree to announce your conference, magazines and journals that would add your conference to their calendar, and other potential marketing possibilities.

These days many special interest group members connect via listservs, public and private Internet-based groups (available for free via providers like Yahoo! and Google), and email distribution lists. If a steering committee member is a member of one of these groups, it's easy to send a conference announcement electronically to the entire group at no cost. If email attachments are allowed for the group (check first) the announcement can include a PDF version of your conference brochure. Just be sure that your mailing to the list is appropriate, and follows any required posting rules. If in doubt, ask the list moderator for permission.

If your conference is elaborate or a repeated event, consider creating a conference website. Sometimes conference information can be added to the website of an allied or sponsoring organization. If you are ambitious, or have appropriate technical expertise on hand, you can set up conference registration online too.

A dedicated website can be overkill if your conference is small. In this case, a conference wiki is an excellent tool for publicizing, planning, and annotating your conference. Small wikis can be set up for free on publicly available "wikifarm" services. There's more information on using wikis for your conference in Chapter 21.

Promoting your conference

Unless steering committee members have publication design expertise, I suggest you engage the services of a professional designer for printed conference promotional materials. If your conference brochures look amateurish, prospective attendees are less likely to register. This is particularly important when you are soliciting attendance from people who have not met in a similar context before. They are likely to judge your conference offering primarily through the quality of your promotional materials. On the other hand, a group of people who mostly already know of each other may be comfortable with more casually produced materials.

Allow plenty of time to promote your conference. How much time is plenty? It depends on your audience. Busy professionals usually need to know the dates of a conference months in advance, so they can fit it into their schedules. On the other hand, if your attendees are primarily self-employed or retired, they may be able to block out time on shorter notice.

Consider using a two- or three-tiered promotional strategy. This will help remind prospective attendees about your conference, and turn an initial positive impression into a conference registration. Start with a short "save the date" conference piece, and follow up with your main promotional material that includes full conference information. Finally, a "places are filling up fast" postcard reminder mailed just before the close of early registration is an effective way to jolt the memory of those who added the conference information to their "get to this soon" pile.

For a small conference with a tightly defined target audience (e.g., "local childcare providers"), one-on-one marketing via telephone by someone who knows the potential attendee is often practical and effective. A few volunteers can quickly call a significant number of likely attendees with a few hours work.

Conference promotion considerations

Provide a clear registration timetable and fee schedule in your conference promotional materials. Be sure to state your *refund policy* for registrations. Include a closing date for refunds, minus a processing fee that reflects a reasonable processing cost. After this date, state that refunds cannot be provided. You can always stretch your refund policy for a hard-luck cancellation if your conference accounting is healthy.

One question you'll need to address is whether to offer *discounts for early registration*. The financial implications of this are discussed in the chapter on conference budgeting. From the promotional point of view, I recommend a single price for short conferences, and a three-tiered price structure (early, standard, and late) for long ones.

For a short inexpensive conference, an early registration discount is generally not worth the additional bookkeeping hassle. Such conferences have a short promotional timeline, and there's little benefit in offering a discount in order to receive registrations a few weeks early.

With no incentive for early registration, it can be unnerving hoping for a last-minute flood of registrations at a conference costing \$400–\$600. Offering discounts to attendees who register early can reduce this uncertainty. Consider providing discounts in the region of 25 percent for early registration, and 12.5 percent for standard registration. Include a statement that late registration is subject to space available, and that late registrants should contact the conference host before making travel arrangements.

It's not unusual for an organization to offer to sponsor the entire cost of a small conference, especially a one-day local conference where the conference site is donated and lunch and refreshments are the only significant costs. In this case, I recommend that you still require registrants to pay a small conference fee. The psychological commitment made in paying even a token fee makes it less likely that people will register but not show up for the conference.

Be sure to provide clear directions for travel to the conference, plus information on nearby airports, train and bus stations, and shuttle services when appropriate. Unless you're running a local conference, include this information in your conference promotional materials, as it will help prospective attendees clarify their travel requirements.

Marketing materials examples

For a one-day local conference, a simple letter and agenda may be all you need.

> January 3, 2006
>
> Dear Chickpea County Early Learning Provider,
>
> In April of 2005, Childcare of Chickpea County conducted a Community Assessment to better inform our community about our most pressing needs. One of many findings was that our region's need for childcare was not being met. At that time the *Chickpea County Childcare Needs Assessment* was not yet

published; however, since its publication, our subjective information has been confirmed. As with all things in life, though, solutions are complex.

We want to offer an opportunity to embark on one of our first service area consortiums. Let's talk about the strengths, challenges, and issues of the Chickpea County childcare delivery system.

We invite you to a conference on Monday April 9, from 9 AM to 5 PM at the Chickpea Community Center. The conference will:

- Give you an opportunity to meet other childcare providers in the area who are facing the same challenges as you are;
- Provide opportunities to discuss with your peers issues that concern you;
- Give participants the chance to talk about new forms of support that could increase collaboration between early childcare and education programs in our area; and
- Feature a keynote presentation by Mary Will-Harmon of the National Families and Children Association.

The agenda for the day is enclosed.

The conference fee is $50, which includes lunch and morning and afternoon refreshments. Waivers for fees and substitute reimbursement funds are available.

To attend, please fill out the attached form and return it, with payment, before March 15.

If you have questions, please contact Tom Ferdinand at (802) 555-1789 or tferdinand@cccdsys.org. We also invite you to extend this invitation to any colleagues who may be interested in participating.

Thank you for this opportunity to work collaboratively to strengthen the system of early care and education in Chickpea County.

Sincerely,

Tom Ferdinand   Trina Mollinas
Resource Specialist   Executive Director
Childcare of Chickpea County   United Way of Chickpea County

You could use the following to introduce the peer conference approach for a three- or four-day conference:

Have you attended a conference about *X* recently? Then you probably sat in room after room with scores of other attendees listening to outside experts talk about topics that weren't quite what you were interested in. You were sure there were some interesting people to talk to, people who had the same questions you did (and maybe even some answers)—but how could you find who they were and meet them among the swirling crowds? Did you come away frustrated, feeling that only a small portion of the time you attended was valuable to you?

If so, you're not alone.

Our *X* conference is different. It is small, responsive, and peer-centered. Small, because the conference is limited to 100 attendees. Responsive, because most of the conference is spent discussing topics chosen by attendees through a careful first-day process. Peer-centered, because we believe that, collectively, we are the experts.

Our conference is designed to make it easy for attendees to share what they want to discuss, the problems they need help with, and the answers they have learned from their own experience. The conference provides a supportive environment for a learning and teaching experience that is tailored by and for the individual attendees. Does this sound like the kind of conference you'd like to attend? If so, we'd love to see you at the *X* conference. Register today!

On the first day of every conference, all attendees join a facilitated roundtable discussion. Each participant has the opportunity to briefly introduce themselves, their institution, their experience, and their hopes for the conference. Our roundtable provides an opportunity early in the conference to discover other attendees with similar interests and relevant experience, and helps to determine peer session topics.

At our conference, participants generate the peer sessions! Using the roundtable discussion, attendees create a list of peer session topics and conference organizers find attendees qualified to lead popular discussions. This process allows the conference to meet the expressed needs of participants, and helps attendees to get to know each other through informal discussion. Our peer sessions are widely acclaimed and a perennial conference highlight. Here are some examples of peer session topics from recent conferences:

And finally here's the text for a double-sided single page brochure for a day-and-a-half conference.

Did you ever stop to consider that:
- **You are an expert at what you do?**
- **You have a tremendous amount to offer!**

Wickham County is home to 273 nonprofit organizations. If we took the population of Wickham County (every man, woman, and child) and divided it equally among nonprofits, each organization would serve only 162 people.

There are a lot of us!

So . . . let's capitalize on our numbers and come together to get to know one another, share ideas and woes, and get those creative juices flowing. Take a day and a half for some well-deserved time away from the office. We guarantee this will be time well used in the interest of your mission and you'll feel great afterwards!

The conference is designed to:
- **Give you an opportunity to meet your peers from around Wickham County who may be pondering the same issues, ideas, and worries that you and your agency are currently considering;**
- **Offer you structured time to capitalize on others' expertise, experience, and thoughts; and**
- **Give you a place to think about and plan for your agency relative to your conversations and possibly your new partners!**

Adrian Segar will facilitate the conference, using an innovative and creative format that he has developed and led over the past 15 years.

The Sponsoring Organization of Wickham County invites you to join your peers for a relaxed and rewarding week's end in July.

When: Thursday, July 13, 2:15 PM–7:30 PM and Friday, July 14, 8:30 AM–4:00 PM

Where: The West Wickham Meeting House, West Wickham

Who should attend:
- **Professional service providers from nonprofits in Wickham County**
- **Nonprofit directors and board members**

- **Nonprofit volunteers**
- **Anyone interested in participating more fully in the Wickham County nonprofit community**

The conference fee is $30, which includes dinner on Thursday evening and lunch and morning and afternoon snacks on Friday. Waivers for fees are available. **It is important for the process of the conference that participants stay through the entire event.** Your peers need your full participation!

The conference will be limited to 60 attendees. To attend, please fill out the attached form and return it, with payment, before July 1. Call Rick Parmenu at 555-3864, with questions or email rparmenu@wickham.co.us.

Please feel free to pass this invitation along to your colleagues.

Thank you for this opportunity to share your experience and work collaboratively to capitalize on the tremendous expertise we have right here in Wickham County!

CHAPTER 18
Budgeting and Accounting

P eer conferences, like opera according to Bing, are not in the business of making money. On the other hand, neither are they events of such prime importance and artistic merit that they should be allowed to lose significant sums. Emerson's rough equality of income to outgo is the goal to strive for. To be successful in this endeavor you need a budget.

> "The opera always loses money. That's as it should be. Opera has no business making money."
>
> —*Rudolf Bing*

Budget building principles

Use the following general principles as a starting point when constructing a peer conference budget. They help to define useful financial constraints on the conference planning.

Begin with a worst-case scenario—your conference is cancelled at the last possible moment due to events beyond your control. What will the financial repercussions be? What could you afford to lose? Answering these questions requires you to think about initial and ongoing conference funding and cash flow. I'll describe possible sources for "priming the conference expenses pump" later in this chapter; but, early in your budget process, it's important to consider the financial risks and exposure that you may, if unlucky, incur.

Next, think about how many attendees you'd want in order to feel that the conference was a success. Come up with a range, and, from a financial standpoint, concentrate on the lower end at this stage. Perhaps 20 attendees would work fine for your topic; perhaps you feel you'd really need 40 for the conference to be worthwhile. You'll build your budget using the lower number of attendees as your break-even point, the accounting term for describing that delicious moment when your revenues cover your expenses.

> "The secret of success lies never in the amount of money, but in the relation of income to outgo."
>
> —*Ralph Waldo Emerson*

Finally, make conservative assumptions when constructing your budget. Despite your best efforts, you'll usually encounter some unexpected expenses. Aiming for a small profit when designing your budget will give you a cushion against unanticipated costs.

Conference start-up funding

Your conference will normally incur expenses before any income is received. Marketing costs are a common early outlay—anything from $100 or so for a small mailing to several thousand dollars for designing, printing, and distributing a high-end color brochure. You may need to supply a deposit when contracting for the conference site. Where will this up-front funding come from?

The most common source of peer conference funding is a sponsoring organization of some kind. Usually one of the steering committee members works for the organization or has a strong connection with it. A nonprofit with a mission related to your conference topic, a club, an association, or even a friendly local business will often be willing to bankroll initial start-up costs, and may also provide a bank account through which to run conference funds. I once had such an arrangement that lasted for 10 years of annual conferences, until the business's comptroller gently pointed out that it might be better for our group to incorporate and manage our finances ourselves.

A sponsoring organization can cover initial conference expenses and absorb minor overall conference losses, or it may be open to subsidizing a portion of the conference costs, allowing you to charge a reduced attendance fee. If you have an organization in mind, prepare and share a preliminary conference budget so that everyone involved has the information to make a well-informed decision.

An alternative approach, suitable for a small conference, is to have steering committee members fund up-front expenses themselves. If you go this route, be sure to have a frank discussion on how any resulting conference profit or loss will be distributed *before* committing to significant spending. Otherwise, there are likely to be bad feelings later on.

If you don't have access to an organization with a bank account that can be used for the conference finances, I suggest you open a separate bank account. Since there's no organization involved, you will have to open a personal account in the name of the steering committee member acting as conference treasurer. You can add an appropriate "doing business as" (d/b/a) account title that will appear on checks and bank statements.

If the conference is a member-funded, one-time event and makes a profit, you can use the proceeds for a post-conference meal for the steering committee as a way of thanking the members for their work and commitment. Or you can donate the profit to an appropriate organization. If it looks like you'll be holding the conference again, bank the profits as a starter fund for the next conference.

Repeating a peer conference on a regular basis can allow you to be more innovative and take greater risks when designing the conference and constructing a corresponding budget. If you build up a financial cushion over time you'll gain some freedom to experiment with your conference design. You may decide to hold the conference in a different region, increase its duration, or spend more on marketing with the aim of expanding attendance.

A financial cushion enables you to make mistakes from which you can learn without suffering unacceptable financial consequences. A reasonable goal is to bank enough funds so you can survive one or two catastrophes, such as conferences that are canceled due to extraordinary events or lack of sufficient registrations. It can take five to ten years to get to this point, but it's great to be able to take a risk to try something new without betting the farm that your vision will be successfully realized.

Building the expense side of your conference budget

Once you've determined the broad constraints of your conference budget, you can work on the details. Generally you'll start by pinning down conference costs and then use the resulting information to decide on your attendance fee structure.

Use a spreadsheet to build your draft budget. Create rows for income items (attendee fees and vendor fees) and underneath list expense items, each in its own row. Determine an upper limit for the number of attendees, and use a series of attendance numbers as column headers. For example, if you are planning a conference for between 30 and 80 attendees, you would create columns headed 30, 40, 50, 60, 70, and 80. The cells at each row/column intersection then contain the budgeted amount for each income or expense item for the column's attendee count.

Obviously it's important to include all necessary expense items in your budget. The checklist in Table 18.1 includes potential expenses for a nontraditional conference site; some of these, such as "cleaning fees" would already be included in the price of a traditional conference center or hotel.

TABLE 18.1 • Conference Expense Checklist

EXPENSE ITEM	NOTES
Accommodations	Attendee accommodations, accommodations for outside speakers and panelists, room linen rental, cleaning fees
Administration	Conference equipment rental (wireless microphones, flip charts, A/V equipment, etc.)
	Conference supplies (flip charts, paper, pens, markers, folders, name badges, 4 × 6 & 5 × 8 cards, printer toner cartridge, printer paper, other office supplies, signs)
	Pre-conference services (wiki hosting, conference calls)
	Conference services (copying, printing, hourly conference staff fees, attendee transportation)
	Credit card processing fees
	Committee member expense reimbursement (telephone, postage, food for site preparation team)
Entertainment	Performer fees, excursion and transportation fees
Facility	Facility rental, cleaning charges, setup charges
Food and beverages	Per capita meals and refreshment charges, additional alcohol (either per capita charge or on an as-consumed basis), steering committee pre-conference meal
Furnishings	Chair and table rental, drapes for vendor exhibit tables
Insurance	
Marketing	Marketing promotion design, printing, postage, and mailing costs; website design, maintenance, and hosting
Promotional items	Shipping costs to the conference site can be significant
Speakers	Honoraria, meals, accommodations, travel expenses
Vendor exhibit	Exhibit furnishings and drapes, provision of power and Internet connectivity, space rental fee, conference meal for vendors

As you identify each budget expense, determine whether it's variable (i.e., dependent on the number of attendees) or fixed. You may be able to control which category some expenses fall into. For example, if you are serving alcohol during your conference, you can either budget a fixed amount or contract to pay for what is consumed. Other expenses may be weakly related to the number of attendees; for example, the cost of the teenagers you hire to help serve food or direct attendees to their rooms. As you establish an expense, enter it in each cell of the corresponding spreadsheet row, using a fixed figure or a formula based on the number of attendees at the head of the column.

Concentrate on accurately defining your major costs first, usually accommodations, food and beverages, and facility rental. For the moment, leave out optional extras, like entertainment and promotional items. Include essential minor costs, but don't agonize about getting them budgeted exactly; instead make reasonable conservative estimates.

Don't be shy about negotiating conference keynote speaker fees. Speakers will often cut their fee for speaking at a smaller than usual conference. Investigate the feasibility of a less expensive virtual presentation, using web-based conferencing software that provides two-way interaction between speaker and audience. And, if you schedule a peer session after the keynote, you may be able to get your speaker to host a follow-up discussion after her presentation at no additional charge.

Evaluating your conference financial feasibility

Once you've come up with a bare-bones expense budget, create a spreadsheet row that shows what you'd need to charge each attendee, on average, to break even. Look at the figure for the smallest acceptable number of attendees and evaluate its reasonableness. Would your steering committee members want to attend the conference at this cost? Do you think you can attract conferees at this price? Is it a good deal; would people pay more to come? Before concluding that it's too high, research the fees charged at comparable conventional conferences. You'll likely find that your conference is a bargain.

If your fee seems too high, you have several options:

- Explore sponsorship opportunities. Perhaps an organization will pay for meals and refreshments, or provide a fixed contribution or per attendee subsidy toward the cost of the conference, or cover a net conference financial loss up to a given level.
- Consider raising the acceptable minimum number of attendees and see how this affects what you'd need to charge.
- See whether you can reduce budgeted expenses. Offer more modest food and drink, spend less money marketing your conference, or reluctantly turn down that expensive keynote speaker and look for a less expensive alternative.
- Investigate the feasibility of a vendor exhibit, which can provide significant income that may be used to reduce attendance costs. See the section on vendor exhibit financial considerations later in this chapter.

After exploring cost-saving opportunities, if your conference still seems marginally affordable, you need to be cautious about proceeding further. Wishful thinking about attendance figures or refusing to face the possibility of a serious conference financial shortfall will not prevent an unpleasant financial reality from rearing its ugly head. Use your budget spreadsheet as a practical tool to predict the range of possible financial futures for your conference, and pay heed to the outcomes shown, bad as well as good.

Fine-tuning your conference expense budget

Hopefully your initial bare-bones budget calculation points to a bargain conference fee. Now you can investigate adding optional expense items to further improve the attractiveness of your conference without making it too expensive. Perhaps you will upgrade your menu, or replace an on-site evening meal with a dinner cruise, budget a few hundred dollars for conference souvenir tee-shirts, or decide you can afford to pay for that conference speaker you're sure attendees will appreciate hearing. Don't go overboard at this point, and don't add unnecessary frills. Scrutinize any proposed additions carefully and decide whether they're really worth the extra cost and effort.

As you rework your expense budget, keep an eye on the break-even registration fee to ensure that it doesn't rise too high. You want your conference to be attractively priced while offering an appealing combination of program and ancillary benefits. If you have difficulty getting to this point, compare your budget to the samples later in this chapter and look for significant discrepancies. I don't claim that your allocations should mirror mine, but noting any major differences may help you pinpoint line items that might benefit from a second look.

When budgeting for promotional items, note that it can take significant lead time to personalize products for your conference or organization, so it's generally better to budget for a fixed quantity rather than an order tied to your eventual number of conference attendees.

Vendor exhibit budgeting

A vendor exhibit at your conference can provide a significant source of income. But don't decide to invite vendors for this reason. Include vendors only if you are convinced that they will be a positive conference addition that attendees will genuinely appreciate, rather than one to endure or ignore and that is only included in order to reduce attendee fees.

Generally, expenses incurred for a vendor exhibit at a peer conference are relatively small compared to the revenue generated. If the vendors find value in meeting potential customers in the relatively intimate environment of a peer conference, it's not unreasonable to charge several hundred dollars for a vendor tabletop or booth fee. Because a peer conference is small, don't offer different exhibit area choices; just charge each vendor a standard fee for a fixed space (usually 10 feet × 10 feet, including a 6 foot × 32-inch or 8 foot × 32-inch table if needed).

A vendor fee of this magnitude is usually a fraction of the vendor's cost to get display materials and staff to the conference site.

Research vendor fee schedules charged for similar traditional conferences and use these as a guide in setting your vendor fees. Because large traditional conferences often charge vendors high booth setup fees, which are rarely a factor for a peer conference, you may be surprised how competitive you can be.

If the conference is a repeat event, and the steering committee is looking to build up a financial cushion to weather an occasional conference financial loss, a practical approach is to set the attendee fee to break even on conference expenses and make a modest profit from vendor exhibit fees. Otherwise, if you're confident that you'll be able to sign up vendors, you can use the anticipated revenue to reduce the registration fee for attendees.

I recommend using a three-tiered fee structure, providing discounts for early registration, to lock in vendor registrations early. There tend to be chicken-and-the-egg conversations between prospective vendors and the vendor coordinator, with the vendors wanting to know which of their competitors will be there. A tiered rate structure gives vendors an incentive to commit early, though in my experience there are invariably those who wait until the last minute.

Use at least a $100 price differential between tiers; a smaller discount than this offers little incentive for an early commitment. Open vendor registration as soon as the conference promotional material is ready. Split the remaining time before the conference into three roughly equal parts, and define them as your early, standard, and late registration periods. Provide a clear refund policy on the vendor application. Typically you'll refund the registration fee minus a handling charge if the cancellation is received a month before the conference.

If you're repeating a conference vendor exhibit, you can use your prior years' financials to determine the percentages of vendors who take advantage of the registration discounts, and design your vendor registration rate structure accordingly. Otherwise, I suggest you assume that half your vendors will register early, one quarter will pay standard registration, and one quarter will register at the last minute.

The vendor registration form should specify an upper limit on the number of vendor representatives staffing a display. If a vendor wants to bring more, charge a small fee, perhaps $50, for each additional representative. Sometimes vendors ask if they can attend other parts of the conference. There's more discussion of this in Chapter 19. If you are comfortable with them attending, I suggest you charge a daily conference attendance rate derived by dividing the conference registration fee by its length in days.

Setting conference registration fees

If your peer conference is held at a traditional conference facility that includes hotel rooms either on the site or nearby, then attendees will usually book their own accommodations, taking advantage of any group rate or discount you're able to negotiate. In this case, the conference registration fee will not include any room costs.

But if your conference site can offer nontraditional accommodation for attendees (e.g. college dormitory rooms), some people will prefer commuting from their homes or arranging for alternative lodgings. How should this situation be reflected in the conference registration fee? Should you make a discounted fee available for people who don't use conference site accommodations?

I recommend against providing a discount for off-site lodging for three reasons. First, the conference site may only offer you an all-inclusive per capita rate that includes a room whether it is occupied or not. Second, the marginal cost of providing nontraditional lodging is generally low, so any discount offered is small. Finally, by not providing a discount for off-site accommodations, you provide an incentive for attendees to stay on-site. In my experience, this can make quite a difference to the social atmosphere at the conference; people staying on-site are more likely to stick around in the evenings and join in group discussions and socializing that form an important ingredient of a successful peer conference.

Sometimes an organization will offer to completely sponsor a small conference, so people can attend at no charge. If this pleasant opportunity is offered to you, I think it's important to charge a nominal registration fee, payable in advance. Shelling out a non-refundable fee, say $15–$25, gives registrants a small but significant psychological commitment to attend. Committing to attend a free conference, perhaps by filling out an online form, is not much of a commitment, and an attendee who hasn't paid a non-refundable registration fee may simply decide the day of the conference that he's too busy, too tired, or has something else he'd rather do. In my experience, pre-paying even a small fee makes it much more likely that registrants will show up.

Unless you're charging only a nominal registration fee, use a three-tiered fee structure for your attendees. Divide the time between when the conference promotional materials are first distributed and the start of the conference into three roughly equal time parts and define them as your early, standard, and late registration periods. Consider providing discounts of around 25 percent for early registration, and 12.5 percent for standard registration. If your conference promotion hits the ground running, I would use an estimate of 60 percent early registration, 20 percent standard registration, and 20 percent late registration. Use these percentages to calculate conference attendance rates that, assuming a minimum acceptable number of registrants, lead to a break-even budget.

Typically, attendees will pay the conference fee with cash or a check. To accept credit card payments, you'll need a merchant account for credit card processing. Unless you already have access to a merchant account, perhaps via a sponsoring organization, I don't recommend offering this option, as merchant accounts are expensive and not, in my view, worth the bother to set up for a single conference. If you do provide a credit card payment option, build the cost into your conference fee structure.

I like to offer steering committee members a special registration rate that represents slightly more than the marginal cost for them to attend—for example, the per capita cost that the conference site charges, ignoring any fixed conference costs. If you decide to go this route, make sure you include the financial impact in your conference budget, since the steering committee can be a significant percentage of the conference attendees.

Another fee you should include in your registration materials is the cost for spouses/significant others who want to accompany an attendee, sharing lodging, joining in meals and any special events, but not otherwise taking part in the conference. This fee can be similar to the steering committee rate described above.

Finally you'll need to set and communicate a clear refund policy for registration fees if a registrant asks to cancel.

Budget review and monitoring

Circulate your budget to the steering committee for questions and comments. After you've incorporated any resulting changes, the conference treasurer must regularly review the budget, comparing it to the financial reality of the money flowing in and out of your bank account. If your budget estimates were conservative, she'll have good news for the rest of the committee. But it's also her job to promptly notify the conference coordinator and marketing committee if deviations in revenues and/or expenses are having a significant negative impact on the budget, so that corrective measures can be taken in good time. A critical issue to monitor is a projected shortfall in conference registrations, something that can usually be corrected by putting more resources into promotional activities.

If the conference's financial viability is a concern, try to avoid significant financial commitment to the host institution until it's clear that the attendance needed for a break-even budget will be forthcoming. Find out from the host site representative the latest date acceptable for a go/no-go decision on the conference, and then concentrate on getting registrants to commit before that date. If the conference site requires a non-refundable deposit to secure the conference time slot, make sure you can handle the resulting financial loss should the conference be cancelled.

Accounting

Although the accounting for a small conference can be done manually, I suggest you use computer accounting software to track your conference finances and provide ongoing and final financial reports. Any personal or small business accounting software will do the job; Quicken® works well for me.

Track the distribution of multitiered registration fees, by assigning a separate subaccount category to each income tier. This will make it easier to estimate your eventual registration numbers, and give you good information for financial planning of any repeat conferences.

If possible, have two people handle accounts receivable; one to process and deposit payments and one to record deposits. This provides some protection against fraudulent activity by a single committee member.

The conference bookkeeper should supply regular financial updates to the conference coordinator, who distributes them to steering committee members as appropriate. A final conference accounting should be given to each steering committee member.

Sample budgets

Use the sample budgets below to help construct your conference budget. The amounts are based on typical 2007 figures for the northeast United States. Every conference has unique circumstances that affect individual budget items, so consider these examples a guide, not a prescription.

Each sample budget shows the financial consequences of a range of conference attendance, plus actual final figures with typical variances you might experience. The budgets assume that volunteers run the conferences, except for hourly paid help for some on-site functions, as noted in the budgets.

One-day sponsored conference sample budget

	Income or cost per capita	NUMBER OF ATTENDEES					Actual	%
		30	40	50	60	70	46	
INCOME								
Sponsorship contribution		$1,110	$1,210	$1,310	$1,410	$1,510	$1,220	51%
Registration fees	$25	$750	$1,000	$1,250	$1,500	$1,750	$1,150	49%
Total Income		**$1,860**	**$2,210**	**$2,560**	**$2,910**	**$3,260**	**$2,370**	**100%**
EXPENSES								
Meals and refreshments	$35	$1,050	$1,400	$1,750	$2,100	$2,450	$1,566	66%
Facility rental		$450	$450	$450	$450	$450	$450	19%
Flyer printing		$100	$100	$100	$100	$100	$92	4%
Flyer design		$150	$150	$150	$150	$150	$150	6%
Postage & mailing		$70	$70	$70	$70	$70	$68	3%
Office supplies		$40	$40	$40	$40	$40	$44	2%
Total expenses		**$1,860**	**$2,210**	**$2,560**	**$2,910**	**$3,260**	**$2,370**	**100%**
Expense / attendee		$62	$55	$51	$49	$47	$52	

This is a sample budget for a one-day sponsored local peer conference with a nominal registration fee of $25. Because attendees come from nearby, no accommodations are included in the conference budget. Buffet-style meals and refreshments are provided by an outside catering service for $35 per attendee. A two-sided conference flyer, distributed by mail and email, is used to promote the conference. The budget shows the sponsor's financial exposure to be between $1,100 and $1,500.

2.5-day pure peer conference sample budget

	Income or cost per capita	NUMBER OF ATTENDEES					Actual	%
		30	40	50	60	70	37	
INCOME								
Registration fees	$325	$9,750	$13,000	$16,250	$19,500	$22,750	$11,865	100%
EXPENSES								
Accommodation, meals, & refreshments	$145	$4,350	$5,800	$7,250	$8,700	$10,150	$4,060	51%
Dinner cruise	$35	$1,050	$1,400	$1,750	$2,100	$2,450	$1,295	16%
Steering committee dinner		$400	$400	$400	$400	$400	$286	4%
Additional alcohol	$8	$240	$320	$400	$480	$560	$315	4%
Brochure printing		$120	$120	$120	$120	$120	$117	1%
Mailing design		$150	$150	$150	$150	$150	$150	2%
Postage & mailing		$300	$300	$300	$300	$300	$376	5%
Conference labor		$400	$400	$400	$400	$400	$492	6%
Promotional items		$500	$500	$500	$500	$500	$587	7%
Office		$300	$300	$300	$300	$300	$360	4%
Total expenses		**$7,810**	**$9,690**	**$11,570**	**$13,450**	**$15,330**	**$8,038**	100%
Expense / attendee		$260	$242	$231	$224	$219	$217	
Profit or (loss)		**$1,940**	**$3,310**	**$4,680**	**$6,050**	**$7,420**	**$3,827**	

Breakdown of attendee income	Fee	Actual number of attendees	Income	%
Early	$300	20	$6,000	51%
Standard	$375	5	$1,875	16%
Late	$450	5	$2,250	19%
Steering committee	$200	7	$1,400	12%
Spouse or s/o	$170	2*	$340	3%
		37	$11,865	

Here's a model budget for a national two-and-a-half-day pure peer conference (no traditional sessions) held at a college campus. The cost of housing attendees on-site is included in attendee conference fees. The college dining service supplies meals and refreshments, and an evening dinner cruise on a nearby river provides an entertaining night out. Marketing is primarily via telephone and email contacts to members of a national organization closely associated with the conference topic, with a simple conference brochure available for follow-up. A free wiki is used to organize the conference. College students are paid to help set up the conference site and guide attendees to their dormitory rooms.

---

*Not included in total attendee count

3.5-day traditional conference site sample budget

	Income or cost per capita	NUMBER OF ATTENDEES					Actual 65	%
		30	40	50	60	70		
INCOME								
Registration fees	$415	$12,450	$16,600	$20,750	$24,900	$29,050	$27,125	100%
EXPENSES								
Meals and refreshments	$145	$4,350	$5,800	$7,250	$8,700	$10,150	$9,823	50%
Wine tasting		$550	$550	$550	$550	$550	$550	3%
Steering committee dinner		$500	$500	$500	$500	$500	$522	3%
Additional alcohol	$14	$420	$560	$700	$840	$980	$649	3%
Brochure printing		$2,500	$2,500	$2,500	$2,500	$2,500	$2,380	12%
Brochure design		$900	$900	$900	$900	$900	$1,000	5%
Postage & mailing		$2,000	$2,000	$2,000	$2,000	$2,000	$1,932	10%
Conference labor		$0	$0	$0	$0	$0	$120	1%
Promotional items		$800	$800	$800	$800	$800	$1,024	5%
Keynote speaker		$1,000	$1,000	$1,000	$1,000	$1,000	$1,125	6%
Office supplies		$400	$400	$400	$400	$400	$421	2%
Total expenses		$13,420	$15,010	$16,600	$18,190	$19,780	$19,546	100%
Expense / attendee		$447	$375	$332	$303	$283	$301	
Profit or (loss)		**($970)**	**$1,590**	**$4,150**	**$6,710**	**$9,270**	**$7,579**	

Breakdown of attendee income	Fee	Actual number of attendees	Income	%
Early	$395	33	$13,035	48%
Standard	$470	11	$5,170	19%
Late	$545	12	$6,540	24%
Steering committee	$220	9	$1,980	7%
Spouse or s/o	$200	2*	$400	1%
		65	$27,125	

This is a sample budget for a national three-and-a-half-day peer conference with a keynote speaker, held at a conference center. Attendees are responsible for choosing and paying for their own accommodations. The conference center supplies all meals and refreshments, except for a steering committee dinner the night before the conference starts. Marketing is via an eight-page three-color brochure mailed to 2,000 potential attendees selected from a commercial mailing list service.

*Not included in total attendee count

197

Vendor Exhibits

Should you include a vendor exhibit?

Conference topics are frequently associated with commercial products and services in which attendees have an interest. If this applies to your conference, consider organizing a vendor exhibit.

One tempting reason to include a vendor exhibit is that it can make a big difference to your financial bottom line. If volunteers organize the exhibit, expenses are generally small compared to what you can expect to receive from vendor fees. (See the sample budgets in Chapter 18 for a typical example.) You can bank the profit to use as a financial cushion for your next conference, or, if you are confident of obtaining a certain level of vendor attendance, you can apply the anticipated profit toward reducing the fees you charge attendees.

Your promotion efforts can also benefit from a conference vendor exhibit. Prospective attendees often greatly prize the opportunity to meet multiple relevant vendors at a single time and place.

Don't hold a vendor exhibit just for financial or marketing reasons. Base your decision on whether an exhibit will be experienced as a win-win activity for both attendees and vendors. If the vendor exhibit is included primarily to make money, it's unlikely that it will be a success.

At a peer conference, the vendor exhibit should run for several hours to be effective for both attendees and vendors. Thus, you should only consider having vendors if your conference runs for at least a couple of days.

Bear in mind that a vendor exhibit generates a significant amount of pre-conference and conference work. I once made the mistake of volunteering for both the conference and vendor coordinator positions at a conference, and exposed myself to a level of work I vowed never to repeat. One person usually does the work of the vendor coordinator; that person should have no other conference responsibilities.

If your conference is long enough, if a vendor exhibit fits well with the interests of your attendees, and if you have a vendor coordinator willing to shoulder the work involved, a vendor exhibit can be a big plus for your conference.

This section concentrates on the planning needed to hold a successful vendor exhibit. The work required to implement the plan at the conference site is covered in Chapters 23 and 24.

Overview of the vendor coordinator's job

The vendor coordinator has plenty of work to do, both before and during the conference. Before the conference, he needs to solicit vendors, organize the layout and facilities for the exhibit space, and provide logistical information to signed-up vendors. During the conference, his responsibilities are to supervise vendor setup, respond to site-related vendor needs, and ensure vendor departure goes smoothly once the exhibit time is over.

Soliciting vendors

The vendor coordinator starts by compiling a list of potential vendors and associated contact information. Conference steering committee members are a good starting resource; additionally, you can send inquiry emails to appropriate mailing lists to obtain additional suggestions. Ask for vendors with which potential attendees already have a relationship, as well as suggestions for vendors that people would like to see at the conference. When you get a referral, ask about any personal contacts the referrer has with the vendor; this is a great way to obtain good information on who to work with at the vendor company.

Vendors need plenty of personal contact to convince them to attend. As soon as conference promotional materials are available, send a copy to vendors on your list and include a marketing cover letter that describes the conference topic, gives information on location, dates, and price, and solicits the vendor's attendance.

The initial vendor mailing should be followed up by phone calls to each vendor. Discovering who at the company decides whether the vendor will attend your conference often takes multiple phone calls. Once you've found the right person, the work of educating him or her about your conference and selling the value of their company coming has just begun. Even if your conference is an established repeating event, you'll often discover that the vendor representative you dealt with last year is gone and the replacement needs to be educated all over again.

As with attendee registration, I strongly advise a three-tiered price structure (early, standard, and late) for vendor fees. Use at least a $100 differential between fee levels, or vendors will tend to ignore discounts and decide whether to attend at the last minute. In 2007 I used vendor fees of $350 (early), $450 (standard), and $550 (late) at conferences with minimal exhibit expenses. If you will incur significant expenses in hosting your vendor exhibit, cover your costs by increasing vendor fees.

Stay in touch on a regular basis with undecided vendors until they either register or decide not to attend. Since vendors usually have a limited number of employees available for staffing conference exhibits, their decision to attend will often depend on whether your conference conflicts with another marketing opportunity. Sometimes vendors will share their decision-making process with you—listen carefully so you can determine when and how it makes sense to follow up with them.

One of your steering committee members, the conference host, or a registrant may be a major client of a prospective vendor. Look for such opportunities, since getting that vendor to the conference can be as simple as the client asking the vendor if they will be attending the conference. This "offer you can't refuse" approach works surprisingly often.

The vendor coordinator should make regular reports of vendor registrations to the conference coordinator, conference host, finance committee, and marketing committee. If you have a conference website or wiki, list registered vendors on it and keep the list up to date so that prospective attendees can see who's coming.

Include a vendor registration form (or provide a link for online registration on your conference website, if you have one) in your vendor marketing materials. Include a clear refund policy with your registration form, and, when necessary, gently remind vendors that they have not registered and reserved a space until they have paid the appropriate fee.

When vendors sign up for the conference and pay the vendor fee, send them a confirmation letter promptly. Include directions to the conference site, directions and/or a map to the building for and entrance to the vendor exhibit area, and specific instructions on the times that vendors are to set up and remove their display and associated materials.

Organizing the vendor exhibit space

If you have a conference host on the steering committee, she will normally work in advance with the vendor coordinator to ensure that the vendor exhibit space is properly equipped before vendors start to arrive. Otherwise the vendor coordinator should attend the site visit to get first-hand information about the vendor exhibit space. If this isn't possible, it's vital that the site visit committee provide detailed information on the exhibit space, as described in Chapter 14.

Peer conference vendor exhibits are small compared to those of traditional conferences—I've never had more than 20 vendors at any conference I've run, and a dozen or so is common. Once you know how many vendors you have coming, create a floor plan showing where each vendor will be located. If there are "prime" spots, give them to the vendors who register first. There are usually one or two companies that, despite every effort on your part, don't commit until the last minute (or just show up on the day), so, if you can, include some unassigned spaces.

To create a workable environment for vendor displays you may need to provide any or all of the following:

- Tables, chairs, and drapes
- Power
- Internet access
- Appropriate access to the exhibit area in advance of the exhibition

I suggest you offer to provide each vendor a 32-inch-wide table, either 6- or 8-feet long, since these are usually available at conference sites, or can be rented inexpensively. Table drapes are optional, but add a touch of class and can also be rented if necessary. Include a couple of chairs with each table. If you have ample space offer vendors a 10 feet by 10 feet exhibit area; if space is limited you can go down to as little as 8-foot frontage by 6-foot depth. Make clear in your vendor solicitation letter the size of the area that will be available. Some vendors may want to bring a booth; these are usually 8 feet by 10 feet or 10 feet by 10 feet and you'll need to figure out whether their booth will fit in your space.

Vendors may need power for their exhibit area. In your vendor solicitation letter offer a power outlet for each display space, and have a place on the vendor registration form where they indicate whether power will be needed. Plan in advance how you will supply power to vendors who request it; you may need to check the capacity of outlets in the vendor area and obtain some extension cords to run to exhibit areas.

From your conference topic, you can probably predict whether vendors are likely to want Internet access. If wired Internet access is available in the exhibit space it can usually be shared through an inexpensive Ethernet hub. Or it may be appropriate to set up an open wireless access point for vendors. Test the availability of any Internet access you commit to providing. If Internet access will not be available in the exhibit area, let vendors know this before they register.

Ideally, the vendor exhibit area should have direct access to an outside entrance where vendors can conveniently bring their display and materials. Conference centers are generally designed for this, while nontraditional conference sites may not offer exhibit-friendly access. If your exhibit space is up a flight of narrow stairs, can only be entered through small doorways, or is otherwise hard to set up, restrict vendors to tabletop exhibits.

I recommend providing a buffet-style meal, usually lunch, open to all who attend the vendor exhibit. Set up the buffet as part of the vendor exhibit. A simple and effective approach is to arrange the booths in a large circle with the buffet tables placed at the center. Include tables and chairs for attendees and vendor representatives to eat together and socialize. Check the practicality of the eating area and food service layout you'd like to use with your food provider.

Program implications of a vendor exhibit

At every peer conference with a vendor exhibit there's a tension between attendee and vendor desires for face-time. Vendor representatives want as much attendee time as they can get, while attendees want just enough time scheduled to see the vendors they want to meet and no more. For years I've been trying to find a satisfactory compromise, but have come to the conclusion that there is no ideal solution; whatever you do, some people are going to be a bit unhappy.

Although the desires of attendees should be given priority, from years of trying various approaches, I suggest a couple of small additions to the program, *vendor introductions* and *vendor presentations*, that inform attendees and keep vendors happy at the cost of a few minutes of attendee conference time.

A short *vendor introduction* session gives every vendor a brief, typically 45–60 seconds, opportunity to introduce their products and services to the assembled attendees. The whole process takes less than 15 minutes, and is best held just before the vendor exhibit opens. Vendors love the chance to connect with all attendees, and the session is short enough for attendees to get a brief overview of what they're about to see without being annoyed at the amount of time taken.

Vendor presentations can be offered during the vendor exhibit. They are optional events for attendees. Vendor presentations provide vendors the opportunity to give a short, typically 20-minute, pitch for their products and services to interested attendees in a quiet private area away from the exhibit space. Ask vendors on the registration form whether they want to give a presentation. Explain that there is no guarantee that attendees will show up.

If vendors agree to give a presentation, ask them for a brief, 100 words or less, description, to be sent to the vendor coordinator before the conference. The vendor coordinator transfers these descriptions into a single document and adds a schedule showing when and where each presentation will take place.

Smart vendors will often showcase their expertise in an area of interest to attendees, only working in how their companies' products and services help solve a problem toward the end of their presentation. Encourage vendors to offer presentations of this kind.

If the rooms you make available for vendor presentations contain potentially useful presentation aids, like video projectors, screens, flip charts, and so on, indicate this on the registration form. Otherwise, advise vendors that they will need to supply any presentation aids they need.

Other pre-conference vendor exhibit considerations

I suggest you limit the number of vendor representatives who can staff each vendor display; two is a reasonable number. Vendors wanting to bring more than two people should clear this with the vendor coordinator first. You may want to charge a nominal amount for additional staff members to cover any increased meal fees.

Vendors often ask whether they can give a presentation at your conference. This is a reasonable request, but it's generally not appropriate for a peer conference. Exceptions can be made for vendor representatives who are recognized experts in a topic that you know is of high interest to attendees.

Vendors occasionally ask whether their staff members can attend conference sessions. Personally, I think vendors who ask to do this are smart—they can learn a great deal from session conversations. However, attendees often have reservations about allowing vendors to be present at sessions. The most common concern is that vendor representatives may try to inappropriately promote their company or products. This is a valid concern; I've seen it happen, and attendees do not appreciate it. In addition, if attendees are discussing personal issues specific to their job or organization, they may not want non-peers to be present at the session. To handle these concerns, see the discussion in Chapter 25.

If you are holding an entertainment event, like an ice-cream social or an end-of-conference raffle, consider asking vendors to sponsor the event. An ice-cream social or a beer tasting may cost them one or two hundred dollars—have the sponsoring vendor present, perhaps with a company banner, and briefly acknowledge their sponsorship. For an end-of-conference raffle, which is a great way to keep attendees around through the final session, solicit all vendors for prizes. Ask for items that are not available as a promotional give-away at the vendor exhibit, and acknowledge the donation publicly if it's not obviously connected to the donor.

Use a database to store information on prospective and attending vendors. This is where you will track who's coming, keep notes on your conversations with vendor contacts, stay on top of power, Internet, and space requirements, and create a list of vendors for attendees during the conference. On www.conferencesthatwork.com you'll find a free, user-modifiable, FileMaker Pro, conference vendor database that provides these capabilities for you to use before and during the conference.

If your vendors are well matched to your attendees' interests, then most if not all of the exhibitors will be pleased by the connections and follow-up sales they make.

CHAPTER 20

Providing Attendee Information: Paper Versus Online

With the ubiquity of personal computers and wide availability of wireless Internet access, it's now possible to hold a peer conference that is completely paperless—registration, schedule, peer session notes, and any other information needed to run and document the conference can be entered, edited, and viewed online. Given the environmental benefits of reducing paper use, if every attendee has a personal computer available at the conference, what can you do to reduce, or even eliminate, the volume of paper consumed at the conference?

A conference wiki provides many opportunities for supplying information to attendees that otherwise would have to be printed and distributed on paper. The structure of a wiki can be modified on the fly to handle new needs as they arise during the conference. The schedule, face book, session and peer session notes, PowerPoint presentations, conference pictures, and any other useful digital files can be uploaded to the wiki, and updated as the conference progresses.

Although I've run conferences where every attendee brought a laptop computer, I still feel there's a place for paper—at least for now. Until software is developed for proposing, signing up, and scheduling peer sessions, for example, it's hard to beat the convenience and flexibility of paper sign-up sheets posted on a wall or tables. When attendees at a refreshment break are deciding which peer session to attend in five minutes, a few copies of the schedule posted around the refreshment area provide a handy reference. And, when noting information about attendees and their experiences on the draft face book during the roundtable, it's difficult to match the simplicity, convenience, and speed of writing on a paper copy, even if every attendee has software for PDF markup, or has a personal copy of the registration database together with the database software needed to edit it, or is running annotation software on a tablet PC.

I expect paper to play an essential role as a low-tech tool for peer conferences for quite some time—perhaps forever. I'd be happy to be proved wrong.

Using wikis to plan and document your conference

Wikis are a comparatively recent addition to the growing number of Internet-based tools. A wiki is an open communal website where anyone can contribute. A wiki is a creation of all its members, rather than the product of a single webmaster or small website maintenance crew, just as a peer conference is a creation of all its attendees, rather than a small conference steering committee. Because a wiki's open design and possibilities mirror those of a peer conference, a wiki is an excellent tool for organizing and documenting your conference.

Some wikis are public; they can be read, and sometimes edited, by anyone with access to the Internet. You should restrict access to your conference wiki to attendees by requiring them to be registered before they can use it. Registered members use a username and password to access the conference wiki; once logged in they can create and edit wiki web pages. Some wiki software supports more elaborate access controls, allowing you to set up private sections on your wiki. Such a private section can be used by the steering committee to plan the conference. Otherwise you may want to use a separate private wiki for your conference planning.

Although each software implementation of a wiki has its own way of doing things, there are a number of features that wiki implementations share:

- Compared to creating and formatting standard website pages using an HTML editor, wikis provide simplified ways of creating and formatting web pages.
- Users can easily create new wiki pages wherever needed by making a reference to them in an existing page, usually using *CamelCase* or a set of brackets.

- Most wikis offer full-text searching, allowing users to quickly find all references to a word or phrase.
- Because wiki pages may be added, removed, or changed at any time, wikis generally include a *Recent Changes* function that shows a chronological list of recent changes made to the wiki's pages.

If you have website committee members with technical skills and access to a web server, they may be able to host and set up your own private conference wiki. Alternatively, there are many free and low-cost *wiki farm* services that provide hosting for wiki websites and which are designed to be easy for novice users to configure and use. Many services are free or offer free trial periods for you to evaluate how well they work for you.

Wikis can be used for many different purposes before, during, and after your conference, including:

- Conference planning
  - Steering committee discussions
  - Site visit notes
  - Marketing ideas
  - Budgets and pricing
  - Conference logistics
- Pre-conference attendee communication
  - Fixed session descriptions
  - Session ideas
  - Conference ride board
  - Attendee preparation
  - Attendee list
  - Registered vendors
- Conference materials
  - Roundtable topics and themes
  - Session resources (web references, articles, media)
  - Peer session schedule
  - Peer session notes
  - Conference face book
  - Photos
  - Spective notes
- Post-conference materials
  - Attendee evaluations
  - Ongoing discussions

Once you've installed your wiki software or chosen a service provider, create a first draft of your key wiki sections. Then organize the sections into a sensible hierarchy. The following suggested contents will help you get started:

- Home page
- How to use this wiki
- Conference
- Registrants
- Schedule
- Vendor exhibit
- Potential peer session topics
- Peer session notes
- Resources
- Keynote
- Traditional sessions
- Recent changes (usually automatically provided by the wiki software)
- Resources
- Steering Committee discussions (restricted to steering committee members)
- Site selection
- Site visit notes
- Site coordination
- Program
- Meals and refreshments
- Marketing
- Finance
- Vendor exhibit
- Site preparation
- Registration
- Entertainment

If you hold multiple conferences, you should extend this structure to include separate sets of pages for each conference.

Building an initial outline of pages will help users figure out where to start posting content. Over time, as people add more pages to suit their needs, the structure may get messy. At any time, users may move things around to clean up the structure, a process called *re-factoring*. Someone on your website committee should monitor the wiki and re-factor it, if needed, so the wiki remains logically laid out and it doesn't become too difficult for users to find what they're looking for.

Promotional conference items

Promotional conference items (a.k.a., *schwag* or *swag*) are optional extras for your conference. Don't feel you need to provide them, especially at an inexpensive one-day conference. At longer conferences, it can be fun to offer swag. But don't commit to an expensive order until you see the registrations rolling in, feel confident that the conference is going to happen, and can see that the conference finances are going to be in good shape.

I suggest you have a short steering committee discussion of possible promotion items and budget, but leave the final choice of item, color, style, and branding to one person. This is because getting a group of people to agree on what swag to buy is a guaranteed time-sink. The person doing the ordering should take into account any existing style or color conventions used by associated group or sponsoring organizations, and choose an item and branding that fits.

Stay away from small items like pens, and gimmicky items like plastic back-scratchers. Give your attendees something attractive that they are likely to use after the conference. Clothing (baseball caps, tee-shirts, and shirts), mugs, and tote and messenger bags are the items I usually stick with. Shirts are popular but a bit problematic because there are always a few left over in the wrong size (my experience is that the standard mix includes too many XL sized items.) Less popular, but inexpensive, items I've tried have been water bottles and fanny packs. Large items can be a pain to transport and store. At one conference we ordered attractive folding sports chairs. People appreciated them, but some attendees who had flown to the conference had trouble bringing their chairs home.

Promotional items should be branded with at least the name of the conference. If there are sponsoring organizations, ask whether they'll underwrite the costs of the swag if their logos are affixed. Companies producing promotional items charge handsomely for express shipping, so investigate lead times for the items you select and place your order early enough to be shipped regular freight. Have everything shipped directly to the conference site if at all possible; even 50 tee-shirts weigh more and take up more room than you might think.

If your conference is a repeat event, you may want to consider ordering badge lanyards branded with the name of your conference or sponsoring organization(s). These can help attendees recognize each other if you're holding the event at a conference site where other events are going on simultaneously. Branded badge lanyards are inexpensive, but most companies will require you to place a minimum order of several hundred or more, so you won't want to order them unless you're confident that the conference will be held at least several times.

What quantity should you order? Because per item costs usually plunge dramatically the larger your order, it's tempting to overbuy. Repeated conferences have a big advantage here;

you can buy enough tee-shirts or hats for a couple of years and cut your annual cost. Until you're confident that your conference will be repeated, and that your finances will be healthy, only order enough items to give every attendee one, plus some extras to hand out to site staff, traditional session speakers and panelists, and a few to spare. Kitchen staff often appreciate swag as an impromptu thank you for a job well done, and so may the business manager or the site coordinator who made that extra effort for you. If finances are tight, order a limited number of items and announce in your marketing materials that you'll give them to the first *X* registrants.

I often set out excess swag for sale, usually at cost or slightly above, for anyone who wants an extra item. You'll probably just sell a few, so don't expect to get rid of significant numbers of extra promotional items this way.

If your conference becomes a repeated event, consider creating an associated logo that you can use on promotional items and marketing materials. Use a professional designer for this, or investigate inexpensive online services like thelogocompany.net. Over time, paying attention to your conference brand will provide your target audience a familiar marketing experience and make your conference an easier sell.

Pre-conference registration

First impressions

Attendee registration is the first contact an attendee will have with your conference's organization. First impressions are important, so be sure you provide a friendly, responsive, and accurate registration process. Because peer conferences are small, attendee registration is an administrative task that's easy to do well. One person can easily handle registrations for a peer conference, although it's advisable to have a substitute available who can take over the job if the normal registrar goes on vacation or will be out of touch for an extended period.

Registration options

There are several common ways to register for a conference, and you'll need to decide which ones you're going to support. Registrants can:

- Register by telephone (attendee calls to register and information is taken over the phone);
- Fill out a paper registration form;
- Fill out a text registration form in the body of an email and either reply via email or by printing the completed form and mailing it;

- Print and then fill out a text, PDF, or Word format registration form; or
- Complete a registration form online:
  - and print it
  - or the website emails it to the registrar
  - or it's added to the registration database by programming on the website.

The online options are listed in order of ease of implementation (and in inverse order of work involved in getting attendee information into the database). It's nice to have online conference registrations flow automatically into the registration database, but it may not be worth the setup work needed. At the time of writing this book, commercial online registration systems are quite expensive to use for a small conference, but they may become affordable and an attractive option in the near future.

Also determine the options you'll offer for receiving registrations: by hand (at an allied event where you promote the conference), mail, fax, email, or directly added to the registration database.

Once you've decided how you'll register attendees, create the forms, emails, or website programming you need, so you're ready to receive and process registrations as soon as prospective attendees hear about your conference and decide to come.

Resist the temptation to ask for lots of attendee information at registration, even if it would be a valuable addition to the face book. Make your registration process as quick and simple as possible, so that someone who has just decided to attend can register without wading through a barrage of questions that may give her second thoughts about completing the registration.

Recording registrations

Use a database to store attendee registration information. Any modern database program should have the functionality you need. The database must be able to hold and display a photograph of each registrant for the conference face book. Bear in mind that you'll need to run the program you choose not only on the registrar's computer, but also on a computer at the conference site. These can be the same computer if the registrar stores the database on a laptop that she brings to the conference. Since this isn't always possible, you may want to choose database software that is compatible with both Macintosh and Windows operating systems, like FileMaker Pro.

I recommend you use separate databases to store prospective and actual attendees. Although it's possible to use a single database for both, having hundreds or thousands of nonattendee records in your registration database will slow down the program and make it harder to find and browse attendee records.

On www.conferencesthatwork.com you'll find a free, user-modifiable, FileMaker Pro, conference database that you can use to create and manage most of the information and reports needed before and during the conference, including badges, a conference face book, attendee reports, fee tracking, mailing labels, conference packet labels, room occupant labels, room reports, attendee vendor reports, and more.

If you add photographs of attendees to the registration database before the conference, be sure to read the important tip on this subject in the section on face book photos in Chapter 24.

Conference attendee registration requests

For conferences lasting more than a day, the registrar should discuss with the other steering committee members, before registrations start coming in, what your policy will be for people who want to attend only part of the conference.

Occasionally you will get a request from someone who would like to come for one day, or one or two traditional sessions. Ultimately it's your choice whether you let them come. If you do, my preference is to quote a daily rate derived from the conference fee divided by the number of days the conference runs. I don't offer a single session price, because it's too complicated to track and encourages people to cherry-pick the conference.

Don't give a reduced conference rate for people who want to arrive late or leave early. If you receive such a request, explain that, unlike a traditional conference, a peer conference includes critical sessions at the beginning and end and that an attendee's conference experience is likely to be significantly degraded if he or she isn't present for the entire event.

Sometimes an attendee asks whether they can sell something at the conference. If you are holding a vendor exhibit, consider treating them as a vendor. If not, and they are selling a book or other small item, you may want to offer them a tabletop to display their wares, together with some kind of deal that benefits the conference—a special price for attendees, or a cut of any sales.

Responding to vendors who ask whether they can attend conference sessions is covered in Chapter 19.

Processing registrations and payments

Registration forms and payments can be sent to the conference registrar, conference host, or a steering committee representative of a sponsoring organization; you choose. Don't have fees sent directly to the treasurer, as it's preferable to have two people handle incoming payments; one to process and deposit payments and one to record deposits. This provides some protection against fraudulent activity by a single committee member.

Copies of the registration information should be forwarded to the conference registrar, conference coordinator, and site coordinator. One advantage of online registration is that attendee registration information can be automatically sent to the appropriate steering committee members.

If online registration is used, you'll need to track the associated payments. When using a multitiered fee structure, send timely reminders to people who have registered but haven't paid as the closing date for the lower payment approaches. Follow up unpaid registrations, since sometimes registrants decide not to attend and don't tell you.

Registration communications

When a registration is received, promptly send an acknowledgment. If payment has been received, include detailed conference information; otherwise, remind the attendee that payment is due and detailed information will be sent when payment is received.

If attendees are staying in nontraditional accommodations, like dormitories, let them know exactly what will be supplied with their rooms, and include a list of items that attendees may want to bring with them, such as toiletries, a towel, a small fan, and a desk lamp.

Your acknowledgment letter or email should also include directions to the conference site, a conference schedule, when rooms will be available for occupancy, which meals are included during the conference, directions for accessing the conference wiki, information on alternative accommodations and communication options such as cell phone reception and Internet access, emergency contact numbers, and any exercise and athletic facilities available at the site.

Make sure that your registration materials introduce the importance and benefits of attending the entire conference. Emphasize that you are using a peer conference process and the attendee will get the most out of the event if she attends the beginning roundtable and stays through the final conference spective.

The registrar provides regular updates on registration numbers to the conference coordinator, treasurer, marketing committee members, site coordinator, and conference host. The steering committee can then take appropriate action if registrations appear to be below expectations or the conference becomes oversubscribed.

As the conference nears, continue to share attendee registrations with the conference host or site coordinator. Decide on a cutoff date, usually a few days before the conference starts, after which last-minute registrants will be processed on-site. After the cutoff date, send a copy of the registration database to the conference host or site coordinator who can then use it to create registrant badges, conference packet labels, room occupant labels, an attendee list, and a room assignment report. Doing this work before the conference gets underway will help reduce stress and mistakes made during on-site registration, which tends to be a somewhat hectic time.

Preparing for the vendor exhibit

My older daughter, a sales manager at a small coffee company, regularly staffs huge natural food trade shows. The most recent show ended at 5 p.m. With forklifts trundling about her on the convention floor, she waited for the pallets needed to pack her booth. To pass the time she played volleyball with other staffers, pounding an empty cardboard carton over the walls of a neighboring booth. Eventually she fell asleep on the floor using a five-pound bag of soup as a pillow. The pallets arrived at 2 a.m.

Luckily, your vendors will not need to endure such tribulations, and they tend to appreciate this. A peer conference vendor exhibit is informal. Most vendors use a tabletop display; a few may bring a small trade show booth with them or, if you so allow, ship it to your conference site in advance. When a vendor registers for the conference, the vendor coordinator should emphasize in her acknowledgment letter that vendors:

- Are responsible for setting up and breaking down their displays;
- Need to let her know in advance if they would like to use a booth; and
- Must discuss in advance any plans to ship their booths to the conference site.

A week or two before the conference, send registered vendors a follow-up letter or email. Include:

- Detailed directions to the conference site;
- A map and/or directions to the vendor exhibit area showing where to unload materials;
- The earliest time vendors will have access to the exhibit area for setup;
- A conference schedule for vendor day, including exhibit, vendor introductions, and vendor presentation times; and
- Vendor coordinator contact information for any last-minute questions.

If you are renting or borrowing any exhibit furnishings, or power or Internet distribution equipment, double check availability and the pickup schedule. Don't feel you have to do the vendor exhibit area setup yourself; arrange for other committee members or some paid help to assist you with any pickup and delivery that you can't handle alone. Providing wired or Wi-Fi Internet access to your vendor area may require technical expertise you don't have on your committee. If so, arrange for volunteer or paid expertise well in advance of your conference.

A few days before the conference, finalize your floor plan and make copies to distribute to vendors when they arrive. If you still have room, decide where any last-minute additional vendors will be placed.

Be prepared for last-minute queries and requests from vendors during this time. Some vendors are overworked, disorganized, or have unexpected events crop up. These realities sometimes turn into cancellations, no-shows, or calls from vendors who had turned you down earlier wanting to come after all. Don't go overboard trying to satisfy every eleventh-hour change of plan, and feel free to stick to your previously announced vendor fee refund policy. Confer with the conference coordinator, the finance committee, and any other relevant steering committee members if you feel the need for a second opinion.

Pre-conference site preparation

Well before the conference, your site coordinator should determine staffing requirements and draw up a schedule for site preparation, collaborating with the conference host if you have one. Traditional conference sites generally have well-defined rules about what can be done with the facilities you are using, and clear guidelines as to who is responsible for setup and cleanup. Nontraditional sites tend to be more flexible, and will normally expect your group to perform most of the work. Whatever your situation, you need to come up with a clear agreement and understanding on who will do what, when, and where.

To get ready for site preparation, first read Chapter 21 for the details of the pre-conference work you'll be doing once you're on-site. Then plan how you'll handle renting any needed furniture or equipment and purchasing supplies like flip charts and markers. Finally, decide who will do the site preparation tasks—steering committee members, local help, or a combination—assign responsibilities, and create a schedule for your pre-conference tasks. Now you're ready to roll!

Pre-conference attendee preparation

A few weeks before the conference, send registrants suggestions for preparation. Adapt the following example to your specific conference needs:

> *A message from Adrian Segar about preparing for the XYZ peer conference:*
>
> *The upcoming peer conference is designed to facilitate and support sharing with and learning from each other. Every participant will have the opportunity to shape the conference to make it personally meaningful and valuable.*

Right at the start, you'll share your interests and experience/expertise. We'll use this information to rapidly determine appropriate peer conference sessions, which may be informal presentations, panels, discussions, workshops, and so on.

So, your preparation for the peer conference is simple. If you have something to share that you think other folks may be interested in hearing about or discussing, bring resources that could be helpful. Resources might include notes, props for interactive exercises, handouts (electronic—we will print or distribute them,) old flip charts, computer presentations plus a laptop that can run them, books, links to web resources, and so on. Please don't spend significant time on preparation— no one will expect something polished.

We'll have computer projectors, screens, and flip charts to use if you need them.

If you'd like to find out more about peer conferences, visit www.segar.com or www.conferencesthatwork.com. If you have questions, feel free to contact me at 802-254-3566 or adrian@segar.com. I'm looking forward to meeting with you on May 1!

Assigning remaining conference tasks

At this stage, most conference administrative jobs and responsibilities will have already been assigned. Before the conference, the conference coordinator must arrange coverage for the remaining jobs, principally those associated with running conference sessions. Go through the following list of conference jobs and agree who will take responsibility for them. If necessary, review the appropriate sections of this book to clarify what each job involves.

- Conference announcer and timekeeper
- Computer and photography staff
- Accommodation and site facilities guide(s)
- Welcomer(s)
- Host site representative
- Introducer of conference staff
- Introducer(s) of conference process
- Roundtable convener
- Roundtable facilitator(s)
- Roundtable scribes
- Roundtable timekeeper(s)
- Peer session sign-up convener
- Peer session determination and scheduling

- Peer session scribe notes collector and poster
- Peer session recording coordinator
- Keynote speaker introducer
- Vendor introductions convener (usually the vendor coordinator)
- Business meeting convener
- Appreciations facilitator
- Personal introspective facilitator
- Group spective facilitator
- Cleanup crew

You'll need a small group, three to six people, to determine and schedule peer sessions. Some of these people can be volunteers from your attendees, but it's a good idea to have a few steering committee members agree to participate in advance, in case volunteers aren't forthcoming.

In general, *peer session facilitators* are found during the conference once the peer session topics are known. However, you should agree in advance on a pool of steering committee members who are willing to facilitate a peer session in the event that no one volunteers to facilitate a group that garners high interest among participants.

Evaluations

Provide a way for attendees to evaluate your conference. If attendees decide they want to get together again, their evaluations will provide you with invaluable information on what worked and what didn't, plus a rich variety of suggestions for positive change. Even if your conference isn't repeated, attendee evaluations provide valuable input you can use to improve any peer conference you run in the future.

You can use traditional paper forms for your evaluations, or you can create online evaluations at survey websites like SurveyMonkey, where, for a "professional subscription" of $19.95 per month (up to 1,000 responses per month) or $200.00 per year (unlimited responses per month), you can create an unlimited number of surveys of any length. One big advantage of online surveys is that their results are immediately tabulated and available in a variety of formats: spreadsheets, web pages, PDFs, or printed reports. Having the online survey site do these summaries for you can save significant time compared to tabulating individual paper forms.

Although online evaluations are preferable, provide the option of paper-based evaluations for attendees who won't or can't complete an online survey. Keep in mind that, in my experience, even with persistent pleading, paper forms do not get filled out and returned once attendees have left the conference site. Online evaluations can be completed on-site and, with a polite email reminder, are more likely to be filled out after the conference is over. Give attendees a clear cutoff time for filling out online evaluations—I'd suggest a week—and send a final reminder a couple of days before your deadline.

Whichever form of evaluation you choose, the content will be similar. I like to provide a three-level ranking system (high/moderate/low) for the usefulness or quality of each conference element, plus space for comments for each item. I also include questions that provide an opportunity for attendees to comment on highs and lows of the conference, and to make suggestions about how the conference could be improved.

In order to maximize the number of evaluations returned, give them to attendees as early as possible. To do this, split the conference evaluation into two parts. The first part covers information on fixed sessions and asks general questions about the conference—provide this at the start of the conference. The second covers peer session evaluations, and is generated once peer session topics are known. Providing the first part at the beginning of the conference allows attendees to work on their evaluations throughout the conference, which increases the amount of information you'll get back as well as the likelihood that evaluations will be returned.

Conference evaluation survey content

Use the following content suggestions as a guide. Evaluation paper forms used at a 2006 conference are reproduced in Appendices 11 and 12. At the beginning of each form or online survey include a statement along the lines of the following:

> *Thank you in advance for filling out this survey. We sincerely hope that this conference has been a valuable use of your time. Please feel free to make any comments that would make our next conference more helpful to you and your institution. Please rate the following conference items and activities in terms of their usefulness to you.*

At the end of the survey, include a space for the attendee's name and organization. I usually indicate that this is optional, though if you follow my example, the number of people who stay anonymous, even if they give highly positive feedback, will probably surprise you.

Evaluation survey part 1 possible content (sessions and issues known in advance)
For each of the following topics, include space for a topic rating: High/Moderate/Low/No Opinion rating, and for written comments.

- Pre-Conference Mailings
- Pre-Conference Wiki
- Roundtable Discussion
- Keynote
- Traditional Session #1

- Traditional Session #2
- Traditional Session #3
- Vendor Presentations
- Business Meeting
- Personal Introspective
- Group Spective
- Informal Discussions
- Other

Supply space for written answers to the following questions:

- Which session or topic was most useful to you? Why?
- Which session or topic was least useful to you? Why?
- What topic(s) were not discussed that you would like to have discussed?
- Our main goal and purpose of this conference was *X*. Do you feel that we were successful in this? Why or why not?
- What did you learn at this conference that will assist you and your institution?
- What could we do better?
- What one thing would you change?
- Would you attend a future conference of this type? Why or why not?
- What could we do at future conferences that we don't do now?
- Do you have any comments on the facilities, meals, and so on?
- Additional comments (feel free to include new directions/programs/event suggestions)

Conference evaluation survey part 2 content (peer sessions)

For each peer session or *ad hoc* session:

High/Moderate/Low/No Opinion rating + space for comments

Space for comments on peer sessions in general

Take a breather!

Attendees are registering and you've passed the point of worrying whether enough people are going to come or your peer conference is going to be financially self-supporting. This conference is going to happen! What do you do now?

Relax, and do whatever is necessary for you to be well rested when the conference starts. Administering a peer conference is intense work. I enjoy it immensely, but it can be exhausting keeping everything running smoothly. So, do yourself a favor and take a breather before the event begins. You'll be glad you did!

PART
III

Running Your
Peer Conference

CHAPTER 22 Introduction

Just before the beginning of every conference I feel the same mixture of emotions, best described as *nervous excitement*.

I know that every conference is different, and I know that there is a very real likelihood that wonderful possibilities will emerge for both the individual attendees and the group that will shortly be gathered together. This knowledge and sense of unknown possibilities feeds my excitement.

I also realize that I don't know what may happen, I'm not in control, and I'm indirectly responsible for only a small part of each person's conference experience. Nevertheless I feel anxious: anxious that I'll screw up somehow, that I'll get in the way of other people's experience, that people will reject the concept of a peer conference when they experience this one.

Then the conference starts, and at that moment what I was feeling becomes irrelevant; I'm not conscious of it any more. Instead I'm part of something much bigger than me. I do my part; I lead, follow, listen, respond, and learn in the moment. The next thing I know, two or three or four wonderful days have gone by. Another conference is over.

It wasn't always this way. I used to plan more, fret over possibilities, and feel responsible for group outcomes. Sometimes I felt stressed, frustrated, hot, and bothered. As I became more confident in my conference process, I felt more comfortable with unexpected happenings at conferences. It has become easier for me to learn from new experiences, from new successes and mistakes. And I expect there to be plenty of learning still to come.

These feelings and experiences I've shared are not unusual. If you're about to run your first peer conference, you may be feeling something similar. You have at least one advantage over me. You have this book, which contains my learning from innumerable successes and mistakes made over the last 20 years. In this final section, I explain how to run your peer conference.

I know that the peer conference approach works; you are about to discover its magic as well. Enjoy the journey!

CHAPTER 23 · Pre-Conference Preparation

Timing

Allocate ample time in your pre-conference schedule for site preparation. If you don't, you're likely to find yourself rushing around trying to get everything ready at the last minute. I much prefer to arrive on-site early, finish site preparation, and have a few hours to relax before registration starts, than arrive at the conference site half a day later and be running about trying to borrow a digital camera that works or installing signs in the rain as the first attendees drive up.

In general, the shorter the conference the harder it is to prepare the site. If you've paid to use a facility for a single day, you may need to pay extra for access the previous afternoon or evening so you can set up. It may even be impossible to get access the day before, because the space is booked by another event. Under these circumstances, a morning start may require your steering committee to rise at an early hour and participate in a somewhat frantic, but hopefully disciplined, rush to get everything ready on time. If you're running a short conference, meticulously plan how you'll accomplish your site preparation in the time available.

If I'm running a multiday conference I like to arrive on-site, together with a few steering committee members, about 24 hours before the conference starts. This gives us plenty of time to complete the site preparation described in the following sections, and allows for a leisurely steering committee dinner or lunch before the conference starts.

Preparing conference signage

There are two kinds of signs you'll need for your conference site, *navigational* and *informational*. Make sure signs are easily readable and that outdoor signs will withstand wind and rain.

When creating *navigational* conference signs, put yourself in the position of an attendee who has never visited the conference site. Start with the directions to the conference site you distributed to registrants. As they drive through the school gates, turn into the churchyard, or pull up to the hotel entrance, where should you place signs and directional arrows so attendees know they've arrived at the conference site and can see where to go next? Once they've parked their cars in the correct parking lot, are there signs pointing to the conference registration location? From registration, they'll need directions and appropriate signage so they can find their rooms and make their way to the conference welcome and roundtable. Finally, attendees will need signs that direct them, in either direction, between any two conference session locations.

Some *informational* signs remain fixed throughout the conference, like signs showing the name of a session location ("Vendor Exhibit Area," "Dining Hall," "Peer Session Room A"). Others, like the schedule and location of peer sessions being run on a given day, should be posted in a timely fashion once their content is determined. Planning in advance where and when signs need to be posted, with a steering committee member responsible for carrying out the plan, will greatly reduce attendee confusion, questions, and annoyance.

Setting up on-site registration

First impressions

On-site registration can be a hectic time. You have no control over when attendees show up, and invariably there will be times when there are people waiting in line to register. A one-day conference, when most people show up at the last minute, is particularly challenging.

On-site registration involves many tasks:

- Welcoming attendees as they arrive
- Providing refreshments
- Verifying attendee registration information
- Handing out the conference folder and name badges
- Registering "at the door" attendees
- Collecting unpaid registration fees

- Taking attendee photographs for face book
- Distributing swag
- Providing directions to on-site accommodations
- Answering attendee questions

Once on-site, an attendee's first experience is invariably the conference registration process. Following the suggestions in this section will help you provide a welcoming and pleasant registration experience to incoming attendees, and will minimize your stress and mistakes.

Physical setup

During your site visit you decided on a suitable place to hold on-site registration. Now it's time for setup. First think about the traffic pattern for the registration area. You want a layout that promotes a smooth flow for incoming attendees, as shown in Figure 23.1.

FIGURE 23.1 • On-site Registration Flow

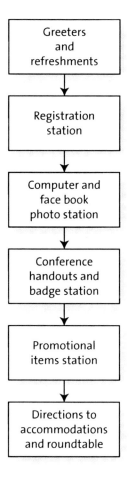

Make sure there's room for a few steering committee members to meet and greet incoming attendees—this is very important. There should also be a place for attendees to relax while waiting to register. Set up some seating there and arrange a refreshment table nearby.

If you're holding a one-day, wintertime conference in a single building, provide a place for people to hang their coats.

Provided you have scheduled enough time for on-site registration (see Table 16.1), you'll only need one registration station. A registration station includes:

- Computer loaded with the registration database and any necessary camera picture transfer software;
- Attached local printer, for printing registration reports;
- Attached digital camera, for taking face book photographs;
- Blank, light-colored wall or other vertical background suitable for posing face book headshots; and
- One or more staffers with the necessary skills and training to run registration.

In addition, you'll need access to a laser printer to print copies of your face book. *A copying machine will not produce acceptable reproductions of attendee photographs and an ink jet printer will be too slow.*

The conference face book

In my view, a conference face book is an essential peer conference tool. Few people have a photographic memory that can infallibly associate faces with names or organizations, especially when meeting a large number of people in a short period of time. The face book provides an invaluable reference to conference participants, both during the conference and afterwards. I can't tell you how many times I have referred to a conference face book to find the name of the person who was so knowledgeable about a subject during an earlier session, or, six months later, to retrieve contact information for an attendee to whom I needed to talk again.

A conference face book contains a photo of each attendee, plus associated relevant information. At a minimum, this should include each participant's name, organization, address, phone, and email. Other items appropriate to the theme of the conference can be added, but only include information that is likely to be of interest to a significant number of attendees. Figure 23.2 shows a sample face book entry.

Because the face book is so useful, it should be completed, printed, and distributed at the conference as quickly as possible. This requires careful organization. I suggest you have at least

FIGURE 23.2 • Sample Face Book Entry

Name:	**Adrian Segar**				
School:					
Title:	**Conference Facilitator**				
Address:			School type:		
			Number Students:		
Email, phone:	adrian@segar.com;				
School computers:		Faculty/teaching:	IT Staff/faculty:		
Student computers:		Faculty/non-teaching:	IT Staff/non-faculty:		
		Staff/non-faculty:			
Questions:					
Expertise:	not taking myself too seriously				
User environment:					
Network OS:					
Network Topology:					
Client OS:					
Admin S/W:					
Academic tech:					
Twitter:					
Linkedin:					
Facebook:					
Other:					

one person, preferably two people, whose sole job during the conference is to complete, print, and distribute the face book.

Capture face book information from pre-conference registration. There's enough going on at on-site registration without the additional work of entering information. If you do this, you'll only need to take participants' photos at registration time. I say only, but getting an acceptable photo of every participant requires careful preparation and a certain amount of persistent follow-up to capture photos of the one or two attendees who have yet to face the camera.

It's important to plan the printing of your face book before the conference, because most copying machines will not create a decent copy of a laser-printed photograph. Such copies are usually very unflattering and seriously detract from the value of the face book. I once made the mistake of relying on the conference hotel to make copies of the face book. The resulting reproduction was so poor, it would have been better to skip the photos entirely. Do a test run of any copier that you plan to use. If a high-resolution copier isn't available, you will need to print the entire face book on a laser printer. Printing at an off-site print shop might be an option, but it hasn't worked for me because of the need to get printed face books into attendees' hands as quickly as possible.

If you print the face book on a laser printer, make sure that you print the book *uncollated* (i.e., with the software set to print multiple copies of each page before starting the next). This is usually a checkbox option "Collate" in the print dialog that appears right before printing; make sure the box is unchecked. If you print a collated face book, your printer will have to download new photographs for each page printed, and your printing speed will slow to a crawl. I've made this mistake too!

Include a footnote on each page stating that the information contained is confidential and may only be distributed to conference attendees.

If a significant number of your attendees have laptops with them, you can offer them a PDF file of the face book to store on their computer. To avoid creating a very large file, make sure that the digital photos used aren't too large. JPEG images that are 50–100KB in size work well and the resulting PDF file will be a few MB. The PDF file can be made available on the conference wiki or shared storage space. Paper copies can be printed only for those attendees who request one. A PDF file can display attendee photos in color, something that may not otherwise be possible unless you have a color laser printer to make your printed copies.

Create at least two versions of the face book. A paper copy of the first draft must be given to attendees before the start of the roundtable session, so they can make notes about what they hear directly onto the relevant person's face book page. If printing the copies with photographs will take too long, omit photographs from the first draft. To be sure that you'll get copies of the first draft printed in time, testing face book printing and copying times in advance is essential.

At a one-day conference, immediately after the roundtable post a paper copy, including photos, of the first draft of the face book in a central spot. Pin up every sheet separately, with attendees sorted in alphabetical order. Ask attendees to check their face book information by 30 minutes before lunch ends, and legibly make any corrections or additions or write a check mark if it's complete. Announce when missing photos will be taken. Before lunch ends, chase down those who haven't signed off on their face book information or been photographed.

At a longer conference, use a similar procedure, adding the printing and display of a second draft of the face book and asking attendees for a final review to catch errors and omissions.

As soon as the face book is finalized, print and distribute copies as necessary to attendees. Create a PDF of the finalized face book and post it on the conference wiki and/or shared network space.

Once you have paper copies of the face book available, don't leave them in a pile in a public space. Make every effort to limit distribution of face books to conference attendees. If you are holding a vendor exhibit, take special care to keep face books out of vendors' hands.

Preparing the vendor exhibit area

Preparing the vendor exhibit area involves obtaining and setting up any and all of the following items: tables, drapes, chairs, power, and Internet access, as per the floor plan you've already prepared. If at all possible, it's best to do this the day before the conference starts, though the morning of a conference that starts after lunch may offer enough time.

Transporting furniture and setting it up in the right place is an exhausting job that seems to take forever if the vendor coordinator tries to do it all himself, and relatively easy if he has a few people to help. Don't be a martyr; make sure that you get the help you need for this task.

If you need to run power or wired Internet connections to vendor tabletops or booths, install extension cords and cables in zero- or low-traffic areas and use gaffer tape to secure them to the floor.

Post navigational signs to guide attendees between the vendor exhibit area and the rooms where vendor presentations will be held. Also post copies of the vendor presentation schedule around the exhibit area and on the doors of the presentation rooms.

Initial conference seating

At the conference welcome and introduction, two or three people speak, one at a time, to the audience. This is a standard scenario for using a classroom-seating format, and with 60 or more attendees that's how you should set up your opening session.

If you have fewer than 60 attendees, and will be running a single roundtable session, start your conference with people seated in the roundtable circle. This avoids having attendees move around after the opening session, breaking the conference flow, and emphasizes that the roundtable is the key session at the start of the conference.

Roundtable setup

The roundtable setup you use depends on the number of attendees at your peer conference. At most peer conferences a single roundtable is all you need. But if you have more than 60 attendees you should run two simultaneous roundtables. If your pre-conference registration count is around 60, prepare for both possibilities, since at-the-door registrations may increase your roundtable attendance, while no-shows and/or late arrivals may reduce it.

If for some reason you cannot hold your roundtable in a room that is large enough for a circle of chairs for the roundtable, the next best alternative is a single block of square or rectangular tables around which everyone sits. Everyone can easily see at least the people on the other three sides with this arrangement, and it has the advantage of giving each attendee a writing surface for making face book notes. In my experience, this arrangement creates a more informal roundtable atmosphere, which can be successful with a small group, particularly if most people already know each other.

You'll need:

> *For every attendee:*
> • A chair
> • A 5×8 card listing the three roundtable questions (see Appendix 6)
> • A draft copy of the conference face book (produced right before the conference starts)
>
> *For each roundtable session:*
> • Two flip chart stands and pads. Masking tape, if the flip chart sheets aren't the kind with a self-adhesive strip OR a plentiful amount of wall-mounted whiteboard space
> • Two roundtable scribes and a timekeeper
> • A place to hang completed flip chart sheets
> • Two boxes of pens
> • A timing device (see below)
> • A digital camera (optional but recommended)

Roundtable layout

When I started running conferences I paid little attention to the configuration of the rooms in which we met. Eventually I noticed that seating arrangements had a subtle yet profound influence on the intimacy and effectiveness of group sessions. For traditional sessions with a speaker or panel, classroom seating was fine.

But for peer conference sessions, where everyone has an equal opportunity to contribute, I realized how important it was that everyone could see everyone else's face, and that individuals weren't emphasized or de-emphasized by virtue of where they sat. Multiple rows, wavering lines of chairs, or chairs scrunched into a too-small room all significantly reduced the intimacy and power of peer sessions. For the roundtable, I discovered that a circle of chairs worked best.

To prepare for a roundtable session, set out a circle of chairs, with a few gaps so people can arrive and depart. If the space in which you're holding the roundtable is much larger than the circle of chairs, position one point of the circle near a wall where flip chart sheets can be hung.

FIGURE 23.3 • Classroom Seating

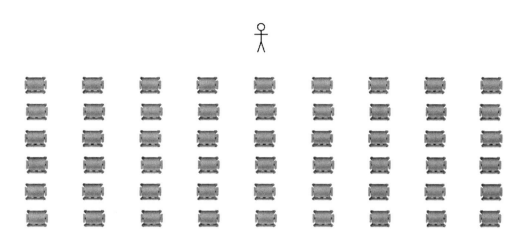

FIGURE 23.4 • Roundtable Seating

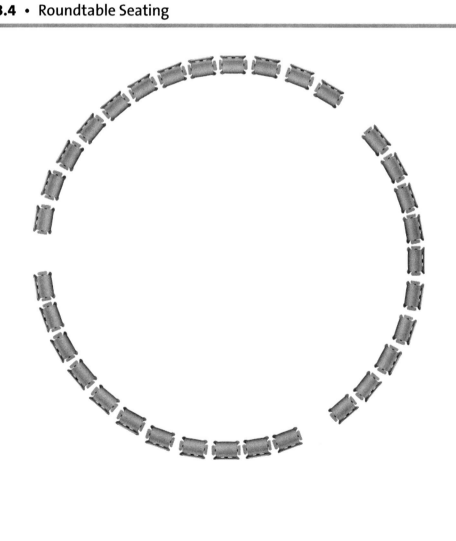

Set out one chair for each registrant, and *make the resulting circle as tight as possible*. Take time to make the circle as round as possible.

You want the smallest comfortable circle, with as few empty chairs as possible. I like to leave gaps in the circle and put out slightly too few chairs, with a pile of extras nearby. Then, late-comers can take a chair from the pile and put it in one of the gaps. This way, the circle is complete during the session, with no empty chairs at any time.

Unless you have a large expanse of nearby wall-mounted whiteboard available, place two flip chart stands near each other, just outside the circle. The flip charts should be near a wall where completed chart sheets can be hung.

Print enough roundtable questions cards to give one to each attendee. Give the cards and the pens to the roundtable scribes, for distribution at the end of the Four Freedoms introduction. If you're using masking tape to hang the flip chart sheets, tear off short strips and store them on the flip chart stands.

Use a digital camera to photograph the flip chart or whiteboard topics recorded during the session. The digital photographs, or a PDF containing them, can be posted on the conference wiki or on the conference file server, easily available for reference during the conference.

Capturing topics and themes

At each roundtable session you'll need two scribes who stand at the flip charts or whiteboards and alternatively record shared conference topics and ideas. Choose people who have some conference subject expertise so they can summarize attendee responses accurately and concisely.

Provide each attendee with a draft copy of the conference face book at the start of the round-table session. Attendees can use their copy to make notes as the roundtable progresses.

Timekeeping

It's important to share the time allocated to a roundtable session equitably between attendees. This is the timekeeper's job. She does this by sounding up to two alerts; the first, 30 seconds before each attendee's allocated time expires, the second when the time is up.

Table 23.1 shows the duration of the roundtable session (minutes) and Table 23.2 shows the amount of time (minutes and seconds) available for each attendee's sharing. So, for example, at a one-day conference with 40 attendees you would sound an alert for each attendee after 60 and 90 seconds.

TABLE 23.1 · Total Roundtable Session Time (minutes)

		NUMBER OF ATTENDEES							
		30	40	50	60	70	80	90	100
CONFERENCE DURATION	1 day	60	75	90					
	1½–2 days	75	95	115	135	115	125	135	145
	> 2 days	90	115	140	150	132.5	145	150	150

←——— 1 roundtable ———→ ←——— 2 roundtables ———→

TABLE 23.2 · Roundtable Time Allocated to Each Attendee (minutes and seconds)

		NUMBER OF ATTENDEES							
		30	40	50	60	70	80	90	100
CONFERENCE DURATION	1 day	1:30	1:30	1:30					
	1½–2 days	2:00	2:00	2:00	2:00	2:00	2:00	2:00	2:00
	> 2 days	2:30	2:30	2:30	2:15	2:30	2:30	2:20	2:00

←——— 1 roundtable ———→ ←——— 2 roundtables ———→

When I decided to use timekeeping for roundtables it seemed, at first glance, to be a simple affair—something that any attendee given a watch or an inexpensive digital timer could easily do. Unfortunately, I quickly found out that attendees using such equipment found it very difficult to do the job well while simultaneously maintaining close attention to what the attendees in the roundtable were saying. Eventually I came up with three strategies that enable an attendee to be the timekeeper and still concentrate on the roundtable proceedings: (1) a small high-end digital timer that is convenient to use, though limited in minor ways; (2) Macintosh computer-based timing software that provides straightforward and flexible roundtable timekeeping; and (3) prerecorded alert tracks played on a digital music player.

The ideal timer for our purposes has the following characteristics:

- Provides the two roundtable time warnings needed in a single unit;
- Can be quickly set up to signal the passing of any desired time periods;
- Automatically resets to the original countdown times after it has counted down to zero;

How to use FlexTime for roundtable timekeeping

FlexTime, version 1.2.2 at time of writing, is available for download from Red Sweater Software (www.red-sweater.com/flextime/), requires Macintosh OSX 10.4 or above, and works on both PowerPC and Intel Macintoshes. You can try out FlexTime free for 30 days, after which you will need to register the program, at a cost of $18.95 (in 2009), for it to continue to run.

Because FlexTime can play any Macintosh alert sound, you can use any sounds you like for your roundtable alerts, as long as they are in AIFF format and installed correctly. The Apple article available at *http://docs.info.apple.com/article.html?artnum=106409* describes how to convert a sound to the AIFF format using iTunes, and explains how to add the sound as an alert to OS X. There are many sources of suitable sounds available on the Internet. You can obtain chimes and other sounds from *http://freesound.iua.upf.edu* (registration is required).

Use a different sound for the warning sound and the "time's up" sound, so attendees can know whether they need to wind up their answers, or stop.

I use FlexTime with two scripts, one that I use to demonstrate the sounds when introducing the roundtable, and one to play the sounds at the right times for each attendee. It's easy to create two alerts by adding a second timer after the first.

The first script, *Demo sounds*, plays the warning sound when started, waits ten seconds and plays the "time's up" sound.

To use the second script, *Roundtable timer*, the first timer is set to the time required before the 30-second warning. When started, the timer waits for this time before sounding the warning sound, and then plays the "time's up" sound 30 seconds later.

FIGURE 23.5 • FlexTime *Demo Sounds*

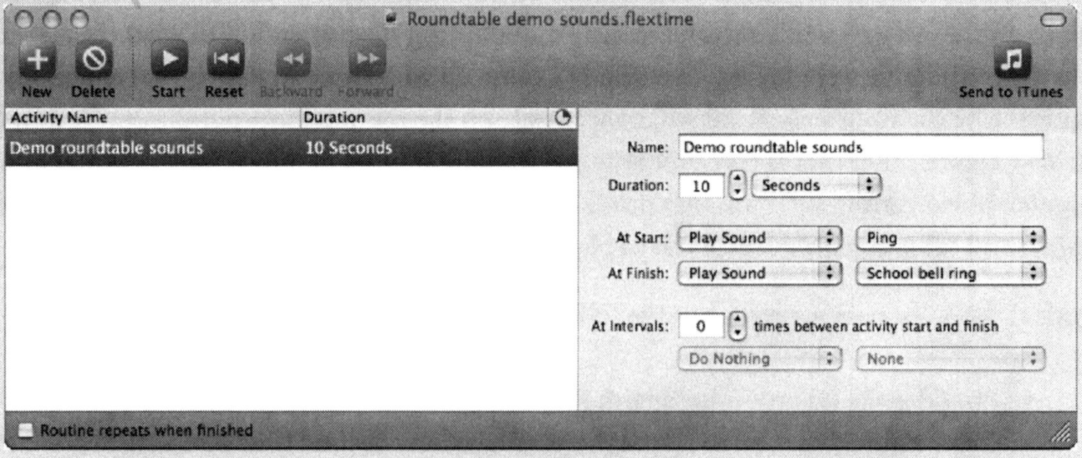

The scripts are available from www.conferencesthatwork.com, or can be quickly constructed by viewing the three screenshots in Figures 23.5–23.7.

You can export the audio from these two scripts to iTunes and then transfer the audio to an iPod or other music player.

If you create a set of *Roundtable timer* audio tracks, each using a different attendee speaking time, you can use an iPod and small portable speakers to provide timed chimes for your roundtable. A set of these audio recordings is also available on www.conferencesthatwork.com.

FIGURE 23.6 • FlexTime *Roundtable Timer* Window 1

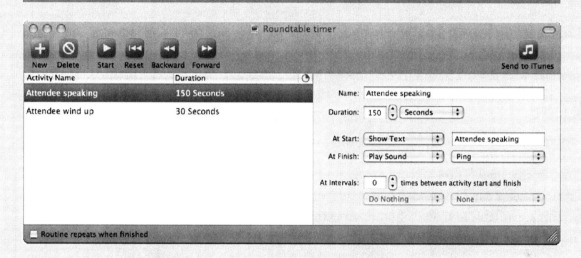

FIGURE 23.7 • FlexTime *Roundtable Timer* Window 2

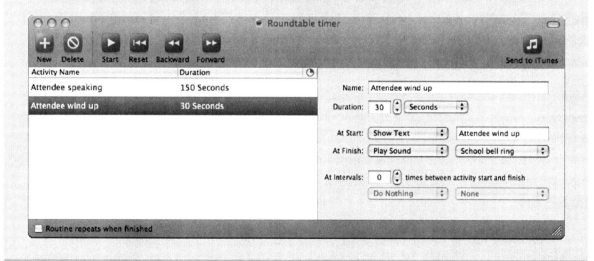

- Easily resets to the original countdown times at any point;
- Makes no noise when being set or reset for the next attendee;
- Provides pleasant and appropriate warning sounds that can be changed in nature and volume as desired; and
- Is easy to use, so that it doesn't distract the timekeeper from the roundtable sharing.

The high-end digital timer and the computer-based timer I currently use satisfy these criteria. Because you may not have access to either of these, I'll also outline the older approaches that use a watch or two digital timers, and describe a method of roundtable timing using prerecorded chimes on a digital music player.

A watch with a seconds hand plus manually made warning and "time's up" sounds. This is the simplest method, but requires the most attention, and so should be given to a conference staff member who doesn't have a direct interest in the conference topic. As an attendee starts to talk, the timekeeper notes the position of the second hand and figures out when the two alerts should be given. Because the timekeeper must keep looking at her watch, it's hard for her to concentrate on what attendees are saying.

You can use small Tibetan hand cymbals or a struck chime to make the alert sounds. I prefer a chime, since it can be sounded with one hand, while the cymbals need two. If you don't have anything available to make a sound, an extrovert timekeeper can usually be found to say "beep" or something similar.

Two inexpensive digital timers. You can use two inexpensive digital timers to provide audible alerts. Both must have the capability to count down in minutes and seconds (some timers can only count down minutes). Timer A is set to count down the time until the first attendee warning. Timer B can either be started at the same time as Timer A and count down the full attendee time, or it can be set to 30 seconds and started when Timer A sounds. I prefer the second approach, with only one timer running at any moment.

Managing two digital timers is less distracting than using a watch, since once a timekeeper sees that a timer is counting down she doesn't have to keep checking to see whether an attendee's time is up. Unfortunately, most digital timers beep annoyingly while being reset and do not reset themselves to the original countdown time if they are stopped before the time period has expired. This can lead to a lot of distracting beeping whenever an attendee does not use his full time.

A multiple event digital timer. There are a number of digital timers that provide timing of multiple events in a single unit. Most are not well suited to timing a roundtable. Common problems include: having to press multiple buttons to start and reset two event timers, a small display, buttons that become unreliable after a short time, and timers that start to count up after time is up. One unit that can provide the timing flexibility needed is the *Invisible Clock II* from the *Time Now Corporation*. This small unit, which costs about $40, has a countdown timer mode that includes alerts that can be set to go off at any time during the countdown. Its display is tiny, the unit is very complicated to set up, and it has a limited number of alert sounds that it can produce, but it does provide all the timing functionality needed in a compact package.

A computer-based timer. If you have access to a computer, preferably a laptop, you can use it to run timing software that provides all the ideal functionality I listed above. There are plenty of timer programs available for computers running the Macintosh and Windows operating systems, but few provide exactly what we need for roundtable timekeeping. An exception is the Macintosh program *FlexTime* from *Red Sweater Software*. FlexTime, which costs $18.95 and can be evaluated for free for 30 days, allows you to quickly create a custom sequence of a 30-second warning sound and a "time's up" sound. You can use any sound sources you want for the sounds. See the FlexTime sidebar for more details on how to use this program.

I'm not aware of a comparable program for Windows computers. Please contact me if you find one (or write one)!

Digital music player and pre-built audio timing recordings. I have used the FlexTime timer to create a series of audio tracks, available on www.conferencesthatwork.com, that can be played on an iPod or other digital music player through some small portable speakers. This is a convenient way to provide correctly timed alerts for your roundtable. If you are using an iPod, once you have chosen the correct timing track, I suggest you place it in an On-The-Go playlist by itself (highlight the track and press and hold the Select button until the title flashes) so you don't play other neighboring tracks by mistake during the roundtable.

Preparing for two simultaneous roundtables

If you have more than 60 attendees, it's best to hold two simultaneous roundtable sessions. Although this means that each attendee will be able to hear directly from just half of the attendees, the alternative is either a marathon session lasting three hours or more, or unacceptably abbreviated sharing time for each attendee. Short pre- and post-roundtable pair sessions, as outlined here and described in detail in Chapter 25, allow attendees to gain most of the benefits of a single roundtable without being overwhelmed with information.

The ideal setup for running two simultaneous roundtable sessions is to have three rooms, one with classroom seating for the whole group, and two each containing a circle of chairs for half the group. If you don't have this much space available, two rooms will suffice but you'll need to move chairs about in the initial room, changing the seating arrangement from classroom to circle. Don't hold both roundtables in the same space, no matter how large; it's too distracting.

At the end of the conference welcome and introduction, attendees will still be arranged in classroom seating. Use the following outline to prepare for the seating and room changes that will be needed.

- Once attendees have written their answers to the three questions, explain the process for two simultaneous roundtables.
- Pair up people from the same organization and remove them from the classroom seating. Have each pair decide who will be in Group One and Two.
- Split the remaining group into pairs by counting off "A-B." If you have movable seating, the pairs can spread out around the room.
- Have pair members share with their buddy their answers to the three roundtable questions (6 minutes).
- Have the two roundtable groups, A and B, move to separate rooms with circle seating.
- Hold separate roundtables, during which each attendee adds a very brief summary of their pair buddy's answers to questions 2 and 3.
- Return to the initial room and have the pairs get together again.
- Have each pair member summarize for their buddy their roundtable's responses, especially those relevant to their buddy's interests and experience, and share any topics of special interest (8 minutes).

After the roundtable session

The roundtable is usually the longest conference session. When it's over, attendees need a break! If you're holding a morning roundtable, make sure that refreshments are available immediately following the roundtable. Follow an afternoon roundtable with a break and a social with appropriate refreshments.

Preparing for peer session sign-up

The timing and location of peer session sign-up are linked. If sign-up is scheduled during a conference activity, such as lunch, dinner, or an evening social break, the topic sign-up sheets must be posted near the physical location of the session, preferably in the same room or space.

If you're planning to hold peer session sign-up during an outdoor social, you can use free-standing notice boards placed close to where people are gathered. Be prepared to switch to an appropriate indoor location if the weather doesn't cooperate.

Keeping a conference logbook

Maintaining a simple logbook during your conference creates a valuable resource if attendees decide to repeat the conference or you plan to organize more conferences in the future. The logbook needn't be elaborate; a simple ruled notebook will work just fine. For each conference, paste in the conference schedule, and note session timings, protocols and procedures used, problems, ideas for improvements, and what worked, what didn't, and why. Somehow, my memories of such things fade faster than I anticipate, and my conference logbook provides me a way to capture fleeting, and often, in retrospect, important learnings for later review.

Decide how you're going to display the 8.5 × 11 topic sheets. They can be:

- thumbtacked to wall-mounted or freestanding notice boards
- taped to smooth walls
- laid on tables

You'll need *at least* five horizontal inches of notice board or ten inches of tabletop width for each attendee. This provides space for one topic sheet for each attendee, which is usually enough. I prefer to play it safe and put out two sheets for each attendee.

Sign-up tables and notice boards should have at least 10 feet of open space in front of them to allow attendees to mingle and see topics easily. With notice boards, pin up two rows of topic sheets with the dividing line between them about five feet from the ground so they're easily accessible. For tables, remove any surrounding chairs and lay out a single row of sheets around the accessible perimeter of the tables.

Put out plenty of pens, at least one for every two attendees. When using notice boards, hanging the pens from strings keeps them conveniently at hand during sign-up.

Preparing for peer sessions

During the site visit you chose four rooms for holding peer sessions. I've never needed more than four, but, if for some reason you do, you can always use the main roundtable/spective space for an additional group. Setting up these spaces for peer sessions is a matter of making sure that there's adequate seating and a blackboard/whiteboard/flip chart with appropriate working markers. If some of your peer sessions might benefit from computer, overhead, or video projection, set up and test any such equipment that you've arranged to have available.

Set up the initial peer session room seating to encourage discussion. Use chairs set in a circle or rounded square, or around one or more tables in the middle of the room. If a peer session is a presentation or panel, attendees can always rearrange their chairs to support this format.

Also figure out where you'll post peer session schedules once they've been established. Posting locations should include the door of each peer session room, plus refreshment and other gathering areas where attendees may want to know which session is being held in which room.

Steering committee pre-conference meal

The steering committee pre-conference meal—dinner the night before for a morning-start conference, or lunch on the day of an afternoon-start conference—is a time for steering committee members to enjoy good food, drink, and conversation while making any last-minute arrangements and decisions. Take everyone out to the nicest place your budget can afford. This pre-conference time is one of the few perks you can offer steering committee members. Providing a fine meal in pleasant surroundings and good company is small compensation for all the preparatory work and tasks your committee will perform during the conference.

The conference coordinator should create an informal agenda. During the meal:

- Confirm that everyone understands their conference jobs, and that all jobs have people assigned. In particular, determine who will greet incoming attendees at on-site registration.
- Decide whether you'll use a volunteer to start your roundtable session(s), to provide a good model for attendees to follow.
- Make any last-minute practical arrangements.
- Ask and answer any outstanding questions.
- Remind committee members who are facilitating and convening sessions of the importance of starting and keeping the conference on schedule.
- Relax and have fun!

CHAPTER 24

Attendee Arrival

Greeting arriving attendees

Just before conference on-site registration opens, station several steering committee members in the registration area. Their work is to greet incoming attendees, and break the ice. The people who do this should be warm and have a genuine interest in meeting conferees as they arrive and getting to know them a little.

Greeting work is important. A few minutes of friendly conversation with attendees who are waiting to register can make a dramatic difference in their initial conference experience. Just about everyone arriving at a conference is feeling a certain amount of nervous excitement. By simply paying some individual attention to new arrivals, your registration greeters can greatly reduce that initial nervousness. And by showing curiosity and genuine interest, the conference greeters model the kind of interpersonal interactions that a peer conference is all about.

Greeting attendees should be a simple and genuine interaction. Introduce yourself, and ask attendees their names, where they're from, and their organizational affiliations. Asking about how their trip to the conference site went, or how they heard about the conference, or why they came will normally get you started on a pleasant conversation.

Look for opportunities to introduce attendees to each other. When you discover that two people waiting in line come from the same town or have something else in common, let both of them know the potential connection, and let them take it from there. I've seen chance connections made in the registration line turn into friendships lasting throughout the conference and beyond.

Greeting an attendee

It was the black leather jacket that caught my attention. He was helping himself to coffee and a yogurt. Alone, and he didn't look familiar. I noticed that his badge sported a green dot, so he was a first-time attendee, and that he was from a school in North Carolina. I smiled and introduced myself.

"Hi, I'm Adrian Segar and I'm on the steering committee," I said. "Will Carter," he replied, shaking my hand.

"How was the flight?" I inquired.

"No flight—I rode all the way here." The leather jacket suddenly made sense.

"Wow, you biked all the way here from Chapel Hill! I'm impressed!"

And we were off and running. The conversation soon turned to why he had come, and the issues he was trying to deal with at his school. I told Will about other attendees who I knew were in similar situations and might be able to give him some advice and support. One was nearby, and I introduced them. They started to talk and I moved on, scanning for more green dot badges.

Twenty minutes later, it was time for the welcome and roundtable to start, so I started to shepherd attendees into the large adjourning room. I saw Will again, in the center of an animated group, each person so intent on the conversation that it took me several attempts to get them seated in the waiting circle of chairs.

Will sought me out several times during the rest of the conference, briefly bringing me up to date on his experiences. He was having a great time. I realized that he was grateful to me for breaking the ice and inviting him into the shared world of our conference. I hadn't done much; a few minutes of conversation at the start, but it had made all the difference.

A year later Will sent me an email. He was leaving his job, making a career change, so the annual conference wasn't relevant for him anymore. He told me how sorry he was that he didn't have an excuse to return, that he would miss us, and he wished the group well. I was touched.

If your conference is a repeated event, then greeters will often know returning attendees and the welcoming conversation gets even easier. In this case, however, avoid concentrating on people you already know. Otherwise there's a real danger that first-time attendees will feel like outsiders. Instead, be an equal-opportunity greeter, providing everyone with a similar amount of attention. Also, be sure to introduce first-time attendees to returning attendees— this really helps to jumpstart first-time attendees' integration into an existing peer conference community.

A little low-key effort in this area can quickly build a warm, invitational, friendly social atmosphere that significantly improves your conference.

Running on-site registration

If you've prepared for on-site registration as described in Chapters 21 and 23, you should be ready to smoothly and efficiently handle a steady stream of incoming attendees. Here are some additional suggestions to further enhance your attendees' initial conference experience.

The conference coordinator should hover nearby, available to make decisions on any unusual situations that arise. What if an at-the-door registrant arrives with a purchase order rather than a check? How about a vendor who turns up wanting to attend the conference? The conference coordinator should deal with these kinds of issues so that registration staff can continue to process waiting arrivals.

Occasionally, someone may turn up at registration with no payment or purchase order, and promise to pay later. In my experience, collecting a conference fee after the event from such people is rarely easy. If you do decide to admit the individual, have them sign and date a written statement that includes their contact information, the amount that will be paid, and the date when the fee will be paid in full. Give them a copy of the statement, and make a note to remind them of their debt immediately after the conference.

The conference coordinator should also be prepared to step in and greet attendees during peak registration times.

Registration staff handing out name badges should ask attendees to wear them throughout the conference.

After the last step of on-site registration, whether it be taking the attendee's photograph or handing out swag, remind attendees of the location and starting time of the conference opening session, and emphasize the importance of being there on time when the conference begins.

Face book photos

You have a number of possible ways to set up photographing attendees for the conference face book. The most elegant I've seen, devised by a smart high school student, used *two* computer monitors connected to the registration computer, one facing the registration staffer, the other the attendee. The camera was mounted on a tripod, at the right height and distance from a blank wall behind the attendee. The staffer displayed each attendee's registration information, and the attendees checked it directly from their monitor. Once any corrections were made, the staffer used software to remotely control the camera so that it displayed the attendee's live headshot on the monitors. When the attendee was ready and the shot composed, the picture was taken via computer command, and then inserted directly into the attendee's registration record. This ingenious setup allowed the entire registration process to be handled by a single staffer.

If you have the know-how and equipment to create such a setup, this approach is strongly recommended. Otherwise, you'll need at least two registration station staff, one to operate the computer and one to take attendee photographs. If your on-site registration time is limited, having two staff taking photos is recommended—one to operate the camera, and one to create a list of names, in the order that registrants were photographed, so the pictures, when downloaded from the camera, can be matched to the correct attendee records in the registration database. If the registration period is short, you may not get an opportunity to download the photos from the camera into the conference database until on-site registration is over and the conference starts. If this is the case, it's important to use a camera with enough memory to store every participant's photo, or have sufficient camera memory cards that can be quickly swapped.

Unless you have a generous budget and access to a high-speed color printer, black-and-white photos are fine. Check that the camera is set to a picture resolution high enough to ensure adequate quality reproduction of photographs when printed on the high-resolution laser printer you use. If you print attendee photographs at a size of around 2 inches by 2 inches, camera JPEG images that are 50–100KB in size will print well. Using larger images will not significantly improve printed quality and downloading them to the computer will take longer than necessary.

You'll need a light-colored wall, close to the registration booth and with good natural lighting for the photo taking. If a suitable wall isn't available, hang up a sheet of flip chart paper for a background. The most common mistake I see is to take photos from too far away. The photographer should take photos with *the face of the subject filling the frame*. If flash has to be used, make sure that the camera's red-eye reduction flash setting is active.

Before the conference starts, do a dry run of your photo-taking procedure. Check how long it takes you to take a photo and transfer it to the database, and see whether you will be able to keep up with the flow of attendees at registration. If not, you may need to schedule photo shoots during the first conference break for those attendees who missed getting their picture taken.

Here's an important tip when using FileMaker Pro (and possibly other database software). *Use the option "store only a reference to the file" when inserting photographs of attendees into the database.* Create an attendee picture folder in the same folder in which the database file is stored, and link each attendee record to the corresponding photograph in the picture folder. *Don't store the actual photograph itself directly in your conference database.* If you do, your database file size will get very large, even with as few as 30 records, and navigation through the database will become unacceptably sluggish.

Handouts

At registration, provide attendees with a set of handouts that answer common questions about the conference and conference site, and prepare them for what is to come. The sets of conference handouts should be prepared in advance of registration, with a last-minute up-to-date list of conference attendees added the evening before or the morning of the conference. I like to use a two-pocket file folder, one pocket containing administrative information, the other holding handouts used to explain and support the conference process.

Conference administrative handouts should include:

- Conference site map, showing buildings and rooms used during the conference;
- One or more site information handouts, containing information on:
  - site accommodations (location, access, any restrictions)
  - access to site facilities: recreation, athletic facilities
  - local resources such as a nearby convenience store
  - site telephone locations; emergency information, numbers, and contacts
- Any necessary instructions for accessing:
  - the Internet
  - a conference wiki
  - shared file server conference space;
- Conference schedule that includes session locations; and
- Alphabetized list of conference registrants

The conference process handouts I use are gathered in the Appendices. Your handout folder should contain the following handouts:

- Four Freedoms
- Peer Session primer
- Facilitator primer
- Fixed sessions evaluation form

with the following additions, if relevant:

- Information about any sponsoring organization(s) and/or their activities
- Vendor list, if you're holding a vendor exhibit

It would be wonderful to be able to provide a comprehensive and accurate face book, complete with attendee photos, by the time the conference starts, but this is rarely practical. There are almost always latecomers and people who don't spot errors in their face book information during on-site registration. Consequently you should plan to distribute draft paper copies of the face book at the start of the conference roundtable, so that attendees can make notes directly on their copy as they hear each attendee's responses to the roundtable questions. A copy of the draft face book should also be posted on the public information board, so that attendees can make corrections for the final version.

If you're holding an organization business meeting during the conference you can also include an agenda, financial statements, and any other relevant information, though I prefer to distribute such handouts at the meeting itself.

Make and attach a name label to each handout folder. People tend to misplace their handouts during the conference, and the name label will ease reuniting a lost set with its owner. Make a few extra sets of handouts to distribute to unregistered, last-minute arrivals. Sort the handout sets by attendee name so you can quickly find the right set during on-site registration.

Badges

I recommend that participants wear their name badges throughout the conference. Prepare name badges before the conference, using a badge report layout in your conference database. To encourage participants to wear their badges I strongly advise lanyard-style badges and avoid stick-on and pinned badges. Print your badges directly onto badge card stock, insert the printed cards into transparent badge holders, and attach the lanyards.

Badges should display the attendee's name and any relevant affiliation in as large print as possible, bearing in mind that the longest name and affiliation need to fit without truncation. I generally avoid including job titles on attendee badges.

I like to add small colored dots (blue) to steering committee badges, so that attendees can find organizers when they have questions. If I'm running a repeat conference, I put a different colored dot (green) on each new attendee's badge, and a third colored dot (yellow) on the badges of returning attendees. This allows greeters to see who's new and give them special attention to smooth their integration into the conference community.

Promotional items

Set up a staffed display of conference promotional items on a table that attendees will pass by once they have registered and picked up their badge and handouts. The display staffer's job is to make sure that attendees receive items that are included in the conference fee and to take money for any items for sale.

If your conference is being held in a fairly private location and your promotional items are not too valuable, you can choose to leave the swag table open during the conference and ask attendees to settle up with conference staff for items they want to purchase. If you're worried about leaving swag out while no one is around, display it in a room that can be locked and announce the times during the conference when it will be available for purchase. Bring a cash box to store payments for additional purchases.

Running Your Conference

Your conference is about to start! The following chapters show you how to run each session. You'll notice that I've included session narratives that cover everything a facilitator needs to say. To help you print and adapt your own versions without destroying this book, I've put downloadable copies of all the session narratives in the resources section of www.conferencesthatwork.com.

Conference facilitation

What's it like facilitating a peer conference? Try this.

Imagine yourself as a tour guide leading a group through an ancient castle. First, you gather the group in the courtyard, introduce yourself, and welcome everyone to the tour. Next, you caution people to stay together, hold onto the handrails while they climb and descend the winding stairs to the battlements, and tell them to ask questions at any time. Having covered the necessary guidelines, the tour begins. At each stop along your route, you introduce the group to what they are seeing, wait and let everyone experience the surroundings for him- or herself, and patiently answer questions. At the tour's end, you bring everyone together back in the courtyard, give people the opportunity to share their reactions, and finally escort them from the castle grounds.

Starting and staying on time

Every peer conference needs a *conference announcer and timekeeper*, usually, but not necessarily, the conference coordinator. It's his job to remind attendees of what's next on the schedule, make announcements of any unexpected changes, and keep the conference on schedule. It's this last duty that is the hardest. Attendees at peer conferences love to talk to each other, and often some people simply *won't* break off their conversations around the refreshments table or at a peer session to arrive at the next session location by the time it's scheduled to start.

There are four things you can do to eliminate, or at least minimize, the otherwise seemingly inevitable tendency for conference sessions to start late.

Begin your conference on time!

An opening session that starts late is disrespectful to the people who were there on time and sends an implicit message that the other conference sessions are likely to be late too. This can lead to major schedule slippage as people continue to straggle between sessions. Conversely, an opening session that starts on time sends a clear message to latecomers that they will be the losers if they continue to be late, and the on-time participants won't wait for them to get started.

Explain your timekeeper role during conference introductions

Emphasize the importance of keeping to the conference schedule. Point out that if the schedule slips, sessions late in the day will have to be unfairly shortened in order to fit everything in. When I'm the timekeeper, I tend to adopt a humorous tone and explain that I may become somewhat unpopular by interrupting important conversations to remind people it's time to move on. Nowadays I'm used to hearing good-natured groans when I interrupt with announcements during the conference; if this happens to you, be assured, you're doing a good job.

There are lots of ways to get people's attention when you need to make an announcement or remind folks that a session is about to start. Here are three I like.

Some timekeepers like to use a warning sound before announcements. Small Tibetan hand cymbals make a pleasant resonating chime that cuts through any hubbub. Timsha Bells that are around two and a half inches in diameter work well and are available from many sources for $15–$30 a pair. You can also use a chime; I like the large Nino Energy Chime, which costs around $15.

Another way to get attendees' attention is to play a short piece of music, right before the next session starts. Emphasize that each session will start as soon as the music ends.

A surprisingly effective way to get attendees to quiet down is to use an old elementary school technique. Simply raise your hand. When attendees see that your hand is raised, they raise their hands too. Hands up means stop talking and pay attention. As each person notices the cue and quiets down more notice and follow, and the room will soon be quiet.

Whichever of these methods you decide on should be introduced and clearly explained at the opening session. I suggest you add it as a ground rule for your conference, to be agreed to by attendees.

Help attendees make it to sessions on time

Provide timely, helpful reminders to attendees when they need to make their way to the next session. Keep a careful eye on the time and know how long it will take attendees to get from where they're currently congregated to where they need to be next. I make two announcements before each session starts; the first giving a five-minute warning, and the second informing the remaining attendees that if they don't leave right away they'll miss the start of the next session. Leave for the session yourself right after the second announcement. You've done your duty.

Begin every session on time

Have the session convener or facilitator of every session start on time, even if you think that some people haven't arrived yet. The majority of attendees who arrive promptly will appreciate not being penalized by the tardiness of a minority. If attendees perceive that the printed schedule is just wishful thinking, it quickly becomes difficult to get the conference back on track. Conversely, once people see that conference sessions start on time, regardless of whether they are present or not, they will realize that it's *their* choice whether to be prompt or late.

The conference timekeeper will be at his busiest just before each set of peer sessions is scheduled to start. Because most peer session facilitators are not steering committee members, they'll need individual encouragement to start on time. Between his two warning announcements, he must find the session facilitators and remind them to be in the appropriate room, ready to start promptly. Immediately after the second warning he goes to each room in turn and asks the facilitator to begin.

Following these guidelines will go a long way toward ensuring a smooth-running conference. But don't be a total slave to your pre-planned schedule. During the conference someone may have a great session idea that enjoys significant support and requires a change in the conference program. Be open to this possibility, take it seriously, and see if it can be accommodated via acceptable changes to your existing schedule. In adapting the program in this way, you're staying true to a key goal of any peer conference—providing a conference that is maximally useful and meaningful to its participants.

The opening session—the big picture

Traditionally, a conference opening session comprises one or more sets of welcoming remarks plus some practical "housekeeping" announcements about conference organization, schedule, and locations. These activities are both necessary and appropriate, but they are often thought of as formalities, tasks that must be done before the "real" conference can start. If you treat an opening session casually then you'll send attendees the message that the conference experience will be superficial. If you rush through an opening session, treating it as a set of have-to tasks to get through as quickly as decently possible, then you'll send attendees the message that the conference experience will be hurried and tense.

Begin as you mean to continue

To create the best possible conference experience for all, you must begin your conference as you mean it to continue. A good way to think about the opening session of a peer conference is to view it as the start of a transition away from the everyday world experience of each attendee and toward the "conference trance" that is the hallmark of a successful immersive conference. I use the phrase "conference trance" to describe an attendee's intense concentration on and involvement in the conference experience—a creative state in which a person is immersed throughout much of the conference, no matter how long or short it is.

To successfully move to an intimate conference space you must do two things. First, prepare for the opening session; don't leave its organization to the last minute. In particular, plan in advance who will cover each opening topic, and make sure that introductory remarks are clear and unhurried. Second, show by your own example how to be involved in and connected with your conference. When you share yourself openly, honestly, and with engagement, you model the behavior you want from attendees, and this encourages them to follow your lead. Create a conference environment that feels natural to you, that reflects who you are. I aim for a relaxed, friendly, and focused ambience, but that's me. Don't be fake; be yourself. If you're nervous about how your first peer conference is going to work out, then say so, and move on. If you and your fellow participants are passionate believers in a common idea that can change the world, then show and invoke that passion.

Nuts and bolts

Despite best intentions, the opening session is often somewhat chaotic. Latecomers arrive and break the flow, a sponsor representative who is slated to give a brief welcome arrives five minutes late, conference housekeeping information is inadvertently omitted, and questions are asked that require some quick research. Keep your cool through the session, expect the unexpected, and don't rush through the practical information and answers that attendees need.

The people who welcome attendees and make announcements should be part of the circle. They can sit in their chairs or stand up to speak, or, if they are a host site or sponsoring organization representative who won't be attending the conference, they can stand in one of the gaps in the circle of chairs. This helps to reinforce the idea, right from the start, that people who contribute do not have a special status at the conference.

A few minutes before the conference starts, make your best estimate of the number of attendees who will be at the roundtable session, use Table 23.2 to determine how much time to allocate to each attendee during the roundtable, and give the timekeeper this information. If it's clear that there will be significantly fewer attendees present than the number of chairs set out, remove surplus chairs and ask people to tighten up the circle, keeping it as round as possible so that everyone can see everyone else.

You may want to have someone volunteer in advance, perhaps a steering committee member, to start the sharing at the roundtable(s). This can help the session by providing a good model for attendees to copy.

Start on time!

Unless there's a genuine emergency, *be sure to start the opening session promptly at the scheduled time*. If a site host or representative of a sponsoring organization is going to welcome attendees, have them agree beforehand to be available at the specific time they're needed. Starting your opening session on time models what you want to occur throughout the conference.

Welcome

How you welcome people to your conference is up to you. Pick one or two people who are genuinely excited about the conference, and have them speak. Perhaps a steering committee member tells the story of how the conference came into existence. Perhaps the head of the sponsoring or conference site organization shares how glad she is to be able to support the gathering. Whatever you decide, keep your welcome short—five minutes at most. Thank everyone for coming, and move right on to housekeeping announcements.

Housekeeping

Every conference will have its own unique set of housekeeping announcements. Use the following list as a starting point.

> *Badges*: Ask everyone to wear their name badges during the entire conference. I usually tell people that I am not good at associating faces with names and

having everyone wear their badge would help me, and probably others. (It's a good idea to repeat this reminder at the end of the first day of a multiday conference.)

Face book issues: Explain that the draft face book can be used to take notes during the roundtable and that a final copy will be made available by [a time you have decided]. Ask attendees to verify their information on the posted copy, make any needed corrections, and sign off on their data by [a given time]. Ask any attendees who have not had their photo taken to attend a photo session at [a given time].

Staying on time: Ask attendees to be at all conference sessions on time.

Cell phones, beepers, and so on, off, or, at most, on vibrate: This is particularly important during group sessions like the roundtable and closing spectives. But electronic devices ringing and beeping in any session is disruptive, and I recommend you ask the group to turn them off except for emergency situations.

Announcements: If you plan to use them, this is a good time to explain and demonstrate your Tibetan chimes, or other attention-getting technique, that you'll use for announcements.

Facilities: Briefly describe the locations of and directions to buildings and rooms you will be using, referring to the conference site map if included in the attendee handouts. Explain any idiosyncrasies (hidden bathrooms, construction to avoid, other groups using the site, etc.).

Handouts: Ask attendees to read the two peer session handouts in their conference packet, *Peer Session Primer* and *Peer Session Facilitation*, before they attend their first peer session. Draw their attention to the fixed evaluation form in the packet, ask attendees to fill it in as the conference progresses, and explain that an evaluation form for the conference peer sessions will be made available as soon as their topics are known. If an online conference evaluation is available, explain to attendees how to access it.

Badge dots: If you're using colored dots on badges to indicate steering committee members, new attendees, or returning attendees, explain your color-coding scheme.

Photography: If you or any attendees (ask them) are planning to take photographs, check to see whether anyone would object to being photographed at the conference. Ask photographers to respect people's wishes, including specific occasions when people don't want their picture taken.

Stand up, sit down!

Here's something I like to do at the end of the housekeeping announcements as a bridge to the roundtable session.

If this is the first time you're holding the conference, have the steering committee members stand for five to ten seconds. (Note: People who have difficulty standing can be asked to raise their hand instead.) Ask attendees to note who's standing, and encourage them if they have any questions or concerns to talk to any steering committee member.

If a conference is a repeat event, ask all new attendees to stand. Invite the seated returning attendees to look around and make the new folks welcome during the conference. Then say "Everyone standing sit, everyone sitting stand!" Encourage the new attendees to see who's standing and use them as resources during the conference. Finally, have everyone except the steering committee members sit down, and have people note who they can contact with questions, suggestions, or concerns about the running of the conference.

Once you've made your housekeeping announcements ask for attendees' questions. Fully answer any questions, and make sure that everyone with a question has been given the opportunity to ask it.

Once questions have subsided, it's time for the roundtable facilitator to get to work.

Describing the conference format

Now is the time to introduce attendees to the structure and processes of a peer conference. It's important to provide the right level of detail at this point—enough so that people can see the general direction they're going and can move forward with confidence, but not so much that they get bogged down in the minutiae of exactly how they're going to get to their individual and group destinations. Here's an example of what you might say:

> "I want to welcome you to our peer conference. This conference is quite different from the traditional conferences that you've probably all attended. In traditional conferences the program is largely determined in advance—you go to sessions and listen to "experts" talking about various aspects of the conference subject. At the end of each session you get to ask questions and then you probably go off to a meal or social event where you meet and talk to some of your fellow attendees, looking

for people with whom you have something in common and discussing topics of common interest. The emphasis at a traditional conference is on passive reception of knowledge from a small number of people who, hopefully, know a lot more than you do about a topic that, hopefully, you're interested in.

That's a traditional conference.

A peer conference has a very different approach. A peer conference is designed and built around the core observation that, if you bring together a group of people with a common interest, the group contains tremendous knowledge and experience about the subject—more in many cases than any small group of "experts" can provide. A peer conference provides a set of processes for effectively discovering, exploring, and sharing this knowledge and experience appropriately among conference attendees, as determined by each individual's interests and needs.

Instead of a well-meaning organizing committee doing its best, before the conference, to figure out what attendees may be interested in hearing about, a peer conference uses a simple and direct approach. At the start of the conference we ask you what you want to hear about, what you want to learn about, and what you want to share. We then use a peer conference process to set up the requested listening, learning, and sharing experiences. So a peer conference is self-organizing, and focuses on providing a meaningful and useful experience for every attendee.

How does all this work? Well, in order for a peer conference to work, you, the attendees, need to learn more about each other early on in the conference; you need to find out who's interested in talking about what, and who has experience or expertise that you're interested in learning more about. All this initial learning about each other happens in the conference roundtable, which we'll be starting in a few minutes.

You also need a way to propose topics you want to talk about or hear about, and a way to turn those topics into actual sessions we call peer sessions, where people can meet, share, and discuss. You need a way to organize the peer sessions so there are people responsible for facilitating and recording what happens. We have these tools for you to use. And then, after the peer sessions have been held, we have two closing peer conference sessions that attendees have found, over the years, to be very valuable. One, the personal introspective, provides each of you an opportunity to integrate your overall conference experience into your life. The other, the group spective, provides a place for group sharing and initiatives to be born and discussed.

That's a brief outline of a peer conference. The primary goal of this peer conference is to provide each of you with the most meaningful and useful experience possible. A secondary outcome of many peer conferences is the discovery and discussion of group initiatives—future activities that significant numbers of attendees wish to pursue. Such initiatives tend to have a lot of energy behind them because they arise naturally from the group process. But, at a peer conference, group initiatives are a bonus; they may appear, they may not. The core purpose of this peer conference is to create an environment for optimum individual growth and learning for each one of you.

> *[PAUSE]*

That's enough talking about what we're going to do during the next few days. Let's begin! We're going to move right into our first session, the roundtable."

The roundtable session

Move directly from the opening session into your roundtable session. Don't include a break; keep the pace flowing. Don't split the group into two roundtables yet.

Right away, while everyone is still together, cover the following:

- Four Freedoms
- Safety
- Staying on time
- How the roundtable works
- The three roundtable questions

Here's what I might say:

On the Four Freedoms . . .

> *"Before we start our roundtable sharing, I'm going to introduce you to Four Freedoms. You have a copy of them in your conference packet. These freedoms provide some ground rules for us during this conference. Let's go through them.*
>
> *Number One. You have the freedom to talk about the way you see things, rather than the way others want you to see. If you feel your voice is not being heard, this freedom gives you the right to speak out and say what you need to say.*
>
> *Number Two. You have the freedom to ask about anything puzzling. If you don't understand what is going on, what someone said or did, or what someone is proposing you do—anything that puzzles you—you have the freedom to ask questions.*

Number Three. You have the freedom to talk about whatever is coming up for you, especially your own reactions. *You'll undoubtedly experience different emotions during this conference—you may feel happy, angry, excited, sad, interested, uncomfortable, curious, and so on. You are free to talk about how you're feeling here, whatever comes up for you.*

Number Four. You have the freedom to say that you don't really feel you have one or more of the preceding three freedoms. *This last freedom provides a check on how we're each doing with the first three freedoms. You have the right to talk about these freedoms directly, how much they are present, or not present, for you.*

I've found these four freedoms encourage an intimate and empowering atmosphere at peer conferences. It is my hope that this conference is no exception. You can help each one of us by exercising your four freedoms while we are together."

On safety . . .

"I have a couple of ground rules to add for our conference. The first is about safety: What we discuss at this conference will remain confidential. What we share here, stays here. *We want this conference to be a safe place for you to share. By respecting everyone's confidentiality you make this possible."*

On staying on time . . .

"The second ground rule is about staying on time. We're going to be developing a schedule for this conference, and, whatever we come up with, sessions will be short-changed if earlier sessions overrun their scheduled time slots, or people arrive late for any reason. To treat everyone fairly, we ask that you start and end all sessions on time."

Describe here the method(s) you will use to make announcements and keep the conference on schedule. Then ask:

"Any questions about the Four Freedoms or our ground rules?"

Answer any questions.

"I would like all of you who commit to using Four Freedoms, maintaining confidentiality, and staying on time to stand."

(Note: People who have difficulty standing can be asked to raise their hand instead.) As the attendees stand, have the roundtable scribes start to distribute the roundtable question cards (and pens if needed).

Wait for attendees to stand. To date, I haven't had anyone balk at making this commitment. Thank the attendees and ask them to sit. If anyone doesn't stand, say "Everyone standing sit, everyone sitting stand!" Then ask those standing to explain what they feel they can't commit to, and, if necessary, work on an agreement as to how to proceed.

On how the roundtable works . . .

> *"Let me explain how the roundtable works. It provides a structured and intimate way for us to learn more about each other right at the start of this conference. During the session, we'll discover why people came and the topics that interest them. We'll also get a feeling for the depth of interest in these topics, and we'll find out who has experience and expertise that we want to connect to and explore."*

Add the following sentence if there will be two roundtables:

> *"By the way, this group would be a little overwhelming to work well as a single roundtable, so, shortly, we'll split into two groups, reseat ourselves and hold two roundtables."*

> *"We hold a roundtable by going round our circle, and answering, in turn, the three questions that are on the cards you've been given. Before I go over these questions, I want to emphasize something that's important for you to keep in mind.*
>
> > *There are no wrong answers to these questions!*
> >
> > *The first question is: How did I get here? What brought you here today? We want to hear a story about how you come to be sitting here, in this room. Tell us your name to start. Then there are countless stories you could tell us. You could tell us that you got here on Interstate 91 in your Subaru. You could tell us how you heard about the conference from your good friend Bruce and that it sounded interesting. Maybe you'll tell us about yourself and how, when you heard about the topic and style of this conference, something important fell into place. Tell us your name, your affiliation if relevant, what you do, what you want to do, what you're passionate about, and how that all plays into your being here. Help us know you a little, help us understand you a little, tell us about where you came from to get here."*

For repeat conferences, add the following sentence:

> *"If you've attended this conference in the past, you may want to talk about how this conference worked for you in the past and why you've come back."*

> *"It's your choice how deep to go, how far to go, what to say. Don't feel constrained by what others share or the way they share. Feel free to go outside the box. Remember, there are no wrong answers.*
>
> *The second question is:* What do I want to have happen? *The first question was about the past; this question is about the future. What do you want to have happen here, while we are together? What do you want to learn about, what do you want to discuss, what puzzles do you want help in solving or investigating, what journeys do you want to make? As you answer this question, themes and topics will appear; we have roundtable scribes who are ready to capture and summarize them on flip charts. This is a time to tell us what you really want from this conference. Don't be afraid to ask for anything. There are no guarantees, but, collectively, we possess tremendous resources, and asking for what you want is the essential first step for getting it.*
>
> *The third question is:* What experience do I have that others may find useful? *We're asking for information about the experience, knowledge, and wisdom you possess and that you can share with us. Many of you will have some clear responses to this question, but I encourage you to dig deeper. I have found that all of us have experience that is of value to others, but we are often surprisingly unaware of the richness of resources that each of us has to offer. If there's something you know something about, or have experience of, that's relevant to [the topic of this conference] please mention it in your answer to this question. I've repeatedly seen an attendee casually mention some experience and be totally surprised to discover that half the people in the roundtable want to find out more.*
>
> *Any questions about the three questions?"*

Answer any questions.

> *"OK, I'm going to give you five minutes to come up with your answers to the questions. Use the card, if you want, to write down what you're going to say."*

Attendees may need less than five minutes. Watch them preparing their answers. When most people seem to have finished, announce that you'll provide another minute for everyone to finish. Then ask if anyone needs more time and wait for anyone who does.

"I have four guidelines about sharing your answers.

First, if someone shares before you do and mentions some of your own interests, desires, needs, experiences, and so on, please don't omit these items from your answers. It's important for all of us to get a sense of the levels and intensities of interests and experiences represented here.

Second, if the person sharing asks for specific assistance on a topic along the lines of 'does anyone know the answer to X,' and you can help, it's OK to stick your hand up for long enough for them to notice you and to say your name and 'I can help with that.' Don't start giving the help there and then, just make the connection between you and the aid you're offering.

Third, if you have to leave before the end of the conference, please mention when you're leaving. This will help us avoid scheduling a peer session involving your experience when you're not around. Scribes, please make a note of early leavers.

Finally, a lot of information is going to come flowing from everyone during this session. Don't expect to remember everything people say—you'll notice what's useful and meaningful for you. As each person responds to the three questions, I encourage you to make notes right next to their entry in your draft face book so you can keep track of who said what."

If you're running two simultaneous roundtables (more than 60 attendees) there are some additional steps required before the roundtable session can start, and these are covered in the next section. If you are running a single roundtable, skip ahead to the timekeeping section.

Additional procedure to use before holding two simultaneous roundtables

Using the procedure described here adds some complexity to the roundtable session. However, by following all these steps you'll maximize the sharing among the whole group, despite the lack of true one-to-entire group sharing that a single roundtable allows.

Here are the steps needed to prepare for two roundtables:

- Explain the process for two simultaneous roundtables.
- Divide attendees into two groups and create attendee pairs with one person from each group.
- Pair members share with their buddy their answers to the three roundtable questions.
- Seat the two roundtable groups in two circles in separate rooms.
- Hold separate roundtables, during which attendees add a brief summary of their pair buddy's answers to the roundtable questions.

- Return to the initial room and have the pairs get together again.
- Have each pair member summarize for their buddy their roundtable's responses, especially those relevant to their buddy's interests and experiences, and share any topics of special interest.

And here's how I might lead attendees through the process:

"When possible, I like to hold a single roundtable session at a peer conference. Unfortunately there are too many people here—we'd either have to stay here for three or four hours or give each of you less time than you deserve. So we're going to hold two simultaneous roundtables. In order that you don't miss out on what goes on elsewhere, you're now going to get a buddy who will act as your representative and your eyes and ears at the other roundtable."

If you have attendees who come from the same organization, say:

"First, if there are other people here from your organization, please stand, move over there [point to a place away from the classroom seating], and stand with your associates."

Pause while people move, and then address the people who moved.

"Put your hand up if there are just two of you from the same organization." [Pause.] *"You folks will be buddies. One of you will be in Roundtable A, the other in Roundtable B. It doesn't matter which one you choose. Please decide which roundtable you're in now."* [Pause.]

"Groups of three people from the same organization—please raise your hand." [Pause.] *"Two of you will be buddies, one in Roundtable A, the other in Round-table B. The third person should return to his or her seat. Please decide who goes where now."* [Pause.]

"Anyone left? If there's an even number of you, divide yourselves into buddy pairs, and decide who is in which roundtable. If there's an odd number, one of you should return to your seat—the others divide up into pairs and decide on your roundtable." [Pause]

Turn back to the rest of the attendees who are still in the classroom seating.

"OK, you're now going to divide into two roundtable groups by counting off along the rows of chairs: A, B, A, B. Each A-B defines a pair of buddies. As you say your letter, look at who your buddy will be. I'll point at you when it's time to say your letter. Begin!"

Point at the first person in the first row and move along the rows to the next person as each person says their letter.

If there are an odd number of attendees, then the last person will have no buddy. Assign him or her to one of the other pairs. The resulting triplet will have two people going to roundtable A, and one to B. The person going to B will need to be given a little more time to share his two buddies' answers during the roundtable.

If you have movable seating, ask pairs to spread out around the room and give them time to do so.

> *"Now it's time to share with your buddy. Your buddy, who will attend the other roundtable, will be your representative and your eyes and ears there. The buddy from Roundtable A should start; introduce yourself and share your answers to the three roundtable questions. You'll have three minutes to do this. Buddy B: your job is to make notes on what you hear—you can use the back of your card— and provide a brief summary of his or her answers after you've shared your own answers at your roundtable. We'll let you know when three minutes are up. Then swap roles—Buddy B shares for three minutes and Buddy A takes notes. Any questions?"*

If you have a triplet, tell them to take two minutes per person to share their answers.

Answer any questions, and then have everyone begin. Sound an alert after three minutes and ask pairs to swap roles. Wait until everyone has swapped over, and give the pairs another three minutes.

> *"Here's what's going to happen now. We're going to hold our two separate round-tables in [provide locations]. After they're over, we'll come back here and get into the same buddy groups again. You'll then have time to summarize what happened at your roundtable, with an emphasis on what was important for your buddy. Any questions?"*

Answer any questions, and then ask attendees to go to their respective roundtables. Once they're settled, it's time to run your roundtables!

On timekeeping . . .

> *"We have [period of time remaining] for our roundtable. So that everyone gets an equal opportunity, each of you will have up to [time period for each attendee] to*

*share. You'll get a 30-second warning alert that sounds like this [timekeeper
sounds the warning alert] and when your time is up you'll hear [timekeeper
sounds the 'time's-up' alert]. You don't have to finish mid-sentence, but we ask
that you keep to this time limit as much as possible."*

Final instructions

If roundtable sharing will last more than 90 minutes, announce that there will be a brief
mid-session bathroom break.

If you are running two roundtables, remind attendees to add to their answers a brief summary
of their buddy's answers to the three questions, starting the summary with their buddy's
name. Suggest that they start this when they hear the 30-second warning. Also remind them
to take notes on topics and experience that their buddy is interested in hearing about.

You have several options for beginning sharing.

- Start with a prearranged volunteer, perhaps one of the conference organizers, who
  can provide a good model for the attendees who follow.
- Ask the circle "Who wants to start?"
- If you have provided a draft face book sorted by name, start with the first person
  listed and proceed in alphabetical order.

With the first two options, once the first person is done sharing, continue around the circle,
with each person taking their turn. You can ask the first sharer to choose the direction to
continue.

An advantage of using the third option, face book order, is that people don't have to flip
through the book to find each person's entry for note taking. However, there can be awkward
silences when the next person in the book is absent. To minimize these pauses, announce the
next sharer's name when each attendee finishes speaking.

Watch the elapsed time. You want people to take an average amount of time equal to or
slightly less than the time you've announced. Don't allow anyone to continue long after the
second alert. Interrupt them politely but firmly and ask them to end. If there is a significant
trend of people overrunning their time, point this out and ask attendees to be more concise.
If people are finishing too quickly, encourage them to extend their answers, by explaining the
answers you feel they could amplify.

The two roundtable scribes take turns writing down the themes that attendees bring up. Tell
the scribes that if a topic is described too quickly to be written down, they should ask the

person to repeat it. And if a scribe is unclear as to how a topic can be captured in a few words, he should ask the attendee how to summarize what she said.

Check that everyone has shared (late attendees may arrive, or people may be missing from the face book) before wrapping up the roundtable.

Additional procedure to use after holding two simultaneous roundtables

Once all attendees have shared, ask them to return to the buddy seating they were in before the roundtable started. If the other roundtable is still in progress, tell the facilitator that you've finished. Once both roundtables are complete it's time to start a post-roundtable buddy briefing.

> *"The purpose of this post-roundtable briefing is to share with your buddy the people, topics, and experience you heard about at your roundtable. Buddy A, start by summarizing your overall impressions. Then, tell your buddy about the people who came for similar reasons, the topics related to your buddy's interests, people with experience your buddy might want to talk to, if there's interest in hearing what your buddy has to say, and anything else that struck you as worth passing on. You'll have about four minutes to share, and then it's buddy B's turn. Any questions?"*

Switch the sharing to buddy B after four minutes. After another four minutes you may allow a little extra time for general sharing. Then sound another alert. If the buddy pairs are scattered around the room, ask attendees for their attention so you can wrap up the roundtable.

Roundtable wrap-up

> *"The roundtable session is now complete. [If relevant, say 'We will photograph the flip chart sheets containing the topics mentioned and post them on the conference wiki.'] But before we break, I want to summarize how we are going to turn the interests, themes, and experiences we've heard about into conference sessions. During peer session sign-up you'll have an opportunity to propose any sessions you'd like to see happen. Once everyone's session ideas are displayed for all to see, you'll then get to sign up for the sessions you'd like to be part of. Finally we'll choose the popular sessions from the information given and schedule sessions that reflect your wishes. Any questions?"*

Answer attendee questions and provide appropriate directions for the next conference event. Congratulations, your roundtable session is complete!

Why use roundtable question cards?

You may be wondering why you should give attendees the opportunity to answer the three roundtable questions *in writing* before their sharing starts. Providing time for attendees to think about and write their answers is important for two reasons.

First, some attendees may be anxious about speaking up in front of the entire group, especially right at the beginning of the conference. Giving everyone a quiet time to collect, organize, and write down their thoughts will help to reduce attendees' unease.

A second reason involves the concept of personality types or preferences, as expressed by Isabel Myers and Katharine Briggs who devised the Myers-Briggs Type Indicator (MBTI), a popular method of categorizing personality differences. One of the MBTI dichotomies is an individual's introvert or extrovert preference. Most people have an extrovert preference—they tend to develop their thinking while speaking, and thrive on interacting with others. However, around 25 percent of the general population inclines toward introversion. Introverts need quiet time to do their thinking, usually prefer to write their ideas down, and find it harder to think well when others are talking. Introverts greatly benefit, therefore, from providing a time before roundtable sharing begins when they can quietly gather and record their thoughts.

Peer session sign-up

By the time the roundtable is over, attendees have shared a myriad of topics for further conversations. Certain themes will have come up repeatedly, and attendees will have gained a feeling for the popular topics. Peer session sign-up transforms this swirl of ideas into concrete topics for specific peer sessions, and supplies information on the degree of interest in each topic. In this section I explain how to organize and run a peer session sign-up.

Preparing for peer session sign-up

Rather than expending precious conference time on peer session sign-up, I schedule it during the first conference social event—usually a meal or similar activity like an ice-cream social or beer tasting. This strategy supplies an extended time for people to make their needs and wishes known, and, by providing a relaxed environment, minimizes the pressure that attendees can otherwise experience when filling out topic sheets while a crowd of people mill around, waiting their turn. Whatever the social event, make it one where attendees can freely circulate, like a buffet lunch or outdoor dinner cookout.

FIGURE 25.1 • Peer Session Sign-up Sheet

Peer Session Topic: _____

_____

_____

Please . . .

. . . place an (**F**) next to your name to indicate you'd be willing to *facilitate* the group.

. . . place an (**E**) next to your name to indicate you have some *experience* or *expertise* in the peer session's topic.

. . . place a (**P**) next to your name to indicate you'd be prepared to be a *presenter* or *panelist* for the group.

. . . place an (**S**) next to your name to indicate you'd be prepared to *scribe* for the group.

Also, indicate your level of interest in the topic by placing the number **1**—*low*, **2**—*medium*, or **3**—*high* next to your name.

Schedule peer session sign-up to start near the beginning of your social event. At the end of the roundtable, announce the time that sign-up will start, and explain that it's important that everyone is present. Immediately after the sign-up, which typically takes about 30 minutes, you'll start work on selecting and scheduling peer sessions. Arrange to have attendees continue to socialize or dine close by, so your scheduling group can easily consult with individuals if needed.

Hold peer session sign-up at a place where there are notice boards or flat walls to which topic sign-up sheets can be pinned or taped. (If using tape, check in advance with the conference site that it's OK to put tape on their walls!) Some sites have movable notice boards available; these are handy if you want to hold peer session sign-up outside in fine weather, and there are no flat walls around. Or you can lay out sign-up sheets on long tables, first removing any surrounding chairs. Whatever display method you use, be sure that there's plenty of open space, at least ten feet, in front of your notice boards, walls, or tables so attendees can gather and mingle.

You'll need a plentiful supply of sign-up sheets. Initially, provide two sign-up sheets for each attendee. This is usually enough, but have more available should they be needed. On notice boards or walls, attach two rows of sign-up sheets, one row at four feet and one row at six feet off the ground. On tables, place a single row of sheets along the table edges.

Print copies of the peer session sign-up instructions sheet (Appendix 3) and intersperse them every few feet among the sign-up sheets.

Don't assume that pens you provide as part of the conference package will be available; provide plenty of extras. It's best to provide a wide variety of colors, as this will make it easier to look for attendee conflicts while scheduling sessions. On notice boards, put the pens in small boxes pinned to the board, or hang them on strings so that all sign-up sheets can be reached.

Introducing peer session sign-up

Because it's important for selected peer sessions to accurately reflect attendees' needs and wishes, you must provide a clear explanation of peer session sign-up, so that people understand how the process works and what they're supposed to do. Start at the scheduled time. After you get attendees' attention, here's what you might say:

> *"Hello again everyone, it's time to begin peer session sign-up!*
>
> *Peer session sign-up is our key process for shaping what will happen in the heart of this conference—the peer sessions. During the roundtable, each one of you shared your ideas and wishes for topics of further conversations. Peer session sign-up transforms your ideas and wishes into concrete topics for specific peer sessions, and supplies information on the degree of interest in each topic.*

There are two phases to the sign-up process. The first is the topic suggestion
*phase. During topic suggestion, each one of you lists, on sign-up sheets for all to
see, descriptive titles of sessions you would like to attend. Also, please offer interesting topics on which you have experience and which you could help present or
co-present. You can suggest as many sessions as you like, each one on a separate
sheet. Don't be concerned at this point about whether a topic you want will be
popular or not. If you want a session to happen or are offering help, ask for it or
offer it by filling in a topic sheet.*

*Put a little thought into the wording of each topic you propose. Aim to describe
your topic accurately and concisely. If someone else has proposed a similar topic,
but it's not exactly what you had in mind, then create a new sign-up sheet for your
version—don't feel constrained by what someone else has already suggested. Also
think about the scope of the topic you propose. You probably won't want to suggest
a subject that is so limited or specialized that it can be covered in a few minutes.
Conversely, you may want to avoid suggesting a topic that is so broad that you'll
either barely scratch the surface during the time available, or you'll attract people
with such different perspectives that they'll get frustrated listening to conversations
about aspects that aren't interesting to them. Remember the story of Goldilocks
and the three bears, and go for the topic that's* just right.

*We'll provide about 15 minutes for topic suggestion. Then we'll move to the
second phase,* topic sign-up. *During topic sign-up you look at all the sign-up sheet
topics that have been suggested and sign your name under every topic that interests
you. This doesn't obligate you to attend any session, but simply indicates the degree
of interest in each subject.*

*In addition, when you sign your name you have the opportunity to indicate
how you can help with the session—as a facilitator, as someone with experience or
expertise in the subject, or as a volunteer scribe who will create a record of the session. You do this, as indicated on the sign-up sheet, by placing an 'F' (facilitator),
'E' (experience/expertise), or 'S' (scribe) next to your name. If you're willing to be
a presenter or panelist at the session, put a 'P' next to your name.*

*Also, when you sign your name, put the number 1, 2, or 3 next to it to indicate
your degree of interest in the topic. 3 indicates high interest, 2, moderate interest,
and 1, low interest.*

*Once topic sign-up is over, a small group of us will use the completed sign-up
sheets to determine and schedule peer sessions. If you'd like to take part in this
process, which takes about half an hour, please let me know.*

Any questions?"

Answer any questions and tell attendees where the sign-up sheets are.

> *"You have 15 minutes to suggest topics. I'll give you a couple of reminders before your time is up, and we move to topic sign-up. OK, go and suggest topics!"*

Monitor the sign-up area, and put out more sheets if needed. Give a 10- and 5-minute warning, and wait until all have had the opportunity to list their topics. Then move on to topic sign-up.

> *"Now it's time for topic sign-up! Sign your name under every topic that interests you. This doesn't obligate you to attend any session. Add a number next to your name; 3 means high interest, 2 means moderate interest, and 1 means low interest. Don't forget to indicate if you can help with the session—as a facilitator, expertise provider, scribe, or presenter or panelist. Also, if you're open to taking notes on a session you attend, please add your name to the scribe volunteer list—again, no obligation. Finally, if you're offering expertise and won't be around for all the peer session time slots, please note when you'll be available."*

If you have provided an assortment of pen colors, include the following paragraph:

> *"One more thing. Each of you, please grab a colored pen and use the same pen for all your writing on the sign-up sheets. This makes it easier for us to see conflicts when we're scheduling sessions."*

> *"You'll have 15 minutes for topic sign-up. OK, go and tell us what interests you!"*

Once again, give 10- and 5-minute warnings, and wait until everyone has had the opportunity to sign up for topics.

Toward the end of sign-up you can encourage people to browse the sign-up sheets to see who else shares their topic interests, especially if they think a suggested topic is obscure and may not become a peer session. Browsing provides a simple early opportunity to discover the other attendees who may want to discuss a specific issue.

During topic sign-up, ask for volunteers to help create and schedule peer sessions, as described in the next section. At the end, remind attendees to read their two peer session handouts before they go to their first peer session.

Determining and scheduling peer sessions

During peer session sign-up, you'll need to assemble a small group of volunteers to help create and schedule the peer sessions. Your group should include subject matter experts on your conference topic, so you don't get stumped evaluating an abstruse topic from the sign-up sheets. Announce that you are seeking volunteers to help create and schedule peer sessions, which typically takes about an hour. Aim for a group size of at least three people for a small conference, with up to six people for a large conference.

Peer session sign-up is over. You have a large pile of sign-up sheets in front of you. Here's how you transform this pile into a scheduled set of peer sessions that reflect, as much as possible, the wishes and desires of your attendees.

Choosing peer session topics: initial steps

First, assemble your "peer session selection crew" of steering committee members and volunteers. Meet in a quiet place with good lighting, somewhere with enough table space to lay out all the non-blank sign-up sheets so they can be viewed simultaneously. Ideally the other attendees should be socializing or dining nearby, so you can consult with them if necessary about participating in a particular peer session.

Before you begin, estimate the maximum number of groups you can schedule during your conference. Your conference schedule has a fixed number of peer session time slots, so the total number of peer sessions depends on how many concurrent sessions you schedule. Of course, the more simultaneous groups you schedule in each peer session time slot, the greater the likelihood that two sessions someone wants to attend will be scheduled for the same time slot. From experience, I'd recommend scheduling four or fewer simultaneous peer sessions in any time slot. The maximum number of peer sessions then is determined by:

> (number of peer session time slots) × maximum of (the number of peer session locations available or four)

To start determining peer session topics, the selection crew moves the non-blank sign-up sheets into clusters of similar topics. If there's disagreement about where a topic should be placed, keep that sheet separate for now.

Look for topics that can clearly be merged, but don't combine vaguely related topics. Discuss with the subject matter experts in your group whether merging is appropriate, and unless there's agreement, keep similar topics separate at this point. (You may merge them later.) Avoid combining similar topics right away because, sometimes, people with a particular slant on a topic aren't interested in what people with a different perspective have to say. For

272

FIGURE 25.2 • Peer Session Determination and Scheduling

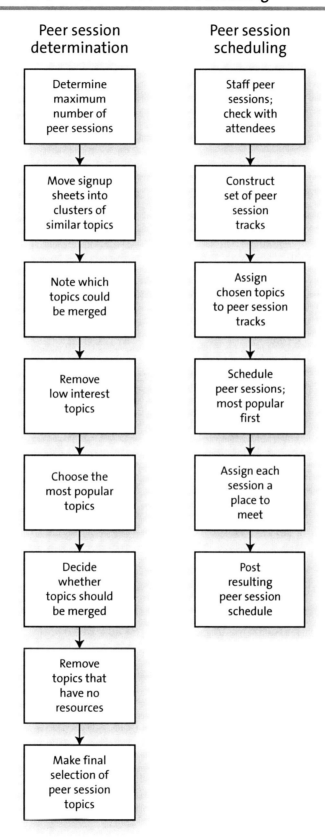

Peer session determination

- Determine maximum number of peer sessions
- Move signup sheets into clusters of similar topics
- Note which topics could be merged
- Remove low interest topics
- Choose the most popular topics
- Decide whether topics should be merged
- Remove topics that have no resources
- Make final selection of peer session topics

Peer session scheduling

- Staff peer sessions; check with attendees
- Construct set of peer session tracks
- Assign chosen topics to peer session tracks
- Schedule peer sessions; most popular first
- Assign each session a place to meet
- Post resulting peer session schedule

example, people who want to talk about the *implementation* of a process may have little in common with others who want to discuss the *possible outcomes* of that same process.

If you decide that two (or more) topics are sufficiently similar to be combined, consider rephrasing the topic with a new title that encompasses the merged topics. Occasionally, from the roundtable comments, you can define the topic better than the versions on the topic sheets, but don't do this unless you're sure that the resulting topic is a genuine improvement over what was proposed and clearly reflects attendees' sentiments.

As you go through the sheets, look for "just right" topics. As in the story of the three bears, just right topics are not too small (specific) and not too big (vague). You are looking for topics on which attendees can have a meaty discussion and share useful information in the time available.

Some topic suggestions are more like specific questions that someone knowledgeable could answer in five minutes. Usually such topics will have few if any names attached and will not make it into the schedule.

Harder to deal with are vague topics that may cover too much ground to be done justice in a one-hour peer session. Often a significant number of people will sign up for vague topics, because they appear to offer something useful for many attendees. The best way to avoid overly broad topics is to describe the "just right" topic at the start of peer session sign-up. However, if one or more seemingly vague topics are popular, don't reject them solely on the grounds of vagueness. Those attendees may know something you don't.

Remove topic sheets with just one or two names attached and put them aside. Sometimes these sheets contain specialized questions that someone at the conference may be able to answer. Consider posting them at a central location and asking attendees to check the postings to see whether they can help.

Now it's time to choose the most popular topics. In my experience, about 90 percent of these are obvious. Count the number of names and write the total on each sheet. As a rule of thumb, any topic with six or more names should be considered as a potential peer session. For the moment, put aside the sheets with fewer than six names. Count the number of topics that remain, and compare this count with the maximum number of peer session time slots available, as estimated in the previous section.

Sometimes one or two topics are extremely popular, with over half the attendees adding their names. This usually occurs when the roundtable uncovers experience with a topic that many other attendees value highly. If you see topics like this, consider giving them an exclusive time slot with nothing else concurrently scheduled. Reduce your estimated maximum number of peer sessions appropriately.

Now that you have a preliminary pool of viable peer session topics, determine whether any of them should be combined into a single peer session. Aim to preserve topic diversity, while minimizing overlap. If you combine topic sheets, count the number of unique names on the sheets and note this count on the combined topic sheets.

Avoiding the dreaded "frustrated peer session"

At this point, you need to detect and prevent potential "frustrated peer sessions." These can occur in two ways. The first is when attendees want to learn about a topic, but no one at the conference has enough experience or knowledge to make a peer session on the topic truly useful. Since there's no in-conference solution for this situation, you should not schedule a session on the topic. A frustrated peer session can also happen if your conference includes attendees with relevant experience, but they don't take part in the session where their experience is needed. With planning and a little cooperation, this impasse can be avoided and the session can be held.

Scan your peer session list, identifying topics where no one has volunteered their expertise via an "E" next to their name and that require specific expertise or experience not mentioned during the roundtable session. If you think there's an attendee who might be able to help out with the topic, ask her if she would be willing to facilitate, present, or provide her expertise to the peer session in question. If the topic implies general discussion in an area where most attendees could contribute, rather than someone with specific expertise, then just a competent facilitator will do.

Sometimes attendees request a presentation from a specific attendee. In this case, check with the potential presenter to make sure he is willing to host the session.

If you are left with sessions that have been requested but lack the expertise or experience necessary for them to succeed, remove them from your peer session topic list. If your conference will be repeated, keep a list of these topics; they may be prime subjects for a traditional session by an outside expert at your next conference.

Choosing peer session topics: the final steps

If there are fewer qualifying topics than remaining time slots, look over the topics on sheets with less than six names and decide whether you should include any of them. Bear in mind that you don't need to fill every potential time slot with a peer session; groups with just a few attendees are rarely found to be worthwhile. Once you've made this determination, you're ready to schedule the topics you've chosen.

On the other hand, if you have too many viable candidates for the number of time slots available, you'll need to prune your list of potential topics. Do this by removing the least popular topics, as determined by name count, from your pool until you have enough time slots for the topics left. You can also use the interest ratings (the numbers from 1 to 3) besides signers' names to decide between topics that have the same number of names listed.

Phew! Congratulations, you've chosen your peer session topics! Now it's time to schedule them.

The peer conference approach to scheduling peer session topics

The final step for determining peer sessions is to schedule the topics you've chosen for specific time slots and locations. While it's conceivable that your list contains the same number of peer session topics as available session times, I have yet to see this occur. People inevitably have more topics they want to talk about than the time slots available. You are thus faced with the challenge of deciding which topics to offer concurrently. How can you arrange sessions to minimize the chance that attendees will have to choose between "must-see" sessions that are, unfortunately, scheduled at the same time?

To minimize attendee disappointment due to scheduling conflicts, it helps to first assign the topics on your list to conference "tracks." Using conference tracks to schedule sessions is a well-established strategy often used by large traditional conferences. The rationale is that most people who attend a conference have a personal bias toward certain kinds of topics. By assigning topics with a common slant to different times, attendee scheduling conflicts are reduced.

At a peer conference, we can do even better than the conventional track solution, because we have significant additional information about attendee interests: the names on the topic sheets. This information makes it easy to see the level of conflict that will result if we schedule particular sessions at the same time. By using this sign-up information together with a conference track approach, it's relatively simple to build conference schedules that work for attendees. As a result, in my experience, frustration about session conflicts at a peer conference is rare.

Scheduling peer session topics

Your first task when scheduling peer session topics is to scan your list of selected peer session topics and construct a set of peer session tracks. Here is an example of tracks we have used at edACCESS conferences, which cover topics of interest to information technology staff at small schools:

- People issues
- Handling institutional issues
- Technical issue discussions and presentations
- Solving specific problems
- Comparisons of different approaches
- Planning

Not all of these tracks have been needed at every conference. Usually I settle on three or four tracks, based on the maximum number of simultaneous peer sessions the conference can handle. Tracks might represent different themes or approaches, or reflect the job responsibilities of attendees, or cover aspects of a burning issue for many attendees. Use the names on the topic sheets to gauge whether there are genuine differences between the track categories you choose.

Once you've sorted your topics into conference tracks, it's time to schedule peer sessions. Clear off your table space, making room to create a grid into which you'll place topic sheets. Initially, the rows of the grid will be the conference tracks you've designated, while the columns delineate the time slots scheduled for peer sessions. Now your task is to place the peer session sheets in the grid intersections so as to minimize conflicts between concurrent sessions (Figure 25.3).

Schedule the most popular sessions first, putting each one in a different time slot so you don't have two popular sessions at the same time. For sessions requiring one or more specific presenters, check with the presenters to ensure they will be available and willing to attend the session. This is especially important for peer sessions scheduled late in the conference if there's a possibility that a putative presenter may be leaving early.

For the rest of the topics, use the topic sheet names to minimize conflicts as you place each topic in the grid. Aim for a mixture of popular and less popular topics in each time slot. Comparing the names between sheets is tedious, but takes less time than you might expect. Minor conflicts are unavoidable, so don't agonize over them. Do the best you can—you'll probably be surprised by how well you do in a brief amount of time.

Once you've placed every peer session in the grid, your next task is to assign each group a place to meet. This can be done quickly. Up to now you've been thinking of the rows of your grid as conference tracks; now, instead, associate the rows with the rooms you've allocated to peer sessions. Shuffle each column, if necessary, so that the more popular sessions are assigned the larger rooms. Check that assigned rooms can handle any special requirements of a given peer session (i.e., Internet access, projection facilities, etc.).

FIGURE 25.3 • Topic Sheet Layout for Scheduling Peer Sessions

	TIME SLOT 1	TIME SLOT 2	TIME SLOT 3	TIME SLOT 4	TIME SLOT 5	TIME SLOT 6
Track 1						
Track 2						
Track 3						
Track 4						

You're nearly done! With peer session topics chosen, scheduled, and assigned to specific locations, all that remains is to staff your peer sessions and publicize the completed schedule.

Staffing peer sessions

At this point you'll have already identified many of the peer session staff through the (E), (P), and (F) notations on the sign-up sheets plus informal consultations with attendees during peer session determinations. Nevertheless, there will invariably be some gaps, and this is the time to fill them.

Start by creating a peer session schedule—a grid of time slot rows by location columns, as in Table 25.1. Include the names of attendees who have volunteered to facilitate, share their expertise, or scribe. If you have one or more presenters lined up for a session, include their name(s) on the schedule too. Next, for the sessions still needing a facilitator or attendees with expertise, brainstorm attendees who might be appropriate, willing, and available to fill these roles. Although it's nice if you have some predetermined scribes, don't worry if every peer session doesn't have a scribe—facilitators can ask for volunteers at the start of sessions. Finally, bring your schedule to the nearby attendee gathering and check that the staff assignments you've made are acceptable. If an assignment proves problematic and you can't come up with an alternative arrangement, announce your dilemma to the group and ask for help staffing the vacant position. In my experience, people willingly step in to fill facilitation positions, and are modestly flattered to be asked to provide their expertise to a peer session. On the rare occasions that you cannot find suitable staffing, consider removing the topic from your schedule.

Getting the word out

Once you've determined peer session staffing, print and distribute your final schedule (see Table 25.2) to attendees. Post the schedule on each peer session room door, in refreshment break areas, and in any other central meeting places where they will be useful reminders for attendees.

You've already distributed your first "fixed session" evaluation to attendees. Now that peer session topics have been chosen, use the list to create a second conference evaluation survey, as described in Chapter 21, as quickly as possible. Create an appropriate paper form and/or online survey, announce its availability, and distribute copies at the next time during your conference that attendees gather as a group. Mission accomplished!

TABLE 25.1 • Tuesday Peer Session Schedule—*Preliminary*

	STUDY HALL	CLASSROOM 27	CLASSROOM 11	CLASSROOM 1
Session 1: 11:00 a.m.– 12:00 p.m.	**Blogging** Michael Moulton (E) Joel Backon (F) Eric LaCroix (S)	**Disaster Planning** Whitney Donnelly (F)	Voice Over IP (VOIP)	**Technology Planning** John Wolter (F)
Session 2: 3:15 p.m.– 4:15 p.m.	**Podcasting** Peter Richardson (F) Dave Lepage (P)	**Backup Strategies** Joe Lorenzatti (E, F)	**Digital Asset Management**	**Digital Language Labs**

(F) facilitator   (E) experience   (S) scribe   (P) presenter

TABLE 25.2 • Tuesday Peer Session Schedule—*Final*

	STUDY HALL	CLASSROOM 27	CLASSROOM 11	CLASSROOM 1
Session 1: 11:00 a.m.– 12:00 p.m.	**Blogging** Michael Moulton (E) Joel Backon (F) Eric LaCroix (S)	**Disaster Planning** Whitney Donnelly (F)	**Voice Over IP (VOIP)** Christopher Butler (F) Peter Randall (E)	**Technology Planning** John Wolter (F)
Session 2: 3:15 p.m.– 4:15 p.m.	**Podcasting** Peter Richardson (F) Dave Lepage (P)	**Backup Strategies** Joe Lorenzatti (E, F)	**Digital Asset Management** Joel Backon (F)	**Digital Language Labs** Ed Curtin (F)

(F) facilitator   (E) experience   (S) scribe   (P) presenter

Running peer sessions

Peer sessions are the core events at a peer conference. They are the sessions where attendees explore, share, and learn about topics that have meaning and energy for them. Peer sessions can have many different forms: presentations, panels, discussions, workshops, case studies, simulations, and so on. Because these sessions are numerous, not pre-planned, and often involve specialized knowledge and experience, it's not generally practical for the conference organizers to provide the structure and facilitation. Running peer sessions is thus a task for the attendees themselves. The question that arises is then: *How do we prepare attendees, with little to no advance warning, to run a peer session well?*

I've found that if attendees follow a few simple rules and avoid some common errors, they can run peer sessions enjoyably and productively. I've summarized this guidance in two handouts, *Peer Session Primer* and *Peer Session Facilitation*, which you should include in attendee conference packets. I've included copies of these handouts in Appendices 4 and 5.

Before the first peer session, remind attendees to read these two handouts. Check with each peer session facilitator to answer any questions or concerns about their role, and ensure that any needed equipment or facilities are on hand. Also, provide an attendance sheet for each peer session (Appendices 7 and 8). If attendees have brought laptops to the conference, ask whether scribes can use them to simplify writing and distributing peer session notes.

The conference coordinator should be available during peer sessions to encourage sessions to start and end on time. Before a peer session starts, make 10- and 5-minute alert announcements to get attendees on their way. This will work for most people, but invariably some attendees will arrive late for their next session. Drop by each session when it's time for the group to start, and ask the facilitator to begin, even if people are still straggling in.

Ending peer sessions on time is particularly problematic—many groups have such a good time that they want to keep going. Of course, this isn't a bad thing in itself, but if allowed it will delay upcoming sessions. When peer sessions are scheduled back-to-back, with five minutes between sessions, you need to be clear and direct when interrupting a session that's in danger of overrunning its scheduled duration. Use a firm but lighthearted announcement, and be prepared to hear good-natured groans as you make it. But do *not* assume that people will stay on time without this reminder—it's vital that you monitor session length and interrupt when necessary.

If attendees badly want to continue their session, let them if it will not conflict with an upcoming session in the same room. When the next peer session time slot starts, announce this to the continuing group, in case there are people who want to attend a different session. If the meeting space is scheduled for another group, insist that people leave, but either offer the group another room that's free, or help them figure out a later time and place they can reconvene and continue.

Notes about scribing

Before each peer session, *remind every peer session facilitator that it's their responsibility to find a scribe, before the session starts*. Otherwise it's all too easy for peer session attendees to rapidly delve into their subject and belatedly realize that no one has taken notes on the session.

Provide a simple attendance sheet (see Appendices 7 and 8) for each peer session. Have attendees add their names to the sheet as it's passed around at the start of the peer session, and pass the completed sheet to the scribe. This makes it easy to record who was present.

Including a peer session topic recap

At a three- or four-day conference, consider including a *peer session topic recap* halfway through the conference. A recap offers attendees an opportunity to confirm and adjust their initial peer session topic choices, and gives topics that were not immediately apparent a second chance to be heard and explored. In my experience, although the majority of peer session topic choices aren't altered by a recap, invariably one or two changes occur. Sometimes a new topic is belatedly suggested and proves to have popular appeal, a low initial-popularity topic becomes more attractive when it's discovered that an expert on the subject is at the conference, and a conventional session may increase or decrease interest in a related peer session. Whatever the changes, if any, the recap provides a check that the remaining scheduled peer sessions continue to reflect attendees' needs and wishes.

When should we include a peer session topic recap?

I don't have any hard and fast rules to determine whether to hold a recap at a long conference. I tend to use one if I'm concerned that topic choices may have shifted as attendees get to know each other and uncover new issues. I did not include a recap until fairly recently, and, in retrospect, saw no great evidence that the choice of topics suffered as a result. At this point, I think of a peer session topic recap as an optional fine-tuning of peer session topics, rather than as a necessary step. If you decide to use a recap, I'd be interested in hearing your experience!

How do I run a peer session topic recap?

If you include a peer session topic recap, schedule it to occur somewhere in the middle of your peer session time slots. I like to run a recap during breakfast of the third day of a four-day conference. Make sure you choose a time when everyone is most likely to be present.

To prepare for the recap, print sign-up sheets that are filled in distinctively with the remaining topics from the scheduled peer session. Use a bright color and a large unique font so it's clear that these sheets contain previously chosen topics. Shuffle these prefilled sheets into a plentiful pile of blank sign-up sheets, and post or lay out the combined pile randomly on your peer session sign-up wall or tables. From this point on, the procedure is similar to normal peer session sign-up. Ask attendees to review the existing topics and add any additional topics onto blank sheets. Remind them that if they want to reframe or change the emphasis of an existing topic, they can enter their version onto a blank sign-up sheet. After this initial topic creation, ask attendees to add their names and potential contributions to the topics they'd like to attend. Finally, determine and schedule the remaining peer sessions using the procedures described earlier in this chapter.

Although I've suggested using one scribe per peer session, if a conference wiki is available, there can be real benefit from encouraging more than one person to make notes on a session. All notes can then be posted on the wiki as is, or combined there into a single summary.

Collecting and posting peer session notes

Choose a steering committee member, *the peer session notes coordinator*, who will be responsible for:

- Finding out from each peer session facilitator who was the scribe for their session;
- Chasing after scribes for their session notes; and
- Posting peer session notes in an appropriate format: on a wiki, via email, or in printed form, as soon as they are available.

Handling vendor representatives attending peer sessions

If you are allowing vendor representatives to attend peer sessions, go over your expectations for appropriate behavior *individually with each vendor representative* before the sessions start, including the need for confidentiality. Either the vendor coordinator or the conference coordinator should take on this responsibility—make sure you're clear who will do this. Usually these expectations include having the representative sit quietly and observe, only providing contributions if asked. In addition, it's a good idea to warn representatives that it's possible the attendees at a group may not want them to be present, though this is rarely a problem in my experience.

Creating audio recordings of peer sessions

A common request from attendees, as well as people who didn't attend the conference, is whether audio recordings of peer sessions are available. Attendees often want to hear what happened at a peer session they missed because they were at another simultaneous session that appealed to them even more, while non-attendees often hear via word-of-mouth about a session and inquire whether a recording is available.

Until the recent advent of cheap digital audio recorders, making audio recordings was a time-intensive task. Now it's become feasible to inexpensively record a conference session and make it available as a podcast or streaming audio over the Internet. Recording devices that attach to an iPod, like the Belkin TuneTalk, available for about $50, can provide high quality digital recordings that can be downloaded (podcast) or streamed (streaming audio) by anyone with an Internet connection.

However, before getting too excited about the possibilities of exposing a wider audience to intriguing peer sessions, you *must* consider the ramifications of exposing what happens in the peer session to the outside world, because of the confidentiality ground rule of a peer conference—*what is shared at the conference stays at the conference.*

To maintain confidentiality, before the session begins, the facilitator must ask whether anyone has an objection to the conversation being recorded, if access to the resulting conversation is restricted to conference attendees. The facilitator should emphasize that it's perfectly OK to ask that no recording be made. If any one person objects to recording, it should not be done.

At the end of each recorded session, the facilitator should again ask for objections to making the recording available to conference attendees. If there are none, the facilitator can ask whether anyone would object to a wider circulation of the recording. Again, any single objection is grounds for restricting the availability of the recording.

Alternatively, the attendance sheet can be used to decide whether and to what extent a recording of the session can be distributed. Include two columns that can be checked if permission is given to distribute the recording to conference attendees and/or wider distribution. Circulate the sheet a second time, at the end of the session, for these permissions to be granted or withheld. See Appendix 8 for a sample attendance sheet that includes permissions and associated instructions.

Once sessions have been recorded and permissions obtained, you'll need to make them available to other attendees, and possibly to the world at large. Typical devices create digital recordings as wav (uncompressed) or mp3 (compressed) files. Converting wav files to mp3 or mp4 will reduce the size of the resulting audio file to around a tenth of its original size. An hour of mp3 will take up approximately 60MB of file space at a bit rate of 128 kb/sec.

If you're restricting access to recordings, host them on an appropriately secured website. You may want to use a commercial site to hold your recordings, as a long conference could spawn 20 or more hours of recordings, requiring hundreds of megabytes of web storage.

Other tasks during the conference

Wearing name badges

Check that attendees continue to wear their badges, and gently remind them if badges start to disappear. It's best to do this via a public announcement, so no one feels singled out.

Announcements

You'll likely need to make occasional public announcements during the conference. The best times to do this are right before the start of sessions, refreshment breaks, and meals.

If possible, avoid the end of sessions, when attendees are expecting to leave. Attendees may want to make public announcements too. They may be seeking a ride to the airport, announcing a trip into town, or scheduling an ad hoc meeting during a social event or other free time. Whenever there's an announcement break, ask attendees if they have any brief announcements to add.

Evaluations

Remind attendees about completing their evaluations regularly throughout the conference. When the peer session evaluations become available, let attendees know immediately.

Cleanup

Sometimes you'll need attendees to help with site cleanup toward the end of the conference. Perhaps the conference site wants people to vacate their rooms right after breakfast on the last day, or strip their beds and dump linens at a central point. If you have such agreements with the conference site, inform attendees well in advance and remind them as the time approaches. Occasionally you'll have other tasks, like returning rental furniture or presentation equipment. Although the steering committee should plan to be able to do this work independently, it may be appropriate to ask if any attendees are willing to help out. Indirectly, you may discover people who have energy for steering committee work at your next conference.

Care and feeding of vendors

The vendor coordinator's job is a hard one. Vendor representatives can be eager, respectful, and accommodating. Unfortunately, they can also be sullen, pushy, and just plain rude. Your vendor coordinator needs to be firm while remaining polite and maintaining a sense of humor throughout the semi-chaos that always seems to erupt during vendor day, when seemingly endless hordes of vendors descend on the conference site with a never-ending rain of questions, suggestions, and sometimes, demands. This chapter describes how to staff vendor day and run vendor introductions and presentations, and answers some common vendor questions.

Staffing vendor day

The vendor coordinator should plan to be present throughout vendor setup time. Because of the wide variety of problems that can occur, it's imperative that the coordinator is available to dream up creative solutions to the issues that can arise. Consider having some paid help on hand during vendor setup to help with peak period vendor problems and requests.

Running vendor introductions

Vendor introductions are best held right before the vendor exhibit opens. Gather all attendees together in one location. If there's a traditional conference session scheduled just before exhibit time, vendor introductions can be given in the same room. Before the vendor introduction session, the vendor coordinator makes an alphabetical list of exhibiting companies. As the previous session ends, he has the vendor representatives line up in the order they will be going in front of the attendees. Then the vendor representatives are asked, company by company, to present their introduction. Keep the total vendor introductions session time to under 15 minutes by informing each vendor they have a 45–60 second time limit. Keep a timer handy to enforce it. As soon as the vendor introductions are complete, announce that the vendor exhibit is open.

Organizing vendor presentations

Vendor presentations, described in Chapter 19, give vendors the opportunity to give a short, typically 20-minute, pitch for their products and services to interested attendees in a quiet private area away from the exhibit space. Before the conference, you should have received brief descriptions of each vendor's presentation. Combine the descriptions into a single document, add a schedule of when and where each session will occur, and distribute the schedule to attendees and vendors before the exhibit starts. You may want to post some copies around the exhibit area too.

Schedule presentation sessions during the second half of the vendor exhibit, so that attendees have the opportunity to visit booths early while the vendor representatives are present. Consider scheduling three 20-minute time slots with concurrent vendor presentations taking place in each one. Divide the number of presentations by three to determine how many sessions to schedule concurrently. Try to schedule vendors with competing products in different time slots.

Providing information on attendees to vendors

In general, peer conference participants want control over whether vendors receive their contact information. Often, vendors will request a list of the conference attendees. Because, unfortunately, some vendors use such lists aggressively, my policy is to provide to vendors a list of attendees' affiliated organizations, with no accompanying contact information. This often satisfies vendor representatives' desires (frequently driven by the demands of their marketing departments) for information on the organizations in attendance, while respecting attendees' privacy. Vendors can, of course, ask attendees appearing at their exhibit display for contact information, and attendees can decide whether to provide it.

Recommended rules for vendors who want to attend the conference

To ensure that vendors who want to attend the conference do not have a negative impact on sessions, enforce the following two rules.

First, each vendor representative must be clearly told, before attending conference sessions, that he must not promote his product, service, or company during any session in any way. In general, he should not speak at the session unless he asks for and receives an OK from the people present.

Second, at sessions where sensitive personal experiences may be discussed, the session facilitator should ask for attendees' permission to allow the vendor representative to sit in. For example a peer session where participants ask for suggestions on how to solve their own personal work issues may be a session that a vendor representative should not attend.

Decide in advance who will discuss the rules with vendor representatives during registration—normally this will be either the vendor coordinator or a steering committee member.

Provided these rules are followed, you should not have significant problems allowing vendor representatives to sit in on conference sessions.

The personal introspective

What is a personal introspective?

A personal introspective is a peer conference session where attendees privately reflect on their answers to five questions that are given at the start of the session. All attendees have an opportunity but not an obligation to share their answers with the entire group. The personal introspective reinforces attendees' learning while it is still fresh, and increases the likelihood of personal change and growth. Interestingly and importantly, the group sharing invariably creates a heightened sense of connection and intimacy among the group members.

When to hold a personal introspective

I like to hold a personal introspective as the first session on the last day of a long peer conference, despite the obvious drawback that the rest of the day's sessions can't be included in the introspective. There are two reasons for this scheduling choice. First, sharing attendees' answers to the introspective questions builds a surprisingly intimate atmosphere during the session, creating a wonderful beginning to the final conference day. The second reason is practical—some attendees leave early, before the end of the conference, and would miss the personal introspective if it was held as the last session. Attendees who haven't experienced a personal introspective tend to underestimate its value until they go through the process themselves. Scheduling the session at the start of the last day can reduce the number of attendees who, not understanding the value of peer conference spectives, decide to leave early.

I'm not enthusiastic about holding a personal introspective at a short peer conference—I think the time is better used for the group spective. If, however, you want to hold a quick personal introspective, divide attendees into several small groups, have them sit in circles, and, after they've answered the introspective questions, have them share their answers inside their circle.

Preparation

Before the introspective starts, you may want to prepare some examples of vague versus measurable goals and actions that connect with your conference's subject, guided by the examples given in Table 25.3. Print a personal introspective questions card (Appendix 9) for each attendee.

Prepare the personal introspective meeting place by setting up the same circle seating arrangement that you used for the opening roundtable session. If you ran two roundtable sessions, you'll need a facilitator and a timekeeper for each corresponding personal introspective. Calculate the average time for each attendee to share by subtracting 15 minutes from the time allocated for the introspective, dividing the result by the number of attendees present, and rounding down to the nearest minute or half-minute. Unlike the roundtable, I dispense with a preliminary 30-second warning chime during sharing; a single signal when time is up seems to work fine.

I've yet to see it happen, but it's possible that no one will volunteer to begin sharing answers during the second part of the session. To get the ball rolling if this occurs, arrange with one of the steering committee members to volunteer to share first if no one else volunteers to start.

Running your personal introspective—answering the questions

Once attendees are seated in their circle(s), begin the session by handing out a personal introspective card, and a pen if needed, to each attendee. Then spend a few minutes explaining the first part of the personal introspective—answering the five questions on the card. Here's what I might say:

> *"Welcome, everyone, to your personal introspective! By now you've had many different learning experiences at this conference. The purpose of this session is to give you an opportunity to explore changes you may want to make in your life and work after the conference is over. This is an opportunity for you: a session to dive into, to*

experience fully. It will work best if you don't think too much; instead, respond from your gut!

You start your own personal introspective by answering for yourself the five questions on the card you've just been given. Let's go through these five questions in detail.

Number One: What do I want to have happen? *Think about what you want to change in your life in the future. These changes could be in any aspect of your life. They could be something mundane, they could be something major. What are your desires, your dreams? What have you just started that you want to keep on doing? What do you want to give up? What are you inspired to do in a different way? What are you inspired to do that you haven't done before?*

These are exciting questions. Think about your answers and write them down!

Number Two: What is the current situation? *Time for a reality check. Before you can go somewhere, you need to know where you are now. So take a minute or two to summarize the current situation, the starting point for the changes you want to have happen. Be as specific as necessary.*

Number Three: What are you willing to do? *This question is about action. To make happen what you want to have happen, you need to do* stuff. *So, what are you willing to do? What are the steps? Write them all down!*

Number Four: How will you know when it happens? *This is an important question, and probably the hardest to answer. Its purpose is to check that you're setting goals, actions, and outcomes that can be measured in a way that's meaningful to you. If your goals, actions, and outcomes are measurable, you can* manage *the process of getting where you want to go,* gauge *your progress toward achieving your goals, and you will* know *when you've succeeded. If you don't have measurable goals, actions, and outcomes, you're going to be frustrated carrying out what you decide here today. So, use this question to review your earlier answers and, if necessary, work on how you can reframe them so they are measurable.*

Number Five: Where and how will I get support? *During this conference you may have discovered resources that can support the changes you want to make. These resources may be reference materials, they may be other conferences, local or online communities you can join, or people you've met here. While they're fresh in your mind, write down the resources you'll use for support as your answer to this question.*

I can't overemphasize the importance of identifying specific, measurable answers to these questions. Ending up with concrete, measurable goals, actions, and outcomes is key to benefiting from this introspective.

Any questions about these five questions?"

288

TABLE 25.3 • Goals/Actions—Vague versus Measurable

VAGUE GOAL OR ACTION	MEASURABLE GOAL OR ACTION
"I'll be more positive."	"The ratio of positive to negative comments in my daily journal will double in the next six months."
"I will get over my fear of public speaking."	"I will join my local Toastmasters club."
"I'm going to learn more about X."	"I will subscribe to the X journal and attend the X conference next July."
"I will treat my direct reports better."	"I will implement weekly one-on-ones with all my direct reports, and give them my undivided attention during the meetings."

Pause for questions. People may ask for examples of measurable goals or actions. Table 25.3 provides some contrasting examples that may be helpful. Adapt them to your conference subject.

When any questions have been answered, continue like this:

> *"I'm going to give you five to ten minutes to answer these questions for yourself. Remember, there are no wrong answers to these questions. Don't think* too *much, get those answers down! Go!"*

Give attendees five to ten minutes to answer the questions. If necessary, ask people who have finished to refrain from talking while others are still writing. I watch for signs that the majority of people are done, then gently announce that a minute or two remains for those still writing. If a significant number of attendees are using computers, you may need to ask for a show of hands to determine who is now surfing the Internet, and who is still writing down answers.

Running your personal introspective—time to share

Once people have stopped writing, start the sharing portion of the personal introspective. How you introduce this part of the session will depend to some degree on your conference topic. You may feel that you don't need to talk much about safety if your conference topic is highly technical and the peer sessions have not been about "people issues." I prefer to play it safe and emphasize that attendees don't have to share with the group. I might say something like this:

> *"I hope this exercise has been useful for you. Now it's time for the second part of the personal introspective. In this part you'll each be given an opportunity for*

sharing what came up for you during this exercise. I want to emphasize that your answers are private, and you can choose whether or not to share. You may not want to share anything. That's OK! You may not want to share everything. That's OK too.

Having said that, I encourage you to talk about whatever you feel you can. Many people find that it can be very helpful to share their answers. We have enough time to give each of you [the average sharing time you calculated]; you'll hear a chime when your time is up.

OK, who wants to go first?"

Pick the first volunteer. When that person is finished, go around the circle, starting with the person to the first speaker's left or right. Don't allow significant interruptions. People may ask for support from others, and a brief agreement from the asked attendee is fine. In my experience almost everyone shares, but this may not be the case for every group. As with the roundtable, monitor the time, and relax or tighten up on the time limit accordingly.

If there's time left over when the sharing is complete, ask whether there is anything else that people would like to share. Ask people to put their hand up if they have something to say. Some who passed over the sharing opportunity may now want to speak; others may want to add to what they said. Because the group atmosphere usually has become quite intimate and intense during this session, it's not unusual for people to make general comments about the session and their experience of it. Let this all happen as it will. When everyone who wants to has spoken or time is up, thank attendees for their contributions and bring the session to an end.

A letter to myself—optional addition

The following exercise can be used to remind attendees of their answers to the personal introspective questions and to reinforce their conference experience. Hand out writing paper and an envelope to each attendee, and invite them to write a letter to themselves from their answers to the personal introspective questions. Suggest they include any changes they want to make as a result of what they have learned. Ask attendees to address the envelope to themselves and insert and seal the letter. When people are finished, collect the letters, store them for an appropriate period of time, perhaps a month, and then mail attendees their letters.

An alternative format for a personal introspective

If your attendees are artistically inclined, here is an alternate way to share answers. I haven't tried this—if you do, please let me know how it turns out! You'll need a large wall, plenty of colored pens or other art supplies, and some large sheets of paper. After attendees have answered the five personal introspective questions for themselves, ask each to draw one or more pictures summarizing their conference experience and/or their introspective answers. Create a gallery of finished pictures and give attendees the opportunity to describe their drawings.

Giving thanks

It's very important to thank people for the work they do to make your conference possible. In a culture that sometimes seems to fixate on mistakes and what's wrong, it's easy to overlook the significant amounts of energy, time, and talent that most people routinely provide to make the world a better place. Without acknowledgment of our contributions, few of us could maintain the desire and drive to offer our gifts and commitment to others. And yet it's surprising how infrequently we thank others for what they do for us, and how weakly we convey our appreciation when we do.

Thank people both publicly and privately. Public thanks, done well, provide a clear acknowledgment by the group of a person's work and efforts. Private thanks build on the group's recognition, and allows the giver to share appreciations that may not be appropriate in public.

Appreciations—more powerful than thanks

Imagine that Susan is standing before the gathered attendees, publicly thanking steering committee members, including you, Bob, for your work organizing a conference. Here are some examples of what she might say. After you read each one, take a moment to notice how you feel.

> [Susan faces audience]
> "The steering committee members contributed a lot of hard work putting on this conference."

> [Susan faces audience]
> "Bob worked hard to get out the face book."

> [Susan faces audience]
> "Thank you, Bob, you worked hard to get out the face book."

> [Susan points to you and then faces the audience]
> "I appreciate Bob, who worked hard to get out the face book."

[Susan asks you to come out from the audience, faces you, makes eye contact, and speaks directly to you]

"Bob, I appreciate you for working hard to create the draft face book in time for our conference roundtable, and for quickly producing an accurate and attractive final version. This helped all of us get to know each other quickly, and gave us a valuable reference for keeping in touch after the conference ends."

Did you find that you felt appreciated more by each successive version, and that the final version had much more power than the others? If so, you're not alone. In the final version, Susan:

- Invited Bob out in front of the room;
- Spoke to Bob directly, making eye contact;
- Used an "I" message—"Bob, I appreciate you . . ."; and
- Described specifically to Bob what she appreciated and why.

Each of these four actions strengthened the power of Susan's message.

When Susan faced Bob and made eye contact with him as she spoke, she had a strong, personal, and direct contact with him—a much more powerful message than when she spoke about him when he was in the middle of a group of people across the room.

When Susan used an "I" message, "Bob, I appreciate you . . . ," it was clear she was giving a personal message about *her* appreciation of Bob. She described specifically to Bob what she appreciated and why, providing explicit feedback about his work and the positive effect it had on her and the conference attendees. Her detailed comments showed Bob that certain clearly defined aspects of his hard work *had* been noticed, *why* they had been noticed, and *what* had been the positive impact of his work.

Appreciations like this are powerful! And, regrettably, they are so rare in our everyday life that, when people receive one, they are likely to remember it for a long time.

By comparison, think about the phrase "thank you" for a moment. It's an interjection—an exclamation that expresses an emotion. "Thank you" by itself is a formality, conveying little without additional information. The phrase's very vagueness makes it a useful and commonplace superficial response for acknowledging something that someone has done for you. As a result, the power of a "thank you" resides not in the phrase itself but almost entirely in the accompanying circumstances—the inflection of the speaker's voice, her body language, and any additional words she may use to define the "thank you" more precisely.

Now compare saying out loud "Thank you Bob" to saying "Bob, I appreciate you because . . ." or "Bob, I appreciate you for . . ." The appreciation phrases create a direct, specific, and intimate connection between the speaker and the recipient. As a result, you can really only use them face-to-face. Conversely, you can say "Thank you Bob" without looking at him; you can even yell it at Bob as he's walking out the door.

Even in writing, the phrase "Susan, I appreciate you . . ." has more power than a "thank you." Remember this if you are writing to thank someone for her contribution to a conference.

Giving thanks during a conference—when to do it?

When should you give appreciations during a conference? As far as *private* appreciations are concerned, the answer is: *at any appropriate time*! By "private" I don't mean "to one person with no one else around"—for me, a private appreciation is simply spontaneous feedback to one or more individuals, given as closely as possible to the time when the need for the appreciation becomes evident. If there are other folks present, so much the better!

Unfortunately, there's no single "best time" to give *public* appreciations during a conference. The end of the last conference session would be the obvious time to pick—*if* people didn't leave early. And at the start of a conference, attendees don't know who anyone is, they don't know which individuals have done what to make the conference possible, and they haven't yet experienced specific conference events (an inspired impromptu workshop, delicious meals, etc.) that they will value.

I suggest you schedule public appreciations somewhere between half and two thirds of the way through your conference when the maximum number of attendees are likely to be present. Possibilities include: during a conference business meeting, early on during an evening social event, during a "morning news" session, or right before a keynote or other fixed session. If you don't feel you have enough time available in any one session, parcel out your public appreciations over several sessions, tucking one or two in before a presentation starts, or during dessert at a conference dinner. Be sure to schedule enough time for public appreciations to the people who have earned everyone's thanks.

Gifts

If your budget allows it, consider providing small gifts to steering committee members and other people who helped make the conference possible. For a one-time conference you probably won't be able to afford customized gifts, since these are quite expensive when ordered in small quantities. If you're running a repeat conference, you can reduce your unit price for a customized gift by ordering enough units of swag to last for several years. Spare swag makes ideal impromptu tokens of appreciation to the custodian who quickly locates and sets up an extra 50 chairs, the electrician who gets you out of an outlet shortage jam, or the food staff who go the extra mile to provide exquisite meals.

The group spective

Introduction

I have always held some kind of closing session at my conferences. For many years, this session was a loosely facilitated open "wrap-up" discussion of issues brought up throughout the conference. Sometimes people were energized and the discussions were intense; at other times people seemed a bit tired and the conversations were subdued.

Over time, I discovered that each wrap-up session was unique—in format, in directions taken, in energy, and in outcomes. I learned to expect the unexpected. Instead of trying to control what happened, I began to see the value of these unforeseen changes from group to group. I also came to appreciate the value of creating an event that provides appropriate closure for attendees.

These days I call the final conference session a *group spective*, as explained in Chapter 8. I find the group spective to be the most unpredictable session at a peer conference—unpredictable in both form and content. In principle, as the facilitator, I get to choose the format, and guide what results. In practice, what happens is rarely what I expected. Sometimes, with a couple of possible approaches in mind, I'll delay choosing the one I'll use, waiting for inspiration to strike at the last moment. The group process can then take a totally unexpected turn, sometimes in the first few minutes, and I'll discover that the group has a different idea of what should occur.

More than any other session, running a group spective requires the ability to adapt to the unexpected, stay flexible, regroup, and go with the direction of the group's energy as it emerges. The spective may evolve into a general discussion, a push to alter the conference format or schedule, a time when bold initiatives are proposed and/or adopted, a critique of the conference status quo, or any of a hundred different combinations of these and other themes.

Engineering and facilitating a group spective that stays open to these possibilities is a challenge. I recommend reading *Project Retrospectives: A Handbook For Team Reviews,* which, although covering a somewhat different kind of spective, contains much relevant and useful material, and in greater detail than I can give here. Particularly relevant is Chapter 9, where Kerth describes skills, lessons learned, and various facilitation procedures to help a spective facilitator improve her art. What follows are my thoughts on and adaptations of his work that are relevant for a peer conference group spective.

Preparing for a group spective

If this is the first time your conference has been held, start with an activity that allows attendees to discover and express their responses to the conference experience. For a small group, a facilitated informal discussion may be all that's required. You can also use the plus/delta assessment technique described later. Or you may decide to begin by using a go-around (whereby you start with one person in the circle and proceed around the circle) with a list of questions that spark comments and ideas. For a larger group, a fourth alternative is to use affinity grouping to discover topics and ideas for later discussion. If you are planning to have informal discussion during the spective, decide on an appropriate set of questions in advance and create copies for distribution to attendees.

For a repeated conference, I usually design a more targeted group spective. There may be clear questions that the group should spend time on: whether to spend money on a conference website update, feedback on the initiative that was started as a result of last year's conference, incorporating the group as a nonprofit, and so on. Under these circumstances, I like to use a focused discussion. Even when there are known issues to cover, time should be set aside in every group spective so that new ideas and perspectives have an opportunity to emerge.

Whatever group spective design you use, set out a circle (informal discussion or go-around) or horseshoe arrangement (focused discussion or affinity grouping) of chairs for attendees before the session starts. Also arrange for one or two scribes to capture ideas and themes on whiteboards or flip charts. A camera for photographing scribe notes is a time saver. If you are using affinity grouping, you'll need large cards or sticky notes, pens, markers, tape, and a wall or whiteboard to capture and organize ideas.

I find a group spective to be the most challenging session of a peer conference. The session is scheduled at the end of a conference, when it's easy for a facilitator's energy level to be low. Perhaps the most important advice I can give on preparation is to ensure that your schedule allows ample sleep the night before, and some quiet time before the session starts for rest, collecting your thoughts, and preparing for the continual intensity of listening and focus that's required for effective spective facilitation.

Facilitating a group spective

To effectively facilitate a group spective, bear in mind Kerth's first lesson (slightly paraphrased):

> "Manage current topic, flow of ideas, and quality by making sure that everyone knows what is being talked about, and that all are talking about the same thing, by channeling the flow of ideas to keep people focused and to keep abreast of people's moods, and by maintaining a high standard for the quality of the discussion."

To channel the flow of a river of ideas you need to build facilitative banks. If the banks are too high, the flow's path will only reflect your ideas, not those of the group, while if they are too low, the discussion will dissipate without traveling anywhere significant. Effectively facilitating a group discussion requires maintaining a judicious balance between overcontrol and under-control of the conversation, and involves the following actions:

- Making continual decisions, based on how the interplay between group members develops;
- Striving for clarity by summarizing discussion when conversations seem to be drifting or disconnected;
- Gently dissuading irrelevant diversions from the broad courses that the discussion takes; and
- Helping the group reach closure when appropriate or possible.

Effectively satisfying these needs, as the group discussion goes through the phases of generating themes, exploring and clarifying them, and then turning them into plans and future actions, is extremely challenging. A good facilitator maintains focused listening to the group conversation, allowing careful attention and appropriate responses to the dynamics of attendee interactions.

As Kerth points out, books will only get you part of the way to developing skill at this work. Studying with teachers, and taking advantage of opportunities to improve your interpersonal skills will bring you further along the path. Above all, practicing facilitation with sufficient courage to trust your intuition, try new approaches, and remain comfortable with the failures that inevitably occur will bring you ever closer toward the goal of becoming a skilled facilitator.

Group spective activities

The remainder of this section describes some activities that you can use in your group spective:

- Informal discussion
- Plus/delta quick evaluation
- Go-around (starting with one person, and going around the circle with everyone taking a turn)
- Affinity grouping
- Focused discussion

Table 25.4 summarizes my suggestions for the activities to use, based on the size of the conference and whether it is being held for the first time or repeated.

TABLE 25.4 • Suggestions for Group Spective Activities

	FIRST-TIME CONFERENCE	REPEATED CONFERENCE
Small (less than ~30 attendees)	Informal discussion, plus/delta, or go-around plus informal discussion	Focused discussion, plus/delta, or go-around plus informal discussion
Large (more than ~30 attendees)	If there's clear energy for future work, affinity grouping, otherwise plus/delta or go-around plus informal discussion	Focused discussion, plus/delta, or affinity grouping

Don't agonize about which approach(es) to choose. What's ultimately important is that you provide a place and time for people to reflect, share, discuss, and perhaps decide on future projects and activities. You'll find that the conference has already prepared the way for an atmosphere where attendees are open for this work.

When to use informal discussion

Informal discussion can be used alone, or following a go-around. Even if informal discussion is not the first activity used at your spective, it usually becomes a part of the session at some point. So, expect informal discussion, and be prepared for the challenging task of facilitating it.

At a small leisurely conference, an initial informal discussion may be all you need to start your group spective, and, at a one-day conference, a brief informal discussion may be the only activity you can squeeze in.

However, because informal discussion is a meeting style that is more comfortable for extroverts, there's a likelihood that introvert attendees will not initially contribute. Only when the session is long enough for introverts to build well-formed conclusions are they likely to speak out. So, if you have more than 30 participants, or have enough time, start your group spective with a plus/delta, go-around, affinity grouping exercise, or focused discussion—formats that provide people more of an equal opportunity to speak.

Facilitating informal discussion

To begin informal discussion, I like to hand out a brief set of questions that get attendees thinking. I include open-ended questions that both invite reflection on what has happened at the conference and also encourage thinking about possibilities for the future. I avoid questions that emphasize problem solving or that concentrate on conference subject-specific issues.

Here are some of the questions I have used over the years:

- What stood out for you at our conference?
- Where were you surprised?
- Where were you challenged?
- What's emerging here for you?
- What do we want to do in the future?
- What opportunities do you see for us?
- What can we do that we haven't thought of yet?
- Would you like to participate in a conference like this again?
- What worked for you that you'd like to continue?
- What would you like to do differently?
- What would you like to change in our next conference?
- How can we support each other in taking the next steps?
- What unique contribution can you make?
- What are the next levels of thinking and activities we want or need to do?
- How do you see us moving forward? What are you willing to do to help make this happen?

Note that many of these questions inquire about the same topic in different ways. Some are concrete, while some invite wide-ranging responses. Think about your attendees; what kinds of questions will make sense to them and spark their interest? If you're not sure, include a range of questions that you think will cover the personalities of the people present.

Create a list of three to five questions that work for your attendees and distribute them at the start of the session. Ask them to think about the questions for a few minutes. Then ask for responses, and facilitate the ensuing discussion. Have one or two scribes capture the ideas expressed on flip charts or whiteboards.

Plus/delta

Plus/delta is a simple review tool that allows conferees to quickly identify what went well and what could be improved. Plus/delta not only provides an evaluation of the conference, but also an opportunity to share and compare experiences, so it is useful even if the conference is a one-time event.

To do a plus/delta evaluation, create two columns on a flip chart or whiteboard, headed with the symbols "+" and "Δ" as shown in Figure 25.4.

I like to brainstorm comments first, before opening them up for discussion. Ask participants for positive comments and list them under the plus column. Next, ask for ways in which the

FIGURE 25.4 · Plus/delta Chart

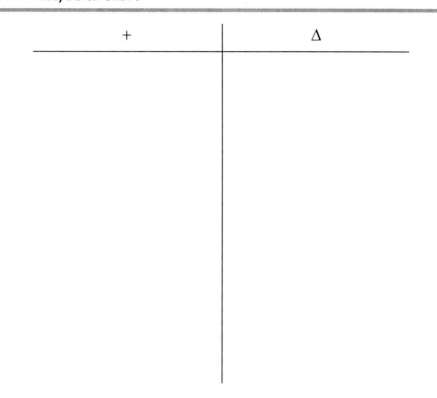

conference could be improved and list them in the delta column. The resulting lists can then be used as a basis for discussion and comments about the group's conference experience.

Using a go-around

One way to ensure that everyone has a chance to speak is to use a go-around, a format similar to the roundtable that starts the conference. A go-around works well with a group of up to about 30, or for a first-time conference when you feel uncertain about the direction the spective may take. If you start with a go-around, make your spective session long enough to allow ample time for discussion after everyone has had a chance to speak. Announce a suggested time limit for each person's sharing, and use a timer to help people keep to it.

Begin a go-around in the same way as the informal discussion format—distribute a list of priming questions and give attendees a few minutes to think about how they'd like to respond. Then, either ask for a volunteer to start sharing, or pick someone. Have one or two scribes capture the ideas expressed, on flip charts or whiteboards. People continue to share, in turn around the circle, until everyone has spoken (or passed). Next summarize the ideas and themes that have emerged and developed. Then facilitate an informal discussion, as described above.

Letting go in a go-around

In my experience, when using a go-around format, the first person to speak can have a significant influence on the subsequent sharing round the circle. His brevity, tone, and emphasis tend to be picked up and echoed by others, in the same way that a boat's subsequent track on a river can, in places, be greatly influenced by a minor current at one crucial spot.

I used to worry that this could pose a potential problem—what if the first person who spoke had little to say, or was very negative about the conference?—and I would pick someone to start who I thought would provide a "good" model of how to share at the go-around.

My eyes were opened at a conference where I thought we had, over the years, arrived at a close-to-perfect schedule. At the group spective, I casually chose the attendee sitting next to me to start the go-around sharing—and listened in dismay as he offered criticisms and made pointed suggestions for improvement. The overall tenor of his remarks was quite negative. Other attendees followed his lead, refining his critique and adding their own judgments. Despite my initial consternation, as I listened I realized that good ideas were being expressed, ideas that could well improve the conference format in ways we hadn't considered. Slowly, my excitement about these new possibilities

overcame my fear of the critical tone of the spective.

During the discussion that followed, it became clear that attendees were also pumped up about these potential format changes. Many felt these could make an already great conference even better. Rather than make spot decisions during the spective, we ended up using an online survey over the next couple of weeks to consider and compare the proposed scheduling alternatives.

At the following year's conference, we incorporated several of the changes suggested at the spective. There was wide agreement that the new design was better than anything we had done before.

It's scary to let go, to let the unexpected happen. It's hard to find the courage to watch without interfering, as an unexpected event leads to a host of consequences. As we sit in our boat, formerly safely floating down the conference river, but now suddenly veering alarmingly toward an indistinct muddy bank, most of us have a natural tendency to want to grab a paddle and attempt to wrest the craft back into the middle of the flow. Yet, if we surrender to the current, using our facilitation paddle merely to moderate our speed and make fine course corrections, we may find that the bank, once we reach it, is full of unexpected delights and possibilities.

Affinity grouping

Affinity grouping is an activity you can use to discover and share ideas that arise from the conference and group them into categories, so they can be organized and then discussed. It's a process that allows and encourages every attendee to participate, sparks creativity as people listen to others' ideas, generates a substantial list of ideas, and provides a way to consensually categorize the idea list.

I use affinity grouping at large conferences that are repeated or where it's clear there's energy for future activities. This is because affinity grouping works best when there's a clear topic for the session. To help decide whether affinity grouping is appropriate, ask yourself whether the focus question *"What do we want to do in the future?"* seems likely to be the key starting point for most attendees. At a first-time conference, such a question can assume too much and it's usually better to begin with an initial informal discussion or go-around. If it becomes clear that there's plenty of interest in future activities, you can switch to affinity grouping.

To use this technique, follow these steps, which are covered in more detail below:

- Describe the affinity grouping focus question, process, and working assumptions.
- Have attendees brainstorm ideas individually.
- Form attendees into groups.
- Discuss ideas in groups and put distinct ideas on cards.
  - Post clearest and different ideas on wall for entire group to view.
  - Sort ideas into clusters.
  - Create names for clusters.
  - Discuss next steps and implementation.

Describe the affinity grouping focus question, process, and working assumptions.

Start your affinity grouping exercise by supplying a focus question. *"What do we want to do in the future?"* avoids naming a specific time frame. If your peer conference is about a topic on which action is limited by time or other considerations, you may want to make your question more specific. Write the focus question on a flip chart sheet or whiteboard so everyone can see it.

Next, briefly describe the affinity grouping process, saying something like this:

> *"Here's an outline of how affinity grouping works. First, we'll brainstorm responses to the focus question individually, and write them onto cards. Next we'll work in small groups to share our ideas with others. Then we'll share our work with the*

entire group, putting our idea cards up on the wall, and consensually categorizing them. Finally we'll reflect on what we've created and discuss next steps and implementation. Any questions?"

Answer questions, and then go over the working assumptions for the session:

"There are three working assumptions I'd like us all to keep in mind for this exercise. One: There are no wrong answers. *Two:* We all have something to contribute. *Three:* Everyone will have the opportunity to hear and be heard."

Have attendees brainstorm ideas individually.

Give each attendee a few 5 × 8 or similar sized cards, and say:

"Please take a few minutes to write down your responses to the focus question. Aim for between five and ten responses. Concentrate on capturing your ideas; don't worry about getting them expressed precisely."

Give a minute's warning when most people have finished writing. Then, ask them to add a star to their three best ideas, however they define "best."

Form attendees into groups.

At this point, divide attendees into random, diverse groups. My suggestions for group number and size are given in Table 25.5. Ask participants from the same organization to join different groups, and have each group sit separately, so its members can talk without disturbing other groups. If you create groups of 8 or more people, consider choosing a facilitator for each group.

TABLE 25.5 • Affinity Grouping Suggested Number and Size of Groups, and Ideas Per Group

NUMBER OF ATTENDEES	NUMBER OF GROUPS	SIZE OF EACH GROUP	IDEAS (CARDS) PER GROUP
20	6	3–4	4–6
40	7	5–6	5–7
60	8	7–8	5–7
80	8	10	5–7
100	8	12–13	6–8

Discuss ideas in groups and put distinct ideas on cards.

Once the groups are settled, hand out 10 cards or large sticky notes to each group and say:

> *"For the next 15 minutes or so, I'd like your group to discuss all the ideas you've come up with. Go around the group in turn, sharing one idea at a time. Start with your starred ideas, and use the rest as needed. We'd like to get [number from Table 25.5] distinct ideas from each group. As you decide on each idea, express it in a short, specific phrase of three to six words and write it in large, clear, bold letters on a new card. When we've finished, your ideas will be shared with the entire group."*

Monitor the groups as they discuss their ideas, checking that everyone is participating and that groups don't get stuck discussing one idea. Periodically remind them how much time they have left. Then do the following:

Post clearest ideas on wall for entire group to view.

When the discussions subside, ask each group to select two or three of their "clearest" ideas. Give the groups a minute or two to make their selection. Have the groups congregate around the wall or whiteboard that will be used to display and categorize the ideas chosen. Ask for the "clearest" cards, shuffle them, read them aloud, and place them randomly on the wall.

When the cards have been posted, give the entire group an opportunity to ask questions that *clarify* what a card's contents mean. If needed, have the card writer explain the idea on the card. Avoid discussion on the *merit* of any idea.

Post different ideas on wall for entire group to view.

Now ask each group to briefly discuss and select one or two of their cards that contain an idea that is different from those that have been posted. Shuffle the cards, read them out, and add them to the wall. Again, give attendees a chance to ask questions to clarify the ideas on these cards.

Sort ideas into clusters.

To start the process of clustering the displayed ideas into categories, say:

> *"Now it's time to group these ideas into categories. We'll do this by first looking for pairs of ideas that have something in common. If you don't agree with this pairing, say so and we'll talk about it.*
>> *Who wants to pick a pair?"*

As each pair is chosen, place the named cards next to each other and draw a common symbol (square, circle, triangle, cross, check mark, star, etc.) on both cards. Ask for more pairs, group the chosen cards together, and add a unique symbol to each new cluster. In what follows, encourage people to refer to a set by its symbol, rather than by an idea in the cluster. This helps to prevent the premature naming of idea clusters.

After several sets of ideas have been paired, say:

> *"If you see other cards that can be added to the existing clusters, feel free to suggest them from now on."*

Continue to create idea clusters with the cards on the wall, until each of the cards is in a set. If an idea is significantly different from the rest, put it in its own cluster.

Once all the cards on the wall are in sets, ask the groups to give you their remaining cards that don't fit the existing clusters. Read these cards out, one at a time, discuss them and either create a new cluster or add it to an existing one. Usually, at this point, you'll have between six and a dozen clusters identified.

Finally, ask the groups to mark their remaining cards with the symbol of the cluster they should be in. Add these cards to the appropriate sets on the wall.

Rearrange the clusters into adjacent columns, one column for each cluster.

Create names for clusters.

Don't be in a hurry to name each set of idea cards. You're looking for a group consensus that captures what the cluster is about, with the cluster name providing, in three to six words, a direction or answer to the focus question.

Start with the largest cluster, and read out aloud all of its cards. Ask attendees to pick key words to describe the cluster. Then, ask for name suggestions. Cluster names are typically a few words, for example, "develop website" or "plan follow-up conference." Look and ask for group agreement. When you've got it, write the cluster name on a card placed at the top of the cluster column.

Repeat this procedure for all clusters. If you have many or time is short, you can assign the job of naming a cluster to each of your original groups. When a group finishes, give them another one to name until all the clusters have names. If you use this small group approach, when all clusters have been named, check each name for clarity with the entire group of attendees. If you don't find overall consensus for a cluster's name, repeat the process for the cluster with everyone's involvement.

Once all the clusters are named, document your work. A clear photograph of the completed, named clusters is the fastest way to do this. If a camera isn't available, have a volunteer scribe the columns of ideas. Make copies, and distribute them to attendees as quickly as possible, and definitely before the spective is over.

Discuss next steps and implementation.

When is the best time to discuss action on the ideas that have flowered during this session? Now! The ideas are fresh, and the attendees are maximally invested in what they have co-created. It's time to discuss next steps, and to build and staff a framework for action. Have a scribe available to document the ideas and commitments generated during this final step.

You might say something like this:

> *"We've done some great work here! There's one more vital step. Let's discuss possible next steps and implementation of these ideas. First, I'm going to read them all out."*

Read out all the cluster names, with a pause between each idea. Next, say:

> *"Now, let's have a discussion that concentrates on three aspects of these ideas:*
> * *Priorities: Which ideas are most and least important?*
> * *Ease of implementation: What kind of effort is needed for implementation?*
> * *Next steps: What next steps could we take?"*

Facilitate a short discussion on these topics. Besides helping to make attendees' opinions explicit, this discussion will also provide information on the energy available for work on the ideas expressed as well as specific attendees who may be willing to work on next steps.

As direction and energy on particular ideas emerge from the discussion, look for a consensus on what should be done next, and ask for volunteers to staff a small committee that will work on the next steps. Agree on what will be accomplished, and a basic timeframe for the work. Don't overrecruit volunteers—it's likely that one or more ideas may reflect longer term goals that attendees are either unwilling or unable to work on at this time.

Focused discussion

One of my favorite formats for a group spective at a repeated conference is the *focused discussion*. Sometimes this term is used to describe a meeting format where discussion occurs between a small number of people seated in a circle, with the rest of the attendees arranged around them, listening. I use a modified version, where the discussion group is limited to three or four people at any one moment, but attendees can join the discussion whenever they have something to say.

When a more targeted group spective is appropriate, a focused discussion works well as the sole activity during the session. The advantage of a focused discussion over informal discussion is that it greatly reduces the cross-conversations that frequently occur when many people want to respond or comment on something that's been said. And it manages this feat without limiting discussion to a few voluble people, as it provides all attendees an equal opportunity to contribute.

To hold a focused discussion, have attendees sit in a horseshoe arrangement of chairs. At the open mouth of the horseshoe, place four or five chairs in a row, as shown in Figure 25.5.

Plan a potential meeting agenda ahead of time. Perhaps attendees have already talked about holding the conference again, or certain ideas have surfaced with energy during the conference, or people just want to have a general discussion on how the conference has gone and what might happen next.

FIGURE 25.5 • Chair Layout for a Focused Discussion Session

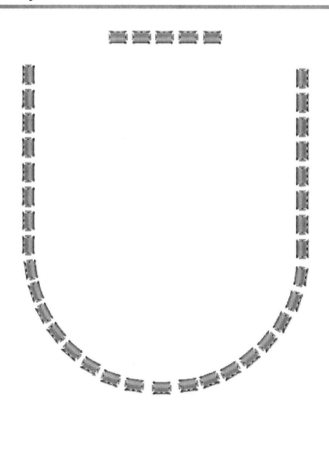

Have someone scribing session notes that will be promptly copied and distributed to attendees.

As facilitator, sit in one of the chairs at the open mouth of the horseshoe and explain how the focused discussion works by saying something like this:

> *"We're about to start a focused discussion. A focused discussion is a facilitated informal discussion, with the difference that, if you want to talk, you must come and sit in one of these chairs next to me. If all the chairs are full and no one has yet spoken, wait a little—otherwise, when you come up, someone sitting here must go back to their chair in the horseshoe. Also, if you're sitting up here and have finished what you have to say, go back to your horseshoe chair. When you're up here, you can talk to someone else in these chairs or the whole group—the choice is yours.*
>
> *I'll facilitate the discussion, and we'll start by discussing a potential agenda. Any questions?"*

Answer questions, outline the potential meeting agenda, and open it up for discussion. You'll probably find that some attendees will want to talk from their chair in the horseshoe. When this happens, gently interrupt and gesture for them to come up and sit next to you. If they've interrupted someone in the front row, steer the conversation back to the folks up front.

Once people get the hang of the focused discussion, everyone's likely to be surprised by how well it works. Participants appreciate how the small group format focuses the discussion, how the contributors change as needed, how simply the front row shows who may talk, and how it's clear when the conversation on a topic has run its course.

Discussing future activities

Be sure to allow time for the group to discuss potential future events and initiatives. It can be a challenge for peer conference facilitators to neutrally solicit participants' desires for follow-up activities. Gently pushing a group to explore future engagements and then respecting the feedback that follows helps to balance the excitement for further engagement with the common reticence to start something new.

Ending the group spective

Make sure that the session scribe notes are photographed or written up and distributed to attendees either before or as soon as possible after the conference ends. If you have scheduled a raffle to entice people to stay until the end of the conference, hold the prize drawing now.

Closure

When your peer conference ends, participants experience an inevitable transition back into their own "real" worlds. *There is no way to avoid this.* Drawing out the ending merely postpones the inevitable. Eventually, the moment comes when people begin to go their separate ways.

> "Is there a fat lady who could sing?"
>
> —*Roy Blount Jr., on Wait, Wait . . . Don't Tell Me!*

I like to give attendees the possibility of some informal time together, if they so desire and their schedule permits. Offering a final meal, which can either be eaten on the premises or boxed for the road, is one way to provide an optional social time for attendees to reflect, share last-minute thoughts, and say their goodbyes.

26 After the Conference

Post-conference tasks

Cleanup

As soon as your conference is over, have your cleanup crew go to work. Make sure you remove any temporary signage you put up before the conference, and return site furniture and equipment to their original locations. Even if you're not contractually obligated to do so, I suggest you tidy up any serious messes that attendees have left, leaving the conference site a little neater than expected. Remember to return any rental items before you leave.

Solicit online evaluations

If you've given attendees the option of evaluating the conference online, promptly send out an email to them with a link to the survey, and a clear deadline date for their feedback (usually a week after the conference ends). Send out a final reminder a couple of days before the deadline.

Share conference evaluations with organizers—and with attendees!

Attendee evaluations are of interest to everyone, not just the conference organizers. It's fine to supply steering committee members with more detail than the summary generated for attendees, but don't ignore the latter; I've learned that many attendees are interested in others' conference experience.

Check in with steering committee members

Contact steering committee members soon after the conference. Share your impressions and encourage additional responses. Ask for feedback on how members handled their specific responsibilities, what worked and what didn't, and what changes they would make in the light of their recent experience.

If you held a vendor exhibit, ask the vendor coordinator for a brief report on her follow-up with vendors.

Document steering committee feedback in your conference archive.

Tie up financial loose ends

Once the conference is over, you may have a few bills left to pay. Follow up on any outstanding bills and settle them immediately. Private schools sometimes take their time to submit a bill for your use of the facility; a polite request for a final reckoning may be needed.

If there are any unpaid conference registrations, send written reminders immediately after the conference, including a date by when payment must be received. I recommend you add interest terms to your reminder, perhaps 1 percent per month, as this can help speed payment. Follow up regularly on any missing payments. If you have not been paid within a few months of the conference, write off the receivable as a bad debt.

If you are paying conference organizers a portion of any conference profit, once all other financial transactions are complete, calculate and pay the appropriate distributions.

Finally, draw up financial statements for the conference. Distribute them to steering committee members. You may also want to post them on the conference wiki or website. Include a narrative providing a succinct summary and explaining any unusual income or expense lines.

Preparing for the next conference

By the end of your conference you'll probably know if you're going to hold the event again. You can save yourself significant work by creating an archive of important conference documents and writing comprehensive notes on issues, problems, and changes that you want to tackle for the next conference. Don't put off these tasks! I find that conference impressions that seemed clear and sharp on the journey home fade much faster than I expect. If my hands and mind are free, I like to write up my notes on the plane or train home. Otherwise, I'll record my thoughts the next day and add them to electronic and paper archives of conference documents and materials.

You should also promptly review conference evaluations. If you are using an online survey, you'll need to wait until the survey deadline you've given attendees. But don't wait a week to record the rest of your conference impressions. Get them recorded right away, and then go back and supplement them with the feedback from the evaluations once they're available.

Here's a list of items to document and archive before memory fades:

- Conference schedule, including locations used for each session
- Attendee registration database
- Site map, showing buildings and rooms used during the conference
- Telephone/Internet/network/wiki access instructions
- Conference site handouts (accommodations, local resources, security, contact numbers, facility access)
- Subcontractor/rental details and contact information
- Conference logbook
- Conference financial statements
- Roundtable topics
- All proposed peer session topics (not just the ones that were held)
- Peer session topics that could not be held due to lack of relevant experience or expertise
- Proposed potential topics/presenters for future fixed sessions
- Site and process glitches; how to avoid them next time
- Session lengths: too short, too long, about right?
- Session schedule details (when scheduled, session order) that worked/ didn't work well; how to improve
- Business meeting notes, decisions
- Vendor coordinator report
- Group spective notes, focus question, responses, proposed activities, action items, resulting committees, timeframes

It's easy to let slide the work of creating a comprehensive conference archive, especially after the letdown in energy you may feel once the conference is over. However, I can assure you that you'll be very glad you put in the effort the next time the conference is held!

CHAPTER 27 Final Words

Thank you for reading to the end of my book. I appreciate you for the time you spent with me.

Now it's time for you to return to your world to put what you've learned to work.

I hope you're excited about the possibility of creating a peer conference around your interest, your passion. Perhaps you're wondering if you can pull it off, not knowing what quite to expect, or feeling a bit overwhelmed.

> "We can lick gravity, but sometimes the paperwork is overwhelming."
>
> —*Wernher von Braun. Chicago Sun Times, July 10, 1958*

Such thoughts and feelings are normal, so don't let them stand in your way! Instead:

- Reach out *now* to the people who will help you make your peer conference a reality. You don't have to go it alone—work together with your peers right from the start.
- Keep in mind that peer conferences are simple human endeavors, and like all social ventures they are messy at times. You can't completely avoid uncertainty, so embrace it! When you do, you will learn something useful.
- Let your peers show up in all their rich complexity of wants, hopes, experiences, personalities, and intuitions. Connect via your common passion.
- And, remember to enjoy yourself along the way!

Wernher von Braun was right, we *can* lick gravity. All we have to do is jump.

The Four Freedoms[1]

In an empowering environment, everyone has the following freedoms:

1. You have the freedom to talk about the way you see things, rather than the way others want you to see.

2. You have the freedom to ask about anything puzzling.

3. You have the freedom to talk about whatever is coming up for you.

4. You have the freedom to say that you don't really feel you have one or more of the preceding three freedoms.

These four freedoms are simple but effective. It is our hope that this conference will provide you with such an empowering environment. You can help us by exercising your four freedoms while we are together.

---

[1] This handout is derived from Virginia Satir's well-known "Five Freedoms," further refined by Gerald Weinberg & Donald Gause in "Exploring Requirements: Quality Before Design" and Norman Kerth in "Project Retrospectives."

Download available at www.conferencesthatwork.com.

Peer Session
Sign-up Sheet

Peer Session Topic: _____

_____

_____

_____	_____
_____	_____
_____	_____
_____	_____
_____	_____
_____	_____
_____	_____
_____	_____
_____	_____
_____	_____
_____	_____
_____	_____

Please . . .

. . . place an (**F**) next to your name to indicate you'd be willing to *facilitate* the group.

. . . place an (**E**) next to your name to indicate you have some *experience* or *expertise* in the peer session's topic.

. . . place a (**P**) next to your name to indicate you'd be prepared to be a *presenter* or *panelist* for the group.

. . . place an (**S**) next to your name to indicate you'd be prepared to *scribe* for the group.

Also, indicate your level of interest in the topic by placing the number **1**—*low*, **2**—*medium*, or **3**—*high* next to your name.

Download available at www.conferencesthatwork.com.

Peer Session
Sign-up Instructions

Please indicate your level of interest in the topic by writing the number **1**—low interest, **2**—medium interest, or **3**—high interest next to your name.

Also . . .

. . . place an (**F**) next to your name to indicate you'd be willing to facilitate the session.

. . . place an (**E**) next to your name to indicate you have some knowledge or expertise in the peer session's topic.

. . . place a (**P**) next to your name to indicate you'd be prepared to be a presenter or panelist for the session.

. . . place an (**S**) next to your name to indicate you'd be prepared to scribe for the session.

Peer Session
Primer Handout

A peer session primer

What is a peer session?

Peer sessions are the core sessions at a peer conference. They provide a flexible, yet somewhat structured, method for conferees to share experience and expertise on subjects of mutual interest. *Attendees determine topics for peer sessions* during the first day of the conference. The typical peer session has five to fifteen participants and lasts around an hour. Peer sessions are often discussion centered, but sometimes a presentation or panel format is more appropriate. You'll be able to tell what's going to work for you.

How do I know that a peer session will provide useful information to me?

Experience has shown that for a peer session to work well, it's important that there be one or more participants who have some knowledge or experience in the topic chosen. Occasionally, no expertise is available, and the peer session becomes a disappointment to all involved. Obviously, there are no guarantees that every peer session will be a success. *You can help! If you have expertise in or experience with a peer session's topic, please consider volunteering to facilitate, or participate in, the group. Our conference will work best when we support each other.*

Who runs a peer session?

Each peer session needs a *facilitator* and a *scribe*.

Ideally the facilitator has some knowledge or experience of the topic, though this is not required. The facilitator is responsible for finding a scribe if no one has yet volunteered, keeping the group focused on the topic, ensuring the session runs smoothly, and making sure that all present have an appropriate chance to contribute and ask questions.

The scribe is responsible for creating a list of attendees and a summary of the meeting in computer readable form. It's important to take notes during the meeting, since experience has

---

Download available at www.conferencesthatwork.com.

shown that memories quickly fade. Resources mentioned at the meeting should be noted in the summary. Please give the summary to the conference coordinator *before* the conference is over!

How are peer session topics, facilitators, and scribes chosen?

You *choose peer session topics!* On the first day of the conference you'll be told the location of the *topic sign-up sheets*. First you'll be given time to propose possible peer session topics. Add as many as you want as headings on the blank topic sheets. When everyone has proposed topics you'll be invited to the topic boards again. You may see topics that interest you. If so, add your name to the list under the topic description. Sign up for as many topics as interest you. Indicate your level of interest in the topic by writing the number **1**—low interest, **2**—medium interest, or **3**—high interest next to your name. In addition, place an:

(F) next to your name to indicate you'd be willing to facilitate the session.

(E) next to your name to indicate you have some expertise on or experience with the peer session's topic.

(P) next to your name if you're willing to be a presenter or panelist.

(S) next to your name to indicate you'd be prepared to scribe for the session.

If you have some facilitation experience, or knowledge or expertise in the peer session's topic, please consider volunteering as a facilitator for the group. Multiple offers of facilitation in a group are very helpful to the steering committee when determining the final peer sessions, because sometimes a schedule conflict prevents volunteers from facilitating. We greatly appreciate offers to scribe for peer sessions, and do our best to share the scribing load.

Once topic sheets are complete, a small group of attendees will pick dominant topics (sometimes combining several themes), find facilitators and scribes, and schedule peer session tracks so that two potentially conflicting groups don't meet at the same time. Feel free to volunteer to help with this process, which leads to a set of peer sessions well tuned to conferees' needs.

Peer Session
Facilitation Handout

Peer session facilitation

What's involved in facilitating a peer session

Each peer session needs a *facilitator*.

Ideally the facilitator has some knowledge or experience of the topic, *but this is not required*. The facilitator is responsible for finding a scribe if no one has yet volunteered, keeping the group focused on the topic, ensuring the session runs smoothly, and making sure that everyone has an appropriate chance to contribute and ask questions.

Peer session facilitation—step by step

- Start on time.
- Make sure there's a scribe for the peer session; ask for a volunteer if no one has yet volunteered.
- Title and circulate the peer session attendance sheet so the scribe can then record who is present.
- If the peer session is a presentation or panel, have the presenter(s) [which may be you] go ahead, and moderate subsequent questions and discussion.
- If a presentation format isn't appropriate (this is generally the case):
  - use a *quick* go-around the group (30–60 seconds per person) to home in on what group members want to discuss, and any relevant experience they possess.
  - briefly summarize the go-around and get a quick consensus on what will be discussed.
  - moderate the ensuing discussion.
- End on time.

Download available at www.conferencesthatwork.com.

Peer session facilitation—tips

Facilitation is an art not a science. Here are some tips that may help you.

- Keep a go-around short! Don't spend more than 25 percent of your time on a go-around.
- Note the themes brought up in the go-around and make time for each of them as appropriate.
- Have your scribe or another volunteer use a classroom whiteboard or flip chart to keep track of ideas if necessary.
- Model the way you'd like to see the group interact. People will follow your lead.
- Keep the peer session on-topic. If the topic wanders, check to see if the group wants to go there.
- If you have contributions to the group discussion, that's fine. But be careful: As facilitator, it's easy to monopolize the conversation.
- Don't allow people to monopolize the discussion. Ensure all who wish to contribute can. It's OK to gently interrupt someone who's talking too much— that's your job!
- Encourage participation. Watch for quiet attendees and check whether they have something to say or questions to ask.

On vendor representatives attending peer sessions
[omit this section if you are not holding a vendor exhibit]

Sometimes vendor representatives wish to attend peer sessions. This can be useful if, for example, the peer session is about a specific product and an expert vendor representative is available. Otherwise it's appropriate to check whether the vendor representative's presence is OK with the other attendees. I generally ask a vendor representative to sit quietly and observe, and only provide input if asked.

Roundtable
Questions Card

I recommend using 5 × 8 cards.

Roundtable Questions

How did I get here?

What would I like to have happen?

What experience or expertise do I have that others might find useful?

Download available at www.conferencesthatwork.com.

Peer Session Attendance Sheet
(no permissions)

Peer Session Topic: _____
_____
_____

Date _____   Scribe _____

Attendees

_____   _____
_____   _____
_____   _____
_____   _____
_____   _____
_____   _____
_____   _____
_____   _____
_____   _____
_____   _____
_____   _____
_____   _____
_____   _____
_____   _____
_____   _____
_____   _____
_____   _____
_____   _____
_____   _____
_____   _____
_____   _____
_____   _____
_____   _____

Download available at www.conferencesthatwork.com.

Peer Session Attendance Sheet
(with permissions)

Peer Session Topic: _____
_____
_____

Date _____ **Scribe** _____

Attendees

	Permissions			Permissions	
	Conf.	World		Conf.	World
_____	☐	☐	_____	☐	☐
_____	☐	☐	_____	☐	☐
_____	☐	☐	_____	☐	☐
_____	☐	☐	_____	☐	☐
_____	☐	☐	_____	☐	☐
_____	☐	☐	_____	☐	☐
_____	☐	☐	_____	☐	☐
_____	☐	☐	_____	☐	☐
_____	☐	☐	_____	☐	☐
_____	☐	☐	_____	☐	☐
_____	☐	☐	_____	☐	☐
_____	☐	☐	_____	☐	☐
_____	☐	☐	_____	☐	☐
_____	☐	☐	_____	☐	☐
_____	☐	☐	_____	☐	☐

Circulate this sheet at the start of the session to obtain attendee names.

Circulate it again at the end of the session. Check both boxes next to your name if you don't mind sharing the session recording with anyone. Check only the first box if you do not want the session recording shared outside the attendees at this conference. If you do not want the recording of this session shared with anyone who was not present at the session, leave both checkboxes blank.

APPENDIX 9 Personal Introspective Questions Card

I recommend using 5 × 8 cards.

Personal introspective questions

What do I want to have happen?

What is the current situation?

What am I willing to do?

How will I know when it happens?

Where and how will I get support?

Download available at www.conferencesthatwork.com.

323

NUMBER OF CHAIRS

	30	35	40	45	50	55	60	65	70	75	80	85	90	95	100
24	34	37	41	44	47	50	53	56	60	63	66	69	72	76	79
26	36	39	43	46	50	53	57	60	64	67	70	74	77	81	84
28	38	41	45	49	53	56	60	64	67	71	75	79	82	86	90
30	40	44	48	51	55	59	63	67	71	75	79	83	87	91	95
32	41	46	50	54	58	63	67	71	75	80	84	88	92	97	101
34	43	48	52	57	61	66	70	75	79	84	88	93	97	102	106
36	45	50	55	59	64	69	74	78	83	88	93	97	102	107	112
38	47	52	57	62	67	72	77	82	87	92	97	102	107	112	117
40	49	54	59	64	70	75	80	86	91	96	102	107	112	118	123
42	50	56	62	67	73	78	84	89	95	101	106	112	117	123	128
44	52	58	64	70	76	81	87	93	99	105	111	116	122	128	134
46	54	60	66	72	78	84	91	97	103	109	115	121	127	133	139
48	56	62	69	75	81	88	94	100	107	113	119	126	132	139	145

SEAT WIDTH (inches)

The above table shows the required minimum room dimensions, in feet, when using a circle of chairs with four gaps of six feet between the circle and the walls of the room on all sides.

Example: If the seat width of your chairs is 28 inches, and you are expecting 45 attendees, you will need a room that is at least 49-feet square.

Download available at www.conferencesthatwork.com.

Sample Conference Evaluation
Form for Fixed Sessions

edACCESS 2006
Conference Evaluation Form—Fixed Sessions

Thank you in advance for filling out this form. We sincerely hope that this conference has been a valuable use of your time. Please feel free to make any comments that would make our next conference more helpful to you and your institution. Please rate the following conference items and activities in terms of their usefulness to you:

Session/Item	High	Moderate	Low	No Opinion	Comment
Pre-Conference Mailings/Wiki	☐	☐	☐	☐	_____
					_____
Roundtable Discussion	☐	☐	☐	☐	_____
					_____
					_____
Keynote: The New Read/Write Web	☐	☐	☐	☐	_____
					_____
					_____
Online Social Networking Tools	☐	☐	☐	☐	_____
					_____
					_____
Course Management Systems	☐	☐	☐	☐	_____
					_____
					_____

Download available at www.conferencesthatwork.com.

Wireless Security ☐ ☐ ☐ ☐ _____

Birds of a Feather ☐ ☐ ☐ ☐ _____

Vendor Presentations ☐ ☐ ☐ ☐ _____

edACCESS Business Meeting ☐ ☐ ☐ ☐ _____

Personal Introspective ☐ ☐ ☐ ☐ _____

Group Spective ☐ ☐ ☐ ☐ _____

Informal Discussions ☐ ☐ ☐ ☐ _____

Other: ☐ ☐ ☐ ☐ _____

Which session or topic was most useful to you? Why?

Which session or topic was least useful to you? Why?

What topic(s) were not discussed that you would like to have discussed?

_____

_____

_____

Our main goal and purpose of this conference was to address various computing issues from the viewpoint of very small schools. Do you feel that we were successful in this? Why or why not?

_____

_____

_____

What did you learn at this conference that will assist you and your institution?

_____

_____

_____

What could we do better?

_____

_____

_____

What one thing would you change?

_____

_____

_____

What could we do at future edACCESS conferences that we don't do now?

_____

_____

_____

Would you attend a future conference of this type? Why or why not?

_____

_____

_____

Do you have any comments on the facilities, meals, etc.?

_____

_____

_____

Additional comments (feel free to include new directions/programs/event suggestions for edACCESS):

_____

_____

_____

(Optional) **Name:** _____   **Institution:** _____

Sample Conference Evaluation Form for Peer Sessions

edACCESS 2006
Conference Evaluation Form—Peer Sessions

Thank you in advance for filling out this form. We sincerely hope that this conference has been a valuable use of your time. Please feel free to make any comments that would make our next conference more helpful to you and your institution. Please rate the following conference items and activities in terms of their usefulness to you:

Session/Item	High	Moderate	Low	No Opinion	Comment
Blogging	☐	☐	☐	☐	_____
Disaster Planning	☐	☐	☐	☐	_____
VOIP	☐	☐	☐	☐	_____
Technology Planning	☐	☐	☐	☐	_____
Podcasting	☐	☐	☐	☐	_____
Backup Strategies	☐	☐	☐	☐	_____
Digital Asset Management	☐	☐	☐	☐	_____
Blackbaud Education Edge	☐	☐	☐	☐	_____
Moodle	☐	☐	☐	☐	_____

Download available at www.conferencesthatwork.com.

Streaming Media	☐	☐	☐	☐	_____
"Getting Things Done"	☐	☐	☐	☐	_____
Faculty Professional Development	☐	☐	☐	☐	_____
Smartboard vs. Tablets	☐	☐	☐	☐	_____
First Class vs. Exchange	☐	☐	☐	☐	_____
Digital Language Labs	☐	☐	☐	☐	_____
Wireless Strategies	☐	☐	☐	☐	_____
Wired Authentication with 802.1X	☐	☐	☐	☐	_____
Wikis	☐	☐	☐	☐	_____
Imaging Options w/Symantec Ghost	☐	☐	☐	☐	_____

Peer Session Comments _____

_____

_____

(Optional) **Name:** _____ **Institution:** _____

Notes

1. What Is a Conference?

5 *World Cafe:* http://www.theworldcafe.com.

5 *The Art of Hosting:* http://www.artofhosting. org.

5 *Everyday Democracy:* http://www.everyday-democracy.org.

8 *Industry Role in Medical Meeting Decried:* Washington Post, May 26, 2002, p. A10 or http://www.washingtonpost.com/ac2/ wp-dyn?pagename=article&contentId= A11056-2002May25.

2. What Are Conferences For?

18 *Future Search:* http://www.futuresearch.net.

3. What's Wrong with Traditional Conferences?

29 *Elinor Glyn: Beginning and Ending Your Story,* http://www.publishingcentral.com/articles/ beginning-and-ending-a-story.html.

33 *Meetings and Conventions Magazine:* August 2008 issue, pp. 66 and 70.

33 *Clay Shirky: A Group Is Its Own Worst Enemy,* speech at O'Reilly Emerging Technology Conference, April, 2003, http://www.shirky. com/writings/group_enemy.html.

36 *Gordon Research Conferences:* http://www. grc.org/history.aspx.

4. Reengineering the Conference

41 *Kevin Kelly: The Technium,* The Bottom Is Not Enough, http://www.kk.org/thetechnium/.

42 *Christopher Allen:* The Dunbar Number as a Limit to Group Sizes, http://www.lifewith alacrity.com/2004/03/the_dunbar_numb.html.

51 *Harrison Owen: Open Space Technology,* Berrett-Koehler, 1997.

5. The Peer Conference Alternative

64 *Etienne Wenger:* http://ewenger.com/theory/.

67 *Cory Doctorow:* http://www.boingboing. net/2006/10/10/disney-exec-piracy-i.html.

74 *"about half the observed decline in life satis-faction among adult Americans over the last 50 years "is associated with declines in social capital: lower marriage rates and decreasing connectedness to friends and community":* Robert Putnam, *Bowling Alone,* Simon & Schuster, 2000. The other half, in case you were wondering, is associated with increased financial worries.

74 *"the magnitude of risk associated with social isolation is comparable with that of cigarette smoking and other major biomedical and psychosocial risk factors":* James S. House, *Psychosomatic Medicine* 63:273–274, 2001.

74 *"Things are the way they are because they got that way"*: Gerald M. Weinberg, "Boulding's Backward Basis" from *The Secrets of Consulting*, Dorset House, 1985.

6. Beginnings

80 *Four Freedoms:* Virginia Satir, *Making Contact*, Celestial Arts, 1976. Donald C. Gause and Gerald M. Weinberg, *Exploring Requirements: Quality Before Design*, Dorset House, 1989. Norman L. Kerth, *Project Retrospectives*, Dorset House, 2001.

86 *Wikipedia article on speed dating:* http://en.wikipedia.org/wiki/Speed_dating as of March 22, 2008.

7. Middles—the "Meat" of the Peer Conference

96 *Merlin Mann:* Comment about traditional conferences, MacBreak Weekly podcast #78, 2/20/08.

96 *Chris Corrigan:* The Tao of holding space, http://chriscorrigan.com/parkinglot/?p= 1040.

8. Endings

101 *Amplifying Your Effectiveness:* http://www.ayeconference.com.

104 *Norman L. Kerth: Project Retrospectives*, Dorset House, 2001.

11. How to Start Making Your Conference a Reality

113 *Group culture, leadership, and your steering committee:* Some of this section is based on ideas from Gerald M. (Jerry) Weinberg's *Becoming a Technical Leader*, Dorset House, 1986.

113 *Ken Flowers:* http://kflowers.blogspot.com/2006/12/my-leadership-philosophy.html.

114 *Dale Emery:* http://www.dhemery.com.

12. The Steering Committee in Action

123 *Self-facilitation Skills for Teams:* http://www.estherderby.com/articles/selffacilitation.htm.

21. Pre-Conference Tasks

208 *your own private conference wiki:* See http://en.wikipedia.org/wiki/Comparison_of_wiki_software for a comprehensive list of wiki software and http://en.wikipedia.org/wiki/Comparison_of_wiki_farms for a comparison of wiki farm services.

218 *SurveyMonkey:* http://www.surveymonkey.com.

23. Pre-Conference Preparation

239 *Invisible Clock II:* http://www.invisibleclock.com.

25. Running Your Conference

277 *"Comparing the names between sheets is tedious, but takes less time than you might expect"*: Scheduling peer sessions using track and name conflict criteria could readily be automated; perhaps someone will write a program to automate this work some day.

294 *Norman L. Kerth: Project Retrospectives*, Dorset House, 2001.

301 *Affinity grouping:* Many of the ideas in this section are derived from R. Brian Stanfield, *The Workshop Book*, New Society Publishers, 2002.

Index

Breinigsville, PA USA
23 February 2011
256255BV00001B/4/P